WILD
LIFE

WILD LIFE

Dispatches from a Childhood of
Baboons and Button-Downs

Keena Roberts

GRAND CENTRAL
PUBLISHING

NEW YORK   BOSTON

Copyright © 2019 by Keena Roberts

Jacket design by Evan Gaffney. Jacket photographs: (background) Image Source / Getty Images; (author) courtesy of the author. Jacket copyright © 2019 by Hachette Book Group, Inc.

Grand Central Publishing
Hachette Book Group
1290 Avenue of the Americas, New York, NY 10104
grandcentralpublishing.com
twitter.com/grandcentralpub

First Edition: November 2019

Grand Central Publishing is a division of Hachette Book Group, Inc. The Grand Central Publishing name and logo is a trademark of Hachette Book Group, Inc.

The publisher is not responsible for websites (or their content) that are not owned by the publisher.

The Hachette Speakers Bureau provides a wide range of authors for speaking events. To find out more, go to www.hachettespeakersbureau.com or call (866) 376-6591.

All interior photographs appear courtesy of the author.

Print book interior design by Thomas Louie

Library of Congress Cataloging-in-Publication Data
Names: Roberts, Keena, author.
Title: Wild life : dispatches from a childhood of baboons and button-downs
   / Keena Roberts.
Description: First edition. | New York : Grand Central Publishing, 2019.
Identifiers: LCCN 2019021573 | ISBN 9781538745151 (hardcover) | ISBN
   9781538745144 (ebook)
Subjects: LCSH: Roberts, Keena--Childhood and youth. |
   Americans--Botswana--Biography. | Philadelphia (Pa.)--Biography.
Classification: LCC CT275.R72253 A3 2019 | DDC 974.8/11092 [B]--dc23
LC record available at https://lccn.loc.gov/2019021573

ISBNs: 978-1-5387-4515-1 (hardcover), 978-1-5387-4514-4 (ebook)

Printed in the United States of America

LSC-C

10 9 8 7 6 5 4 3 2 1

to Laura

TABLE OF CONTENTS

GORILLA MAN AND FIFTY TINY BALLERINAS

I SAT QUIETLY ON the gym floor and wiggled my toes. I wasn't allowed to move, but I was so excited I thought I might explode. I always had trouble sitting still, but today it was much harder than usual. The slippery laminate floor felt smooth under my bright blue sweatpants and I ran my fingers idly along the grooves in the wood, needing something to do with my hands and wishing I was outside instead. My heart pounded and the glare from the overhead lights made my dark hair feel heavy and hot. When was it going to be my turn?

The first pair of girls from my second-grade class were called up to do their dance routine. Their blond hair was tied back with glittery silver ribbons, and under their pink leotards they wore tights with sparkles on them. I looked around the room at the fifty girls from my class all sitting patiently around the blue gym mats waiting for their chance to perform. *They all look like Angelina Ballerina*, I thought, feeling a small swell of pride in my chest. Not one of them had a green bandanna wrapped around her head. *Their* outfits hadn't been borrowed from a real-life gorilla researcher.

The glittering dancing girls shimmied across the gym mats, swaying and jumping in time to Kris Kross's "Jump" and giggling nonstop. They were followed by another pair, who did exactly the same thing to exactly the same song. And another pair. And another.

I elbowed Elizabeth and hissed, "This is so boring. Our routine is going to be so much better." I couldn't understand why she looked so pale and unhappy, her brown eyes wide. "Don't worry," I whispered. "This is going to be so much fun!" She smiled thinly and looked down at her red sweatpants. She'd insisted on wearing red rather than blue because she said she'd look like a Smurf in blue. I tried to cheer her up by offering to wear the blue, but it hadn't worked. I still thought we should have tried to put together a gorilla costume for her, but I didn't want to make her any unhappier. I'd considered bringing her a cookie that morning to make her smile, but I didn't know what kind she liked. I didn't know anything about her, really, except that her name was Elizabeth and she was almost as new to my class as I was. We'd been paired together for the dance routine because neither of us had a best friend to run to squealing when we were told to find a partner for the class. Well, I did have a best friend, but he was a boy and they got to play basketball instead.

The teacher called up the next pair of dancers; there were only a few more kids to go before we were up.

The routine went like this: I was the hero and Elizabeth was the gorilla I was chasing, who (according to the song) had stolen my woman and driven off in a fancy car. The song didn't specify whether the hero ever caught the gorilla, but in order to create a dramatic conclusion, I decided that I would end up catching Elizabeth. We would run around in circles for a few minutes during the "chase," and then the routine would end with me theatrically shoving Elizabeth to the floor and standing over her, victorious. We hadn't practiced the whole routine yet since Elizabeth hadn't wanted to, but I wasn't worried about anything except pushing Elizabeth; she was a lot bigger than I was, and didn't seem like the kind of girl that got knocked over very often.

The song itself is called "Gorilla Man," which my dad told me was written by a Zulu sangoma (healer) in South Africa named Condry Ziqubu. My parents used to play the song while we made dinner, dancing around the kitchen holding my little sister and pretending to be the gorilla to scare her. When I told Dad I wanted to use "Gorilla Man" for my dance performance, he smiled and said, "That's an excellent choice.

Every good story has a car chase." And then Mom lent me her old green bandanna, the one she had worn to work with Dian Fossey with real-life gorillas in Rwanda.

I knew "Gorilla Man" by heart and had played it over and over in my head as we practiced our routine. I'd instructed Elizabeth on where she should go and what she should do as the drama played out. When the synthesizers began their downbeat, we'd square off: me, the desperate protagonist, and Elizabeth, the debonair gorilla who'd stolen my lady love.

"Look happier," I had to remind her. "You've stolen my woman! You're in a fancy car! You're not supposed to look terrified, you're the *GORILLA!*" For the past week of rehearsals, Elizabeth had looked nauseated as I jumped around the blue gym mats, acting out my choreography.

But now the day was here, and I couldn't wait to show everyone how cool I was. My classmates didn't know me very well since I'd only been back in the US for a few weeks, and no one really understood where I had come from. No one knew where Kenya was, so I had to just say, "I'm from Africa," when they asked me where I lived. They didn't know anything about Africa anyway, but just asked whether I had a pet elephant and spoke "African." My classmates had been genuinely surprised when I said that yes, I owned shoes but didn't like to wear them unless it was snowing. And no, I'd never seen a Koosh. What was it for? This was my chance to show them that the music from where I lived was so much better than their Top 40 hits. I wiggled my toes again and grinned. This was going to be so good.

Finally, it was Elizabeth's and my turn to dance. I hopped up eagerly, pulling Elizabeth behind me with one hand. Why did she look so scared? We were about to be the envy of all these boring little ballerinas around us! I squeezed her hand and smiled even wider, nodding to our gym teacher to start the music.

The synthesizers started, then the drums. I started dancing slowly in a big circle, moving my hands and tiny seven-year-old hips with the music, the way my Maasai babysitter had taught me, making sure to hit each downbeat with my right foot and throwing in an extra shimmy here and there with the bump of the synthesizer.

"Tell me where's Gorilla Man," Condry Ziqubu wailed, "No one's found a trace of him...people say he drives a smart car...he looks for beautiful women in town..." Elizabeth half-heartedly mimicked starting a car and started to drive around the gym mat, while I continued to dance. The drums picked up and I danced faster; it felt strange to be dancing to South African music in this school gym in the suburbs of Philadelphia instead of by a campfire in Kenya, but I knew the song so well I let the beat take me away, spinning, stomping, and waving my hands in the air as the bridge chanted, "I'm a, I'm a, I'm a gorilla; I'm a, I'm a, I'm a gorilla!"

After a few short minutes, we reached the climax of the song: the protagonist spots the Gorilla Man driving down the highway and yells, "We gonna find him, catch him, follow that car! We can't stop now! 'Cause he took my woman and drove away!" I danced my way behind Elizabeth, who had stopped driving and now stood in the center of the mat, looking like she might cry. I had timed it such that I reached Elizabeth just as the song got to its loudest point, and as the synthesizers and drums hit their final downbeat, I put my hands against Elizabeth's shoulders and threw her down on the mat, where she landed on her back and lay quietly as the music slowly faded out. I put one foot gently on her stomach and raised my fist in triumph. Gorilla Man had been defeated.

I panted in exhilaration and looked around the room. There was complete silence. No one moved. No one spoke. My classmates stared up at me with wide eyes and open mouths, a look of utter shock on their faces. Elizabeth whimpered and I removed my foot from her stomach. She rolled away and ran to the other side of the room, where she buried her face in my gym teacher's sweatshirt. One of my classmates giggled. Then another. Soon, all fifty second-grade girls were laughing and pointing at me. I didn't know where to go or what to do. I couldn't run away since they were sitting all around the dance area, and I couldn't turn to Elizabeth for help because she was crying in my gym teacher's arms. Bewildered, I stood there, looking from one girl to another in complete confusion.

"You...you didn't like it?" I said softly. The roar of laughter grew louder, and the pointing continued. My face burned and I felt a rush of nausea. Suddenly, my sweatpants didn't feel soft anymore, they felt hot and heavy and wrong. Everything was wrong. My pants were wrong, my turtleneck was wrong, my bandanna was wrong, I was wrong. The blood pounded in my head and my upper lip started to quiver. I heard my dad's voice in my head say, "Stiff upper lip!" but in that moment I hated him. He was wrong too.

I won't cry, I said to myself. *I won't. I won't.* I waded through the crowd of girls and walked slowly through the gymnasium to where my second-grade teacher, Mrs. Elliott, was standing in the doorway, watching.

I reached the doorway and glared up at her. She squatted down and balanced her elbows on her knees, looking me right in the face, ignoring the laughter that had followed me from the gym. My eyes filled with tears but I angrily brushed them away.

"Well that was certainly interesting," she said. I thought she might hug me, but was glad when she didn't. I wasn't about to cry on anybody's shoulder and I just wanted to be left alone. "You know what I think?"

"What?" I mumbled, my sleeve in my fist and my fist over my eyes.

"I think that you're back in the United States now, and not in Africa anymore. And I think it might be time to start acting like the other girls if you want to fit in."

You're wrong, I thought. It would take more than acting and dressing like everyone else to make me fit in; my wrongness was bigger than that, and I knew it from the top of my green bandanna to the tips of my toes, still calloused from the hot sand outside our house in Kenya. If I really wanted to fit in, I'd have to change the inside of me too.

CHAPTER 1

THE FIRST THREE TIMES I ALMOST DIED

THE FIRST TIME I almost died I was six months old. We had just moved to Kenya and were living in a small green house far out in the middle of the grasslands in Amboseli National Park, close enough to the border with Tanzania to see Mount Kilimanjaro. My mother put me down to sleep in my crib with a candle burning on the windowsill since I screamed if the room was completely dark. As the story goes, when she came back a little while later to see if I had fallen asleep, she found me no longer alone in my room but suddenly in the company of a very large, very angry black mamba.

My mother froze. There wasn't anything she could do. She couldn't run into the room without scaring the snake into biting me, so she stood in the doorway, hoping the snake would decide that the flailing baby was too disruptive and leave on its own, which it eventually did, but only after I made an especially loud "coo!" and attempted to grab it by the neck.

I don't remember the incident with the snake, of course, nor do I remember the second time I almost died, a few months later when my parents sat me down to play in the grass in front of our house only to see me immediately swarmed by siafus, or safari ants.

"So what did you do?" I asked, years later when I first heard the story. Siafu bites are very painful, and our Maasai housekeeper Masaku used to tell me how siafus could kill and eat small animals and had jaws so strong that the Maasai sometimes used them for stitches when they had an injury. I couldn't imagine a baby surviving being swarmed by them. Mom looked uncomfortable.

"Well, we got them off you, of course," she said. "Dad brushed most of them off and then we got the rest of them to let go of you by dunking you in the rain barrel behind the house."

"You dunked me in a rain barrel?" I yelled.

"Of course we did! I mean, it was no big deal," Mom said. "Obviously you were fine. It was a lot less scary than the first time you met a baboon."

That one I do remember. I must have been three or so and was again playing outside the house in Kenya. I'd walked a short way down the dusty road that led away from our house and toward the nearby Maasai village, following elephant tracks. I wasn't paying attention to anything around me, just kicking one of the round balls of elephant poop that the other village children and I often used as soccer balls. I squatted down in the road to pick it up when I heard a rustle in the grass behind me and turned around to find a gigantic monkey standing over me.

Even as a small child I knew it was a baboon. The monkeys Mom and Dad studied were much smaller and had black spots on their faces; they were called vervet monkeys, though I'd always called them "fever monkeys" since it was easier to say. The vervets rarely came close to our house, but the baboons were often nearby; Masaku told me these nyani were garbage animals that came into his village to look for food. It was the job of the little boys in the village to chase them away from the cows and goats since, though the nyani were monkeys, they were skilled hunters and often killed baby goats and ate them. I knew this particular baboon was a male because his snout was wider and heavier than the females' and Dad said the male baboons were about the size of a Saint Bernard, whatever that was.

I dropped my ball of elephant poop and stared up at the baboon, which didn't seem all that scary. I smiled at it. Mom always told me that animals aren't dangerous by nature; they're dangerous if you startle them, and if you don't then you're just another animal to them. Then the baboon grunted and took a few steps closer to me.

"Keena," I heard Dad say quietly from the front steps of the house where he'd been watching me play. "I need you to do something for me."

"Okay!" I said brightly, still looking at the baboon.

"I need you to walk backward to me. Do you think you can do that?"

"Yes, Daddy!" I said. I waved to the baboon and began walking backward through the soft sand in the road. As I retreated, the baboon immediately sat down and snatched up my soccer ball, happily picking through it for partially digested seeds and fruits. Fresh elephant poop is one of their favorite foods.

It didn't occur to me that the baboon was any danger to me. Dad seemed relieved when he finally picked me up, but didn't raise his voice or shout in any way that made me think he'd been worried for my safety. Baboons were familiar, and just as much a part of my daily life as the Maasai warriors who trooped down the road singing songs in their bright red shukas or the herds of elephants, buffalo, and zebras that roamed

Me and Dad in the backyard of our house in Amboseli National Park

through the grassland around our house, which Dad drove me out to see in our Land Rover if I'd been good.

We'd been living in Kenya for almost two years by then, all in the little green house in the grasslands under the mountain. I knew that Kenya was in Africa, and Africa was a long way away from another place called America, where Mom and Dad said we had another home that I didn't remember. "Home" to me meant soft wind and waving grass, the smell of zebras and the whooping of hyenas as the sun set over the plains. Home was our housekeeper Masaku letting me tenderize meat with an empty wine bottle before dinner and shaking out my shoes before putting them on in case scorpions or spiders were inside. Home was spending my days wrenching the lug nuts on and off the wheels of our truck and going on game drives with Dad to look at buffalo and watch quietly as they moved through the grasslands like ships on the sea.

America was where I was born, or so they told me. When Mom learned she was pregnant with me, she had driven into the capital city of Nairobi to one of the few clinics that had an ultrasound machine. Shaking his head sadly, the ultrasound tech informed my mother that her fetus was "too deformed" and had "a very, very small head. Too small for a human baby." Mom unsuccessfully tried to stay calm and made arrangements to fly to California to have her child, since my parents' academic affiliation with Stanford University gave her access to the hospital there.

The second I was born I was whisked into the neonatal intensive care unit and a team of doctors descended on me, led by a neonatologist named Dr. Sunshine. When I was finally brought back to my mother, Dr. Sunshine said cheerily, "Her head is fine. Just please promise me: no more backroom ultrasounds."

I also knew I had grandparents in America, though I never saw them. They often wrote us letters that my mother read to me, and sometimes sent me presents, including a stuffed owl I named Bundi, which Masaku had told me was the Swahili word for owl. Everyone gave me stuffed monkeys, since that's what my parents studied, but I liked the owl best because it was different. Masaku said that witches turned themselves into owls at night and that it was very bad luck if an owl landed on your house because it meant that someone who lived there would die soon. He refused to touch Bundi, even though it was just a toy.

My grandparents were furious when my parents brought me back to Kenya only a couple of months after I was born. When my mom had become pregnant with me, my parents had only recently relocated to Kenya from the Karisoke Research Center in Ruhengeri, Rwanda, where they had been working with the famed gorilla researcher Dian Fossey in a camp that was very basic and hardly a place to raise a baby. My grandparents were worried that our home in Kenya might be just as unsuitable.

It's important to specify that these concerns came almost entirely from my dad's parents, the ones who lived in suburban Chicago. His family was (as he later put it) "painfully conventional," and the idea of moving halfway around the world to study monkeys was an unbelievable shock to the country club community he had grown up in.

"I just don't know what to tell them," Dad's mother drawled in a Southern accent she brought with her from Hattiesburg, Mississippi.

"There aren't any monkeys in the US," Dad would say. "If I'm going to study them in their natural habitat I kind of have to go where that is."

"Are you sure you don't want to be an architect?" his father would ask, and Dad, third in a line of Robert Seyfarths and the first nonarchitect, would simply nod.

"This is what I'm going to do," he said. Eventually, they agreed it was fine as long as he didn't take his children with him, whenever they came along.

Mom's mother, my grandmother Sally, was never bothered by Mom and Dad's work. Mom was raised in the Foreign Service, in a family that spent time in Malaysia, the Netherlands, and Nicaragua all before my mom was a teenager, and before her father was killed in a plane crash on an aid mission in the Philippines. No one in her family was bothered in the least by having few modern amenities or not speaking to family members for months or sometimes years at a time because the mail was so slow. When she met Dad in college and decided to follow him into his PhD program in animal behavior so she could go "ask interesting questions about interesting animals in interesting places," as she used to tell me, her mother and siblings barely batted an eye.

"It really was very wet and cold up there in Dian's camp," Mom told me. "We lived in these tiny wooden huts that were heated with wood stoves and were always full of smoke. It was so wet that nothing ever dried and it was very hard to keep our notes and recording equipment from being chewed up by rats. There were just so many rats..." she trailed off. "At night they would sometimes run across my bed and I'd have to hit them with books."

It sounded to me like the entire time at Dian's camp was difficult. First, studying the gorillas was challenging. In order to observe their natural behavior, the scientists had to do everything they could to make sure the gorillas ignored them, including standing quietly as young silverbacks charged them in displays of aggression, and letting themselves be shoved down a hill covered in stinging nettles if the babies wanted to play with them. Back at the camp, Dian liked to slap Dad on the back and call him Bobby, even after he repeatedly told her that he preferred to be called Robert.

"Not to worry, Bobby," Dian would say, throwing her arm around Dad's shoulders. "Auntie Dian will always be there for you."

As Rwanda became more and more dangerous to work in politically, Dian began to show signs of strain. Her paranoia became increasingly odd, and when she eventually confided in my parents that she thought her phones were being tapped, they decided that the time had come to move on to a more stable and comfortable situation.

Kenya, my parents patiently explained to my grandparents, was much safer. Vervet monkeys are small and nonthreatening, and we could live in a real house, far away from the smoking shacks of Dian's mountain camp. But it was no use. To my grandparents, everywhere in Africa was the same and the whole continent was dangerous. One of the first sentences I learned to say on my own was, "I am fine, I am safe," spoken confidently through a phone from a hotel in Nairobi to my grandparents' house in the suburbs of Chicago.

And I really was fine, at least to the extent that I understood what that meant as a toddler. Every day, my parents would leave in the Land Rover to spend the day watching and observing the vervet monkeys, while I would hang out with Masaku as he did chores around the house or took walks to the village to talk with the other mzee, old men like himself. Masaku smelled like wood smoke, and his hands were soft and strong as he held on to mine as we walked.

Masaku taught me the names of all the animals on the plains in front of our house and that each animal has a different kind of track and its own kind of poop. As we walked up and down the road between the village and our house, he would point out crisscrossing lines of animal prints and wait for me to tell him which animals they came from; these small ones were gazelles', these hoofprints were zebras', and this poop was from a hyena—the easiest of all to identify because hyena poop is always white from the bones they eat. How many lobes on the paw of a simba (lion)? I held up three fingers. And do you see claws when you see the track of a duma (cheetah)? I nodded my head yes. Cheetahs' claws don't retract into their paws like lions' and leopards' do.

Sometimes one of Masaku's three wives would help babysit me, though as a child I always had a hard time telling them apart since they never really spoke to me. None of them ever said anything above a whisper. When Dad asked him why, Masaku replied, "One of them cursed the other two so they can only speak in a whisper and the one who did the cursing also whispers in order to hide her identity."

"And you don't mind?" Dad asked.

"Oh no," he replied. "The house is so quiet." And every afternoon, Mom and Dad would come back from work and take me on game drives out through the grasslands of Amboseli National Park to look for animals. The buffalo were my favorite since they moved around in such large groups that they would completely surround the car and make me feel like I was part of the herd. We often saw elephants, zebras, and herds of hundreds and hundreds of wildebeests grazing under the mountain and bleating like cows. My parents and I would sit out there for hours, quietly watching the animals go about their business, while Dad would periodically reach out the window of the Land Rover to empty my plastic bin into the grass. Potty training had to go on, even when there were wildebeests to watch.

Every morning as the sun came up and every evening as it set behind Mount Kilimanjaro, I sat on the front step of the tiny green house and watched the animals move across the land. Birds flew home to roost, elephants rumbled to their babies, and zebras moved out of the trees into the grass where they could see any approaching predators more easily. When it was time for dinner, we ate at a small foldout table in the kitchen, lit by hurricane lanterns and open to the night. Sometimes Mom and Dad told me the story about how an elephant sneezed on their windshield, and sometimes we'd talk about the vervet monkeys and how they were different from the gorillas they studied in Rwanda. When I went to sleep under my mosquito net with my stuffed owl, the thick smells from outside surrounded me and reminded me the animals were still there, just going to sleep as I was, and we'd see each other again in the morning when the sun came up.

Despite the peace of being alone with the wind and the animals, I couldn't help but feel a sense of disquiet creep slowly into my life. Why did Mom and Dad keep telling me my home was not my home? And what were these machines in my books called elevators, escalators, and microwaves? These things were as foreign to me as this place called America, and even though I was told I'd seen them before, I wasn't interested in going back. There was so much to see and do and learn about in Kenya, and Mom and Dad said there were no animals in the US. Why would I want a home that didn't include them? America could stay safely where it was, on the other side of the world; I had all the home I needed already.

CHAPTER 2

A DEAD CHICKEN
AND AN OFFER OF MARRIAGE

WE LEFT KENYA FOR a few months in the summer when I was two and a half years old. My parents had accepted full-time teaching positions at the University of Pennsylvania and had to "make an appearance" in the US in order to reassure the university that they wouldn't be spending all their time in Kenya, though they had every intention of being there as much as they possibly could. They also wanted to be in the States because they were expecting another child and didn't want to risk undergoing the same traumatic experience that they'd had with me. They bought a small yellow house in the suburbs of Philadelphia and, despite my vehement objections about its having "too big an inside and not enough outside," they made me live in it.

The house itself was like nothing I'd ever seen before. Though it was fairly small by US standards, it felt huge in comparison to our house in Amboseli and had all kinds of features that were completely new to me. The front door was not just a door but actually two doors, one on the outside made with heavy glass and one on the inside that was made of wood that was even thicker and harder to push open. I had to open both of these doors to enter the actual house. Once I finally got inside, there was a big room that was called the "living room," even though we lived in all the rooms. The house also had a "dining room," where we ate dinner on special occasions like Christmas or when my grandparents came to visit, and a tiny room off the kitchen where there were two large white machines that made a lot of noise and vibrated against the tile floor like a herd of stampeding buffalo. This small room was always warmer than the rest of the house and smelled clean, like wind after the rain or the grass after Masaku cut it with his machete.

But the house's most exciting feature by far was its second floor. I knew what stairs were, and I'd even gone up and down them a few times in fancy places like the airport or the shopping center in Nairobi, but I'd never had them in my own house, where I could go up and down them whenever I felt like it. The stairs started in the hallway next to the heavy front door and went up exactly twelve steps before they stopped at a small square resting place called a "landing," took a left turn and went up six more steps to the second floor of the house. Mom said the stairs were not as fun as stairs ought to be because they were carpeted and no good for Slinkys, which needed wooden stairs, but I cared less about that than the fact that they also came with a dark wooden bannister.

The bannister was smooth and heavy, much like the front door, but smelled different. If I put my nose right up to the wood and closed my eyes, I could smell dark trees with fluttery green leaves, smoke from a campfire, and just the faintest hint of buffalo. I knew that buffalo often liked to scratch on trees to clean themselves, so I assumed this bannister had come from one of those buffalo-scratching trees.

There were all kinds of things for me to do during the day in the new house. When I got tired of running up and down the stairs, I could put on my socks and slide across the dining room floor, climb the shelves in the linen closet, or find other things to jump off of, like the magnolia tree in the front yard, the hood of the car, or the hot metal contraption in my bedroom that hissed and spat but made the room warm and cozy when it was cold outside. It was cold in Kenya, but never enough that you needed anything more than a campfire. This was a different kind of cold, the kind that somehow got under your jacket where it wasn't wanted.

I distrusted this metal apparatus during the day but was terrified of it at night. That was when the daytime animals and birds went to sleep and the nighttime animals began their silent hunting; it was supposed to be a quiet time. But the radiator in my bedroom didn't seem to adhere to any of the same rules as the rest of the natural world, and that made it dangerous. It pinged and whistled all night long and made it hard for me to sleep. When I closed my eyes, I kept picturing the steamship from the movie *Pinocchio* that took the bad boys away to Pleasure Island to be turned into donkeys. Instead of the comforting familiarity of hyenas whooping and zebras calling, in America the only company I had was the bubbling muttering from the metal monster in the corner of my room, waiting for me to fall asleep so it could turn me into a donkey.

My bedroom itself also became a threat when the lights went out. The house creaked and groaned as the wind blew outside and I wondered how the second floor was supposed to stay attached to the first when all that connected them were pieces of wood and nails. Masaku used to give me bent nails to straighten while I helped him cook and I knew how easy it was to reshape them. At any moment I expected my room to either topple backward off the house and land in the backyard or for the floor to splinter under the legs of my bed and collapse in on itself, crushing the room below it and sending me toppling into the basement, which, naturally, I imagined to be full of snakes and spiders. Sometimes, desperate to hide from the sounds of the wind and the threats of the radiator, I would grab Bundi and crawl under my bed. It felt safer there somehow, and if I laid my head sideways on the floor I could hear the hum from the refrigerator in the kitchen below. This sound wasn't so scary to me since it reminded me of falling asleep on a plane flying to Kenya. Finally, I would fall asleep.

Outside our house, too, I found America to be a terribly confusing place.

"Is that Nairobi?" I asked Mom, pointing to a steeple poking through the trees outside my window.

"No, Nairobi is very far away. That's a church."

"What's a church?"

She rocked back on her heels, taking a pause from helping me tie my sneakers. "Ah...that's a good question. A church is a place where people go when they feel sad or confused and want to sit and think for a while." I considered this a moment and then nodded. I'd never been inside a church before, but since it was built with stone, I assumed it must be something like a cave on the inside, which sounded like a very good place to sit and think.

Every Saturday morning, Dad took me out in our red Volvo station wagon to do errands with him. Our first stop would be the bank, where Dad would take out exactly one hundred dollars in cash and fold the bills neatly in the wallet he kept in his back pocket. If I was being good and not asking too many questions, he would let me push the buttons on the robot that gave him the money. But no matter how nicely I asked, he would never let me smell it. Money was interesting because it looked like it might come from a plant but smelled completely different.

Our next stop would be the farmers market, which was my favorite place in all of America. The farmers market was a large room with four wide aisles in it, all of which were full of people in overalls and old-fashioned hats selling vegetables still dirty from the ground, fancy pastas in the shapes of springs and ribbons, and sticky cakes covered in raisins that smelled like Christmas and made my mouth water. Dad always went immediately to the cheese counter, where he asked a man with a big beard for "one piece of American cheese for immediate consumption." The man would smile and remove a piece of white cheese from a large stack and hand it to me, wrapped in a piece of wax paper. As Dad continued to talk to the man about various cheeses, I would slowly peel the cheese apart in thin strips and dangle them over my open mouth, like prisoners on a pirate ship being made to walk the plank. We never had cheese in Kenya since the Maasai thought fermented milk was disgusting and much preferred to drink it fresh from the cow and mixed with blood to make the warriors strong. I liked it because it felt smooth and slippery.

Other things that Americans ate were different too. Americans didn't drink Ribena or eat the same kind of Smarties that I did in Kenya, the candy-coated chocolate kind that came from a place called Great Britain in cardboard tubes and tasted different from American

M&M's. Americans also didn't take tea in the afternoon or pepper their sentences with British words like "rather," "knickers," and "jolly," the way my parents' friends in Kenya did. Mom told me that Kenya had been colonized by Great Britain before becoming independent in 1963, but a lot of the trade between the two countries continued and that was why so many of the things we found in Nairobi were actually not Kenyan at all, just imports from Britain. Even though Americans seemed to be trying to speak English too, everything they said sounded like it was coming through their noses.

I was too close to the ground to hear much of Dad's dealings with the various vendors, so I stayed tight to his side as I was instructed and people-watched instead. These Americans seemed awfully clean and tidy, which meant that they didn't spend much time outside. Their clothes looked new, without any stains or rips on the sleeves or pant legs, and their hair was combed in neat little lines that fell politely and obediently around their faces. America, I thought as I looked around the farmers market at the staid patrons in their fancy coats and shiny shoes, was a place to behave.

We hadn't been back in the States for more than a month or two before I was rudely dragged out from under my bed in the middle of the night and driven to the house of a family friend where I was to stay while my parents went to the hospital to retrieve my new baby sister, Lucy.

Lucy was a tiny baby, about the size and shape of a small vervet, and had bright blue eyes and a shock of dark, fluffy hair, very unlike my own eyes and hair, both of which were dark brown like my mother's. I remember the dark hair in particular because one day when she was about six months old, all of her hair seemed to fall out overnight and was replaced with the bright, almost iridescent blonde hair she has had ever since.

"What do you think of her?" Mom asked one day when I was helping her give Lucy a bath in the kitchen sink. I was in a grouchy mood because all of my stuffed animals were in the big white cleaning machine and Lucy had been screaming all morning.

"I think," I said, "that Lucy will become smaller and smaller until one day she becomes a plant."

"That so?" said Mom.

"Yes. A plant."

Through no fault of her own, Lucy was an incredibly colicky baby and took up a lot of my parents' time, between calming her down, trying to get her to eat, and then cleaning up the baby vomit from all the creative places Lucy managed to spray it. It was clear that Mom and Dad needed help, though I wasn't sure how I could contribute. Lucy seemed very sick, and I was worried that if we didn't figure out how to make her better, my parents would never have time to play with me again and Lucy might really turn into a plant (which, I admitted to myself, I didn't really want to happen).

While Lucy rocked back and forth in her baby swing, I pulled over my red plastic stool and pretended to read to her. I couldn't read the actual words, of course, but I'd memorized all my favorite children's books to the point where I knew what happened on every page and could recite the stories to her from start to finish, filled with dramatic voices and reenactments of the action scenes.

The story I told Lucy most often was from the book *Babar and Zephir*. When the monkey princess Isabelle is kidnapped from the tree city of Monkeyville, Zephir the monkey goes on a quest to rescue her from a strange yellow beast, a kind of hornless rhino named Polomoche, who hides in a green cloud smelling of rotten apples. Real monkeys don't do this, I pointed out to Lucy; real monkeys sit in trees and talk to each other and eat fruit, but they do not fight sea witches or evil mermaids or whatever kind of animal Polomoche was.

"You'll see," I said to Lucy. "Soon we'll take you to where the monkeys live and you won't cry anymore." No one ever cried when there were monkeys to look at; I knew that for sure.

Back in Kenya, Masaku and the men from the village came by to welcome us home and offer their condolences to my father. Only two children, and both girls? My father was a very unlucky man—my mother should have drunk more liquid goats' fat when she was pregnant; that was the best way to have sons. Dad feigned weariness and shook their hands, agreeing that the best thing for his small girls was to find them husbands as soon as possible.

One of the ladies from the village started coming to the house every day to help look after Lucy and me while my parents were out working. Soila was very kind and patient, and while I found her more nurturing and significantly more snuggly than Masaku or his wives, I was a bit disappointed that her version of playtime was usually of the indoor variety and involved a lot less animal poop identification.

Soila often brought her two sons with her to the house. At seven and eight years old, Njaraini and Ma were slightly older than me, and were already doing things that the big kids did, like guard the village goats from the nyani and visit the truck graveyard, where the long-haul truckers from Rwanda and Burundi abandoned their trucks when they broke down and no one had the money to fix them. The truck graveyard was one of my favorite places to go, but Dad wouldn't allow me to go alone, and only took me on special occasions like my birthday. But when Njaraini and Ma started coming by to play, Dad said it was safe enough for us to go to the truck graveyard by ourselves as long as we stuck together.

Njaraini, Ma, and I visited the truck graveyard almost every day. The trucks were our jungle gyms, and so large that we could spend hours scrambling through the cabins, climbing up the ladders on the sides, and poking around the wheels, all of which were taller than we were. All the best pieces from the trucks had long since been looted and sold, but if we were lucky we could find a lug nut or a spring from one of the engines. Masaku shook his head when he found the pockets of my shorts full of rusty car detritus and stored all the pieces carefully in a plastic bag to give to the boys when they came back to play the next day, as he didn't consider car detritus appropriate toys for a girl.

One afternoon, Njaraini, Ma, and I were running through the village toward the truck graveyard when we came across a small yellow chick.

Njaraini, Ma, another friend, and me sitting in a hole in the truck graveyard

Usually all the village chicks and chickens moved around together to keep them safe from the wild animals, but this one was all alone and looked scared. Ever so gently, I picked the chick up around its middle and cupped it in my hands, being careful not to wrap my fingers around its neck. I'd seen men from the village carry dead chickens by their necks and didn't think that was the proper way to carry a live chicken. I told Njaraini and Ma that we should return the chick to the village, and Njaraini said we should be extra careful because this chick belonged to one of the chief's chickens, and therefore to the chief himself.

Slowly, we walked back to the village, passing the chick between us so we could all have a turn holding it and feeling its soft feathers against our hands. I don't remember how it happened, but by the time we got back to the village the chick had been passed between us many times and somewhere along the way it had died. I was horrified for the baby bird, but Njaraini and Ma flew into a complete panic. As soon as they saw the limp chick dangling in my hands, they said the chief was going to beat them if he found out, and they dashed headlong back toward the truck graveyard to hide.

I felt sick to my stomach and disgusted with myself that this beautiful little creature had died when I was supposed to be taking care of it. I marched resolutely back toward the village and, under the watchful gaze of the mzee sitting around the fire and a number of other children, deposited the dead chick very carefully on the concrete step of the chief's hut. Then I ran home and told Masaku everything.

Masaku told me the next day that Njaraini and Ma had hidden in the truck graveyard for the rest of the day but had in fact been given a beating by the village chief when they returned home for dinner. This felt grossly unfair to me since I was also responsible for killing the chick, and I demanded that Masaku take me to the village chief to receive my share of the beating. Masaku refused, but promised to pass on my outrage to the village chief when he went home. I don't know what Masaku actually told the chief, but he reported to me that the chief had laughed at my request and called me a brave little girl.

"You are not like the other children," Masaku told me. "You do not get a beating." I stomped my foot and glared at him. What Masaku said didn't make sense to me. I was just the same as Njaraini and Ma; why did everyone insist on treating me like I wasn't?

"You are not like Njaraini and Ma," Masaku said. "You are not Maasai; you are a white, American girl. You are very different." This made my stomach hurt, but I couldn't argue with him. I had always known that my skin was a different color than his, or Soila's, or Njaraini's and Ma's, but the ramifications of those differences hadn't been clear to me, at least in a personal sense. I thought through what Masaku said. I knew we were fortunate to have a car, which none of the villagers had, but that Mom and Dad tried to share the car by letting the villagers borrow it and helping to shuttle people to the nearby health center in Loitokitok if someone was sick. I also had more books and toys than the other children did, but tried to follow Mom and Dad's example by sharing them with my friends whenever they asked. These concrete actions were obvious to me in the sense that if my family had something that someone else needed, we shared because that was the right thing to do. But the idea that where I was born and the color of my skin made us fundamentally different from each other—that was new to me. Even though I lived in a house and my parents had a car, we still lived in the same place and loved the same things, so how could we not be the same? My six-year-old mind couldn't figure it out.

I was very sad when Soila told me that Njaraini and Ma wouldn't be coming by to play anymore. I missed their company, and without them I didn't have a soccer ball to kick against the side of the house or toward the zebras in the grass behind the clothesline. Soila said they missed me too, but that didn't matter much if I was never going to see them again.

My family had almost forgotten about the chicken incident when one night a Maasai warrior from the village stopped by the house after dinner. He'd heard about the brave little white girl in the green house and, despite the fact that she was only six years old, was interested in adding her as one of his future wives for the generous price of five cows. Dad politely declined.

CHAPTER 3

DON'T BRING YOUR BEER SHIRT TO SHOW-AND-TELL

WHEN I WAS SIX, we left Kenya for good. My parents' work with the vervet monkeys had been successful, science-wise, but it was becoming increasingly difficult for them to conduct their research. The Maasai herdsmen's cattle ate the undergrowth where the vervets liked to hide and scared them up into trees, completely disrupting their normal behavior and making it impossible for my parents to conduct their experiments.

By 1990, times were changing in the world of primate research too. The three greats of primate research, Jane Goodall, Dian Fossey, and Birutė Galdikas, first brought the world's attention to the great apes in the 1960s and 1970s and documented a great deal about what the animals ate, what their family structures were like, and how they interacted with each other. When it became clear that primates were much more complex than anyone thought, a new generation of primatologists like my parents began asking even tougher questions: How did primates communicate in their social groups? Did they know the difference between their sister, their cousin, and a stranger? And if so, how would their behavior change if they were interacting with a close family member compared to a stranger? How much did they really understand about their world?

Vervet monkeys don't do anything as stylish or intellectually challenging as using stone tools or fishing for termites like Jane Goodall's chimpanzees did, but they do have a number of interesting behaviors.

At the time my parents were doing their research, there was a huge debate going on in the primate world about language, and whether we can take something like a monkey chirp or chatter and call it a "word." Many scientists assumed that animal vocalizations were just involuntary expressions of emotions, like shouting out when something surprises you or touching a hot stove. This wouldn't be considered language. Others took a different approach, focusing less on what primates do on their own and more on what they could be taught to do. There were several famous examples of gorillas being taught to use human sign language in laboratory settings, and many scientists took this as proof that primate language did exist since primates had the capacity to learn it, even if they didn't use language in their own societies in the same way.

My parents ascribed to the idea that if you could teach a captive chimp or gorilla to understand the meaning of a sign, this ability to understand meaning must have been favored by evolution, so we ought to be able to discover how it functions in the wild. In the 1960s, a colleague of theirs named Thomas Struhsaker reported that vervet monkeys give different-sounding alarm calls in response to predators like leopards, eagles, and snakes, so my parents decided to study these calls with playback experiments on the animals in their natural habitat.

My parents hated lab work. They didn't like locking animals up, and despite the importance that others in their field had attached to the idea of teaching primates to use sign language, they believed that teaching an animal to do something wasn't as interesting as looking at what that animal already does in its own natural setting. "You can train a dog to ride a bicycle," Dad used to say. "That doesn't mean that if you put a bicycle in front of a dog he'll just know how to ride." What Dad meant by this is that there's a difference in what a vervet could be taught to do, which demonstrates a certain capacity for learning, and what they do unprompted. Observing this natural behavior (or manipulating it) is what would help show how and why vervets do what they do, and the implications those behaviors have on how human communication has evolved from it.

The vervet monkeys in Amboseli were highly communicative and spent most of their day interacting with each other while they ate and hopped through the acacia trees. They barked and chirped and chattered and screamed. All of this, my parents believed, showed the members of the group engaging in social communication that not only signified intent and feeling but also served to further solidify the social bonds among the individuals.

Building on Struhsaker's earlier vervet communication work, my parents focused their research on the three distinct calls that vervets made when they saw a predator. Each call sounded different from the others, and each produced a very different reaction in the vervet group. My parents showed that the vervets' reactions to the alarm calls weren't just instinctive reactions, but that they really understood what each call meant—that, as Dad would say, "call X" means "response X." My parents proved this by manipulating the vervets' situations to show that pairing "call X" with "response Y" made the vervets completely confused, indicating that they knew the pairing was somehow wrong. Using a classic experiment, they would strategically place a stuffed predator in the vervets' path (like a stuffed leopard they borrowed from a Nairobi museum) and then play the incorrect alarm call for the vervets over a hidden speaker (like the call for "snake"). Some of the vervets would give the "leopard response" and jump into the trees and others would give the "snake response" and stand on their hind legs to look around. Then, all would look at each other as if to say, "What the hell?"

This was a big deal in the world of primatology, and my parents, excited and reenergized by the success of their experiments, were desperate to find another field site where they could continue their work, if not with vervets than with other monkeys. There weren't many realistic options for them, however. They didn't want to go back to Dian's gorilla camp in Karisoke and, because they had my sister and me (then three and five years old) in tow, couldn't go to any of the chimpanzee study sites. Chimpanzees have been known to hunt and eat human children. My parents told me a story of some chimps raiding the research camp of a colleague and chasing their four-year-old daughter around and around the camp, trying to kill her, before being chased off by their research assistants.

"I don't think I like chimps," I declared after hearing this story.

"That's okay; neither do I," Dad said. "I'd much rather stick to monkeys."

Leaving Kenya felt like a punch in the stomach. Mom tried to downplay our departure by telling me it was just a vacation to visit my grandparents, but when she and Dad donated all our clothes and toys to the village and sold the car, I knew we were leaving for good. I sobbed when Masaku left our house for the last time, but he merely grunted and told me I was going home and should be happy about it.

"BUT I AM HOME!" I bawled, wrapping my arms around one of the car tires and pressing my face against the dusty rubber. Mom shook Masaku's hand and pried me off the tire, but I didn't stop crying until we got on the plane and a flight attendant handed me a dinner tray with a bread roll and a little jar of jam. I adored the tiny "jam-jammies" that we got on planes and in hotels, and when Mom handed me hers and Dad's to play with too, I cheered up a little bit.

Back in Philadelphia, Mom said I was old enough to go to school and "might as well give it a try" while she and Dad were busy at the university and toddler Lucy was in day care. I had never gone to school before, though Mom and Dad had taught me how to read and write while we were in Amboseli. There had been a school in the nearby town of Loitokitok, but since the kids there were just working on reading and writing and basic math anyway, Mom and Dad said I could just as easily do that at home. After all, they were both professors. Despite my objections to the idea when I heard that school was an inside activity, Mom applied for me to enroll in a fancy nearby private school to start first grade. She selected this school at the recommendation of some colleagues at the University of Pennsylvania whose children had gone there and because the school administrators were comfortable with the idea of her and Dad taking me out of school if and when they found another field site and moved. Though there were two excellent public schools nearby, neither had agreed to let me join the class if we were just going to leave again, telling my mother I was either in school or I wasn't; Mom couldn't just withdraw me whenever she felt like it. So, private school it was.

I had to take an IQ test in order to be accepted into the school and, when he gave my mother my results, the test assessor shook his head and said, "She meets the Shipley School's standards, I just don't understand why she was talking so much about gold and rubies." (It was because I'd just been sick with a stomach bug and had been allowed the rare privilege of watching a movie; I'd picked *The Hobbit*.)

At the Shipley School, first grade was on the second floor of what my teacher called a carriage house, surrounded by tall, dark trees that were much bigger than the trees we had in Amboseli and also much less interesting because only squirrels lived in them, not eagles or leopards. Though getting up every morning and going to school was a completely foreign experience to me, I found that I liked first grade, largely due to my exceptionally understanding teacher, Mrs. Morgan. After Mom explained where we'd come from and how I usually spent my days playing with car parts or chasing zebras behind our house, Mrs. Morgan made sure I ran around as much as possible at recess and was gentle when she told me not to bring my Tusker beer T-shirt to school after I wore it one day for show-and-tell. Realizing how much I disliked sitting still, she let me doodle as much as I wanted during class as long as I promised I was listening, and even made sure I had a seat by the window where I could watch the squirrels chase each other up and down the trees. Everything was very clean and very orderly and I did my best not to fidget, since I remembered that I had to behave myself in America.

There were only twelve students in Mrs. Morgan's class, and she clustered our desks in four groups of three, so that each student had what she called "desk friends." While she said it was important that we made friends with all the other students, our desk friends were supposed to be our "at-school family," the classmates who would lend you their markers if you left yours at home and hold your hand on the walk to the cafeteria for lunch.

My two desk friends were a boy named Nat and a girl named Meghan. Nat had wavy brown hair like mine and was very quiet. He was nearly as short as I was and was the only other person I'd met who liked the book *Redwall* as much as I did, though he said he preferred computer games to reading if he could choose. Nat taught me how to draw dragons and told me that if there was ever a girl who could be an X-wing pilot in *Star Wars*, it would be me. I liked him immediately.

Meghan was a little taller than me and had soft blonde hair that she pinned back with pink ribbons or a glittery hair band. Her shoes were always tied and she had beautiful handwriting that slanted to the right just the way Mrs. Morgan wanted it to and never sprawled across the page like mine did. Meghan was kind and smart and reminded me of the little girls in *Madeline* who did everything in two straight lines, rain or shine. If she were British, I thought, I would call her "proper," but people in America didn't seem to use that word.

Mrs. Morgan was very pleased that Nat and Meghan quickly became my friends. "Keena is a very smart little girl with a wild imagination," she wrote to my mother after a parent-teacher conference, "but would benefit from spending more time with the other children and less time reading by herself."

"Well, I can't really fault you for reading," Mom said. "Do you bring your books to recess with you?"

"No, I don't," I said. "Recess is for running around!"

She laughed. "That's what you do at recess? You run around?"

"Yes. The boys all want to pretend they're Ninja Turtles but they won't let me be one because I'm a girl. There's only one girl in Ninja Turtles and they always want Meghan to play her. They make me play an evil pig and they chase me."

Here I am behaving in my first-grade school picture. Mom paid me five dollars to wear a dress.

"That makes...some sense, I guess," she said. "Is that fun for you?"

I shrugged. "It doesn't really matter what I'm supposed to be; they never catch me anyway." And if I was being honest with myself, I liked being stronger and faster than they were. At least I knew I could outrun them if some animals appeared.

"I see," she said. "Well...carry on, then."

What Mom didn't tell me was that she actually was growing worried about my reading, since at the time my reading pile wasn't full of books at all, but rather something called the *Wildlife Fact-File*. The

Wildlife Fact-File was a heavy three-ring binder that held more than a thousand cards, each describing everything about a particular animal, from its size, shape, and breeding habits to where it lives, what it eats, and what its social behavior is like (if it has any). In America, I had a subscription to the *Wildlife Fact-File*, and every month I would receive thirty new cards in the mail and could sort them into the right order in my binder: reptiles, insects, mammals, what they called primitive animals, and animals that were extinct. This last category was my favorite because it contained the dodo bird, the passenger pigeon, and all the dinosaurs.

I pored over this binder day and night, memorizing details about each of the animals and tracing the maps of where they lived in the world to see if and where they overlapped.

"*The Wizard of Oz* is wrong," I said to my mother one morning at breakfast.

"Oh?"

"Yes. There is no place in the world where lions and tigers and bears all live in the same place." Mom flipped a pancake and turned to look at me in what I thought of as her "professor face."

"That is true," she said. "And you're right. But remember that Oz is a fictional place, and maybe there they do have lions, tigers, and bears that all live together. And the rules have to be different there anyway; otherwise, how would it be possible that the lions in Oz could talk?"

She was right. My mother, I believed, knew everything there was to know about animals, both real and fictional. She didn't need the *Wildlife Fact-File*; she already knew where all the animals in the world live and what they do and how they eat. If I wanted to be as smart as she was, then I clearly had to study my *Fact-File* a lot harder.

It was very exciting whenever a new set of *Fact-File* cards arrived in the mail, though it was brutally disappointing every time a set arrived that contained the common cards I already had. One afternoon, I burst into tears when I realized, yet again, how far I was from completing my set.

"I already *have* earthworms and llamas," I sobbed into my mother's shoulder. "I'm never going to get a water vole!"

"I know, I know," she said, rubbing my back. "It's terrible, and I know how badly you want that water vole. Maybe he'll come next month."

Mom reached around me and flipped open the *Fact-File* where it sat on the couch next to Lucy, who had been playing in her bedroom but had come downstairs when I yelled. Lucy didn't like it when I was upset. The page Mom opened to was the file for spotted hyenas, a common sight in Amboseli and an animal that I knew well.

"Hyenas actually have a fascinating social structure," she said. "Did you know that in a hyena group the females are more dominant than the males and their whole social network is determined by who their mothers and sisters are? Hyenas are a lot like monkeys in that respect."

I sniffed and wiped my nose on my sleeve. "That is kind of cool," I said. Mom ran her finger down the page, and I knew she was silently fact-checking the information to make sure it was correct. Nothing made her angrier than bad data.

"They aren't primarily scavengers either," she continued. "Hyenas are some of the best hunters in the world, even better than wolves, if you ask me." Her finger paused on the map of spotted hyena distribution in Africa and she looked at me.

"Do you know where this is?" she asked, pointing to a spot near the bottom of the African continent, right between Namibia, South Africa, and Zimbabwe.

"No."

"That," she said, tapping her finger against the page, "is the country of Botswana. We got a letter from a guy who works there who might want to have us take over his study site for him next year." My heart leapt.

"We get to go back to Africa?" I asked. I'd been asking about going back for months, but Mom kept saying she wasn't sure. "What's it like in Botswana?" Mom sat down on the couch and pulled Lucy into her lap.

"I don't know everything yet, but I'll tell you what I do know. It's very different from Kenya," she said. "There are many more animals and the camp is very far away from any other people." I began firing questions at her: If we moved there would we have a house? Would there be a village nearby? Would I have to take malaria medicine again? Could I bring my stuffed animals with me? "I'm sure you can," she said. "The Okavango Delta is a big swamp, but I see no reason why you can't bring your stuffed animals." A big swamp? That didn't sound very appealing.

What I hadn't known before this was that after a year of fruitless searching, my parents had been contacted by a guy named Bill Hamilton, a researcher from the University of California, Davis, who had a study site in the Okavango Delta in Botswana that he was ready to leave. Bill thought it might be perfect for our family since Botswana was a stable place to work politically and the baboons at his site were already habituated to humans. Bill had had enough of fieldwork with primates and wanted to go back to California to study wild turkeys instead. Overjoyed at the idea of starting their fieldwork again, Dad set off to Botswana around the time I had my meltdown about the water vole to check out the study site while Mom, Lucy, and I stayed behind in Philadelphia—Mom teaching their classes at the University of Pennsylvania and me finishing what had turned out to be a fairly torturous year of second grade after my "Gorilla Man" performance.

We didn't hear from Dad at all while he was gone. Even in Kenya we had received the occasional airmail letter from my grandparents, so not hearing from Dad for almost two months made me anxious. Where was this place he had gone and why was it so far away? Was it dangerous? Were there zebras there, and did the wind smell like elephants? Why hadn't he taken me with him and away from the girls at school who kept laughing at me and calling me "gorilla girl"?

We met Dad at the airport on a cold afternoon in December, two months after he left to visit the potential new field site in Botswana and four months after my dance performance.

"DADDY!" Lucy and I yelled, scrambling under the barrier at the arrivals terminal and jumping into his arms.

"My girls!" Dad shouted, hugging us. "You're so clean!" Botswana was, apparently, a very dusty place, and as Dad peeled off his Red Sox hat, sand sprinkled over the floor of the terminal.

Dad reported that the study site was perfect and the camp would be a fine place for us to live as long as we completely rebuilt it, since at the moment there was basically nothing there except a couple of run-down huts and some junk that Bill Hamilton would be leaving behind. Over dinner in the dining room the following day (Dad said it counted as a special occasion since he hadn't had fried chicken in months), Mom and Dad announced that at the end of the year we would be officially moving to Botswana. Mom and Dad had to finish the year teaching at the university and Bill Hamilton needed to wrap up his own work, but after that we would be packing up again and moving to the Okavango Delta.

Mom put down her knife and fork and looked at us seriously, the way buffalo do right before they get angry. She said that they would only be able to do their research and maintain the camp and keep us all safe in the process if everyone worked together. Lucy and I were just as important to the success of this mission as she and Dad were, and they had decided to go because they knew they could trust us.

"You're bush kids," Dad said. "You know the animals and you understand the dangers. We wouldn't be going if we didn't think you could handle it. We know you can. We're all in this together."

"We got you these," Mom added, handing me and Lucy two notebooks with flowers on the covers. They looked like real books, not like the notebooks Mrs. Elliott had us use in school. "These are your journals. Every day you can write in them about what we're doing and what Baboon Camp is like."

"Every day?" I said. Mom gave me the buffalo stare again.

"Yes, every day," she said, adding under her breath, "This is what passes for school now, I guess." She looked at Dad and then back at me and Lucy, now ages eight and five, and clasped her hands on the table in front of her. "This is serious, girls. Are you ready?" I thought back to the year of school that had just finished, and heard nothing but the sounds of the synthesizer, the sound of the "Gorilla Man" song, and the laughter of my classmates.

I straightened in my chair, heart pounding with excitement and trying to banish all thoughts of second graders and swamps from my head. Mom was talking to me like I was a grown-up, so I had to start acting like one.

"Yes, Mom," I said. "I'm ready."

CHAPTER 4

THE AFRICAN NIGHT IS LONG AND DARK

JUST A MONTH LATER, I found myself lying on my back on a tin trunk next to a shallow river in Botswana. The air was crisp and cold and I stared up into a stark blue sky, watching long-tailed shrikes and brightly colored bee-eaters swoop between the acacia trees along the banks of the river, catching flies in elaborate loops. The sun was barely up, and I was freezing. We had to start our trip early because we weren't entirely sure we knew the way and couldn't afford to get lost. Dad and I guarded our small pile of supplies while Mom and Lucy wandered up and down the riverbank looking for snail shells, all of us waiting for our boat escort into the Okavango Delta.

The Okavango Delta is the only wet part of Botswana, which is almost entirely desert. As rains collect in the mountains of Angola to the northwest, floodwater flows south across the Caprivi Strip in Namibia and spills into the dry, dusty expanse of Botswana, creating the permanent and seasonal swamplands of the Okavango Delta. During the winter flood season (generally from April/May to October/November), endless tiny channels snake across the delta in between wooded islands. Although many of these channels are navigable by boat, they can be terribly confusing to all but the most experienced navigator. As the floodwaters recede and the summer temperatures rise (between October and April), the water dries from the floodplains between the permanent islands and leaves behind grassland. Boats are abandoned for cars, and roughly marked roads emerge where channels once ran.

We arrived in Botswana in June, and it wouldn't be until October at the earliest that we'd be able to drive, so on our first trip up to Baboon Camp, we had to go by boat.

Though several tourist lodges were scattered across the Okavango Delta, the delta was largely dominated by the Moremi Game Reserve, a protected area for animals much like the Amboseli National Park in Kenya. The big difference in Botswana, Mom and Dad told us, is that the nearby town of Maun would be more than four hours away from our camp, unlike Loitokitok in Kenya, which had only been a fifteen-minute drive from our house. That meant that doctors, stores, schools, and everyone except the few people who worked at the tourist lodges would also be more than four hours away.

"We also can't have a house," Dad said, "since the government of Botswana doesn't allow any permanent structures in national parks. We can have big tents and build a couple of huts like the ones they have at the tourist lodges, but nothing else. It'll be a lot more like..." He paused. "Well, long-term camping is probably the best way to describe it. You'll see."

I snuggled closer in my jacket, a bright purple Patagonia windbreaker that I'd begged and begged for in the aisle of the Eastern Mountain Sports store back in Pennsylvania.

"This is an expensive coat," Mom had said, pausing while loading our cart full of batteries, oral rehydration salts, and gauze bandages. "If I buy this for you, will you promise to wear it every day?"

"Every day for the rest of my life," I swore, dropping to my knees. She laughed, but added the coat to the already impressive load in our cart. I'd carried the coat in my backpack through two interminable night flights and halfway across the world, but it had made it safely and was now wrapped tightly around my small, shivering body as we waited by the riverbank. The coat felt fancy and outdoorsy, like the coat of an adventurer, which I now supposed I was.

The air smelled like cows, and I could hear cattle moving slowly through the bushes, lowing softly to each other as they ate. I didn't mind the smell; it reminded me of buffalo, and buffalo smelled comfortingly like Amboseli. My stomach lurched as I remembered that even though the smells were familiar, I wasn't back in Amboseli, I was somewhere new. We were half a continent away from our green house in the grasslands, where someone else probably lived now. We were getting ready to move to a place no one but Dad had even seen, and a place that he had already told us was barely habitable. And what did he know about habitation anyway? All he needed to survive was a polo shirt and coffee. Did he even think about where I would put my books and stuffed animals?

I bounced my bare heel on the side of the tin trunk and stared up into the sky, trying to settle my nerves with slow, deep breaths. What were we thinking? This would be nothing like living in Amboseli; we would have no house, no nearby village with people to talk to, nothing except what we brought with us, and I knew that wasn't much—just a couple of tents, some tin trunks to store food, and a few boxes of tools. How were we going to do this? How was I going to do this? I caught the zipper of my coat between my teeth and sucked on it, still tapping my heel against the trunk. I closed my eyes. Could we at least get going?

A low, mechanical hum interrupted the sounds of grazing cattle. I sat up, rubbing my eyes against the change in light and realized I'd been dozing on the trunk. Two boats swung into view down the river. The first was a large blue cargo boat about thirty feet long being driven by a gigantic man with blond hair, a veteran of the Zimbabwean civil war named Dan Rawson, who always smiled and smelled like wood chips. Dan owned a shop in Maun that built and repaired boats, and we'd visited his shop a few days earlier to buy the boat that would eventually accompany us up to camp. The boat, along with an old Toyota Hilux that Bill left on the island, would be our only way to get in or out of camp while we lived there.

I couldn't see the second boat behind Dan's, but knew it was much, much smaller. When Dan had sold it to us, he laughed when Dad told him we didn't need a big boat, just something large enough to get us where we needed to go on the river.

"Whatever you say, Robert, hey?" Dan said. He'd punched Dad in the shoulder and laughed. "If a hippo bites it in half we'll just get you a new one!"

I listened to the higher-pitched whine of our smaller engine and frowned, thinking I'd make sure to ride in the larger boat with Dan.

Our boat, which now looked utterly pathetic when it finally moved into view, was driven by Mom and Dad's old friend Tico, who studied wild dogs in a different part of the delta. I didn't know how they knew him, but it seemed like everyone who studied animals knew each other in some way. When Mom and Dad introduced him, my first question was, "So what do you study?" I assumed everyone they knew was a researcher of some kind.

Tico was from the US and had been working in Botswana for several years already; he had spent the last few days helping Mom and Dad get all our paperwork in order in Maun before we moved to camp. He had also introduced us to some friends of his, Tim and Bryony Longden, who owned an ostrich farm on the outskirts of town along the Boro River. Tim, a white Zimbabwean, and Bryony, from the UK, had two daughters named Maxie and Pia who Tico thought we could play with while Mom and Dad bought all the supplies we'd need to move to camp.

The Longdens' ostrich farm was about ten kilometers outside of Maun, so my first exposure to the town came only in bits and pieces when I accompanied my parents on their errands. Though it looked a bit like Loitokitok, there seemed to be only one of everything: one streetlight, one supermarket, and one bank. Everything was covered in a film of dust, and goats and cows wandered the streets, nibbling the butterfly-shaped leaves of what Tim told me were mopane trees. There were people everywhere, but I didn't get a chance to meet many of them since we were only in Maun for about a week before we were ready to take the boat up to camp.

Tico was the only person other than Dad who actually knew where Baboon Camp was, and I was glad to have him along. Tico looked and sounded like Han Solo, and because of this, I trusted him immediately.

The boats nudged into the muddy bank alongside our pile of supplies, and we began loading them into the two boats: crates of tuna fish, boxes of Corn Flakes, and piles and piles of tools.

Determined not to appear nervous in front of Dan and Tico/Han Solo, I settled onto the canvas-covered bench on the side of Dan's boat and tucked my knees up under my jacket to keep them out of the wind. Mom and Lucy joined me in Dan's boat while Dad rode behind us with Tico.

"No standing, girls, hey?" Dan called and I nodded. Silly, of course I knew not to stand in a moving boat. I didn't know much about the delta but at least I knew that. I held on to the railing as Dan started up the engine and the convoy lurched slowly forward up the river. The riverbank, cows, and birds disappeared behind us, and off we went, into the complete unknown.

The roar of the engine and the wind made it too loud to talk. Mom tried to hold Lucy in her lap to keep her warm but Lucy wiggled free and wormed her way through the piles of building material to the bow of the boat where there was a small, raised area for sitting. She slid onto the seating area on her stomach and placed her chin on her hands, gazing forward. I glanced at Mom, who shrugged. Lucy always did what she wanted; it was impossible to tell her no. Though I desperately wanted to join Lucy in the front, I didn't want to disobey Dan's rule not to stand and so sat stubbornly in my seat, holding on to the railing and watching the riverbanks flash by. Lucy's body tipped left and right as the bow snaked between reedbeds and around floating piles of grasses and bobbing clumps of elephant poop.

Though I'd been thankful we had Dan with us from the beginning, I didn't know how much we needed him until we left the main channel that led back toward town and entered the swamp proper. Sitting on the side of the boat, I couldn't count the number of times I ducked under reeds or shielded myself from spray as Dan navigated the boat around tight corners and down tiny, thin channels, dodging between beds of papyrus and completely ignoring the open, wide channels on either side of the reedbeds. I turned around and glared at him after he made a particularly tight turn that covered me in icy cold river water and pointed at the wide, open channel to our right. He grinned and pointed farther upriver in the channel, where the heads of more than a dozen hippos stared back at me, ears flicking in the early morning sunshine. My eyes widened and Dan laughed, turning us down yet another corridor between the papyrus beds. I knew from my *Fact-File* that hippos were responsible for more human deaths in Africa than any other mammal.

The sun climbed higher in the sky and the air grew warmer. After it became clear that Dan didn't care at all that Lucy was lying on the bow of the boat, I hopped off my seat and inched through the supplies to join her. The metal on the seating area had been heated by the sun and it was actually quite warm once I settled down flat and out of the wind. I stared down into the river rushing past below me. The water was clear and clean, and I could see right to the bottom. In the shallow parts, catfish with giant heads cruised slowly across the sandy bottom and smaller fish darted in and out of the reedbeds. Higher up, islands covered with thick trees dotted the floodplains (which Dan told me were called melapo in Setswana, the most common of the local languages) on either side of the river, full of dark trees and thick bushes. As we sped up the river, white egrets and turquoise kingfishers flew out of the reeds and flashed in front of the boat before disappearing into the melapo. I tried to count the turns in the river but quickly lost track, getting distracted by the beautiful birds and the gigantic crocodiles sunning themselves on the sandbanks with their jaws wide-open. No wonder Mom said we wouldn't be allowed to go swimming.

On and on we drove, past wide-open melapo dotted with palmetto groves and palm trees standing starkly against the bright blue sky. We passed island after island of dense bushes and tall termite mounds placed like wedding cakes on small mounds of dirt. We passed trees half-submerged in the water from where elephants had pushed them over and flattened beds of reeds where Mom yelled that hippos had been sleeping. The wilderness spilled to the horizon in every direction, completely devoid of any sign of human life. As the minutes stretched into hours and we were still moving, I began to understand just how far away we were from civilization; the nearest grocery store, paved road, and doctor were all back in Maun. There would be nothing out here but us and the supplies we carried with us in the boat—no one to talk to but my family and no help if we needed it. I felt a lump form in the back of my throat and consciously swallowed it down.

After almost five hours of driving, Dan turned off the main channel and entered a big lagoon alongside one of the larger islands we'd seen thus far. A narrow path had been cut through the spikey green hippo grass at the far end of the lagoon, and Dan steered his boat down this path, killing the engine and letting the boat drift to the end, where it bumped gently against the sandy shore.

"We're here!" Dad shouted from the boat behind us. I looked around skeptically, not seeing anything that could properly be called "here." My ears were still ringing in the sudden silence that followed the roar of the boat engine and I shook my head to clear it before looking around. Though I knew my parents had described Baboon Camp as "long-term camping," I certainly wasn't prepared for what I saw—or didn't see—on the island in front of me.

I stepped stiffly off the boat and onto the shore. I wanted to show everyone how brave I was by being the very first person to step into Baboon Camp, whatever it looked like. I promised Mom I could do this, and I wouldn't start by hanging back behind my parents. They trusted me to act like an adult, and this was my first test. Aside from a large clearing in front of me, the island looked much like the others I'd seen on the trip from Maun: Tall, gnarled trees filled the thick riverine woodland all around me and the wind blew softly through the branches, rustling the leaves and sending small clouds of dust swirling across the clearing. An enormous fig tree at the edge of the water dominated the forest to my right, towering over the surrounding bushes and leaning far out over the lagoon. To my left, the shoreline curved in a wide loop around more of the island, tightly packed with hippo grass waving in the wind. I was relieved to hear the familiar *coo-coo-coo* of mourning doves—I remembered them from Amboseli. I made a mental note to look at whether the doves in the Okavango were the same species. Maybe my *Wildlife Fact-File* would know. Yellow weaverbirds darted through the high branches of the fig tree and bright, iridescent starlings poked through the dead leaves and branches on the forest floor. I turned my back to the clearing and looked across the lagoon, over miles and miles of melapo to the far distant tree line. The waves lapped gently against the shore, the air was clear and smelled clean, and the midday sun felt warm through my T-shirt, my new purple coat long forgotten on the bottom of Dan's boat. In the far-off molapo I could see the dark, shiny backs of hippos grazing in the grass, and a large crocodile glided silently with only its eyes and nose above the water (*like a battleship*, I thought). The chattering call of a vervet monkey interrupted the birdsong and I grinned. There were monkeys here!

I slowly made my way back to the rest of my family, who were still climbing out of the boats. Dad ran his hands through his hair and straightened his Red Sox hat.

"Well, this is it," he said. "Let's take a look at the old kitchen."

"Kitchen?" Mom said. "You mean the pile of debris over there?" Dad laughed and made a "pooh-pooh" noise.

"Obviously, Dorothy." We walked over to the old kitchen and stood around it in a semicircle. A piece of tin roof lay on top of a pile of rotting reeds, which I supposed had once been the kitchen's walls. The piece of tin looked like it might still be useful, but the reeds were full of insects and smelled like wet hay. I poked the piece of tin with the toe of my black-and-white Samba sneaker and looked up at Mom with my eyebrows raised.

"It will look a lot better once we rebuild it," she said.

No kidding, I thought.

Dad pointed to another structure on the opposite side of the clearing and told us this was the storage hut. It looked dark and sinister, but largely intact. Mom walked over to the hut and tentatively pushed the door open. It swung silently inward, revealing a pitch-black interior with a sandy floor, crisscrossed with delicate, feathery trails.

"Do you know what those are?" she asked me. I'd followed her over to the hut and peered around her waist and into the interior. I shook my head.

"Spider tracks."

I gasped. "But they're so big!" I said.

She laughed. "Yes they are. Big tracks for big spiders! We'll have to keep an eye out for those guys."

"Are we going to kill them?" I asked. The only spiders that big I'd ever heard of were the Mirkwood spiders from *The Hobbit*—famously difficult to kill.

"No," she said, pulling the doors closed and, I hoped, sealing the monstrous spiders inside. "Spiders eat mosquitoes and mosquitoes give you malaria. These spiders are our friends." She walked back to the boats to check on Lucy but I stood a moment, gazing at the storage hut. *You and me—we aren't finished yet*, I silently warned the spiders.

We helped unload Dan's cargo boat and said goodbye as he headed back to Maun. Tico pitched a small tent next to the storage shed, since he was going to stay with us for a few days to help rebuild the kitchen and get our big tents set up.

In the hours remaining before sunset, we pitched two more small tents and made a fire in the clearing in front of the old kitchen. I could see more remnants of Bill's old camp as I foraged through the bushes to find kindling for the fire; some of the trees had clearly been chopped with an ax, and I found a stack of homemade bricks behind the storage shed that we used to line our new firepit. We rolled a few larger logs through the clearing to the firepit, where we positioned them in a circle to sit on.

As the sun sank lower, Lucy and I perched on the logs next to the campfire and tried to stay warm. Lucy was still wearing her sundress and I was still in shorts. Our long pants were somewhere in our luggage but we had been too busy helping out to look for them. I pulled the log closer to the fire and leaned forward, trying to convince myself that the hotter my shins were, the more the warmth would travel to the other parts of my legs, which were freezing.

Dad grilled some chicken and vegetables while I held a flashlight for him. I kept thinking I could hear something rustling in the bushes and I stared intently into the darkness, using the flashlight to look for the eyeshine of approaching animals.

"Keena," Dad reminded me, "I need the light; I'm trying to make dinner here." I was excited but nervous. The camp looked nothing like what I expected a camp to be; it was just an island in a strange new place with no people around. It was so dark and so cold. Some of the night sounds were familiar, but most were not. I didn't know what was out there, and though I felt safe in the warm circle of the campfire, it was impossible to forget how far away we were from electric lights, houses, or other people. I traced the path of the smoke curling up from our fire and saw only darkness and stars. Some of the stars I knew, but most I did not. Dad told me that they looked different farther down in the southern hemisphere, and there were some constellations we would see in Botswana that I'd never seen before. *We're so far away that even the sky is different*, I thought.

After dinner, Lucy and I sat quietly while the adults chatted. I remembered from *Little House on the Prairie* that when Laura Ingalls Wilder's family was camping on the high prairie, the little girls were often given the job of washing the dinner dishes in the creek by their cabin. Determined to be helpful and to continue to show my parents and Tico how unfazed I was by our new surroundings, I raised my chin and said, "Mom? Would you like me to go down to the river and wash up the dishes from dinner?" Expecting gratitude and respect for my bravery, I was surprised when the three adults looked at me in complete shock before starting to laugh.

"Dear God, no," Mom said. "Please don't go down to the water at night. You'll be grabbed by a crocodile or attacked by a hippo."

"Oh," I said, face burning. "Okay."

Dad held the flashlight under his chin and grinned at Lucy and me. "After all, you know what they say, don't you, girls?"

I looked at Lucy and we rolled our eyes. Dad had been asking us this question since we were babies.

"The African night is long and dark," we answered in unison. Dad had made up this phrase to make fun of the overly dramatic nature documentaries in the US that made it sound like no matter where you were in Africa you were always THIS CLOSE to being eaten by something when the sun went down. I knew he was just trying to make us laugh, but it didn't seem so funny this time around. This particular African night really was extremely dark.

After the adults finished their beers, they stored our dishes in one of the coolers, locked it against prying animals, and whisked Lucy and me off to our sleeping bags in a little pup tent we'd borrowed from the Longdens. I fell asleep immediately, too tired to even write my first journal entry in Baboon Camp.

In the morning, the rebuilding of the camp began in earnest. While Dad and Tico began ripping apart the old kitchen, Mom turned her attention to the materials we'd brought with us from Maun, including twelve gigantic logs harvested from mopane trees. Mopane trees grow in the drier parts of the delta and since their wood is very hard and difficult for termites to eat, they are the trees of choice for building material. Though already strong, mopane wood still has to be treated to avoid termite attack (and subsequent collapse of the buildings) and this was done by painting the logs with creosote, a compound of tar and plant material that is incredibly sticky and smelly. While Mom brought the logs from the boat and set them lying between two stumps, Lucy and I painted each log with a thick layer of creosote, trying hard not to get it on our clothes, since it would be impossible to remove. It stained our hands orange and made our noses burn, but I was glad to have something to do. "Just make sure to clean yourselves carefully afterward," Mom added as an afterthought, gesturing at a bucket of water she'd hauled from the river. "On the can it says this stuff can cause cancer."

Once the logs were painted, Dad and Tico arranged them in a circle where the kitchen hut used to be and secured them to the ground with cement that we had also brought from Maun. Between each pole they wrapped thick strands of wire and creosote-treated string overlaid with letlhaka, the bamboo-like reed that grew on the sides of the lagoon. When I realized letlhaka were hollow, I grabbed a couple of discarded pieces and tied them together. I wanted to make a pan flute just like Peter Pan's but succeeded only in partially inhaling a fly from one of the pipes before Mom said that creosote was too poisonous to have anywhere near my face. So instead I sat quietly and watched the adults work.

My parents insisted that every opening in the kitchen's walls be covered with chicken wire, in an attempt to keep out the baboons and vervets. In reality, any animal could have easily ripped the walls apart, but like so many things in camp it was the illusion of impenetrability that mattered, or so we told ourselves. In any case, the hope was that the chicken wire would prevent the baboons from discovering that the kitchen contained food and so deprive them of the motivation to rip the walls apart. Once the walls were sufficiently layered with chicken wire and the tin roof covered with thorn branches, Dad and Tico installed a door with a dead bolt and declared the kitchen reconstruction finished. Since the storage hut was largely intact, nothing much was done to improve it. It remained as dark as the previous day, though I found it slightly less ominous now that it had been filled with the tin chests of food, tools, and other miscellaneous items we'd brought with us from Maun. Though we saw no spiders, I knew they were still there. Waiting for me.

My parents didn't want us to sleep in huts like Bill Hamilton had. Huts weren't particularly clean, first of all, and it was easy for insects to live in the walls and for bats and snakes to hide in the ceiling. The one sleeping hut that remained from Bill's time on the island was down a path behind the storage hut and was always full of bats (Lucy and I were sure a vampire also lived there). As an alternative, my parents bought two very large canvas tents from Maun and set these up behind the

Baboon Camp as seen from the lagoon

kitchen under a light-colored tree with heavy, cylindrical fruits hanging from it by thin vines. Tico said it was called a sausage tree and that we should be careful not to stand under the fruits in case they fell and bashed our heads open.

Down the path from the kitchen and storage hut was an open-air shower, also made from letlhaka with a cement floor. Beyond the shower, the path split in two. The right branch led to a large plastic tank that had been suspended in a tree as well as a petrol-fueled water pump at the edge of the river that pumped water up into the tank. The tank gravity-fed the shower and kitchen through a series of underground plastic pipes that appeared largely broken, since many of them were sticking up from the ground like skeletons rising from a cemetery. The left-hand branch of the path led to the interior of the island (also the start of the road to Maun in the dry season) and the latrine, which we called the choo (pronounced like "cho"). *Choo* is Swahili for *toilet*; Mom said using a different word might make it feel fancier than it was. Behind the choo was a laundry area, made up of a sink in the middle of a clearing with wires running between the trees as clotheslines.

This was the extent of camp when it was fully set up. We tried to keep the "buildings" clean, installed small military cots in our tents to sleep on, and built a few bookcases from two-by-fours we found in the woods, also left over from Bill's time. The kitchen was finished with a small stove and deep freeze, both powered by propane and the largest and most expensive of our purchases in Maun. As a last touch of what she jokingly called "needless extravagance," before we left the States, Mom used some of her savings to purchase a solar power system so that we could have electric lights in our tents and the kitchen. Though small, the solar power system provided more than enough power for us to have lights at night and made the kitchen feel vastly cozier than it had with the candles we had been using. After a few days, Tico returned to Maun and my family was left alone.

The more I walked around the camp and learned where everything was, the more comfortable I began to feel. I didn't have everything I wanted, perhaps, but I had everything I needed: food, clean water, a safe place to sleep, and my family. I hadn't seen many animals yet, but I was beginning to get excited. Though the Okavango didn't look at all like Amboseli, many of the underlying pieces were the same, and the more I began to see the similarities, the happier I felt.

The morning after Tico left, Dad got up early and used the new propane stove to make us pancakes. I sat at the kitchen table (a repurposed door discovered in the woods), eating pancakes off a tin plate and rolling the pieces around in my mouth to savor the taste of the small dollop of maple syrup Mom had given me.

"We only have this one jug of maple syrup to last us all year," Mom said. "But today is a special day and the start of a new adventure. On special days, brave little girls get pancakes with syrup." They were delicious, and I was happy. We were really here, and everything, it had turned out, was okay.

While it had quickly become clear that my parents were capable of running the camp by themselves, there was enough to be done that some tasks inevitably had to be outsourced to the kids, just as Mom predicted. Maybe I wasn't able to help Mom fix the AC/DC line leading from the solar panels or work with Dad to replace all the broken water pipes, but I could do our laundry, bake bread, and keep a fire going under the hot water tank so we could have warm showers at the end of the day. I could also follow Mom's instructions to keep an eye out for any animals wandering through, and let the rest of the family know if I saw anything dangerous.

"An elephant is an elephant no matter who sees it," Mom said. "And if you see one, I want to know about it." I was beside myself with excitement when, the day after this pronouncement, I was sitting at the dining table eating toast when I saw my first Botswana elephant, meandering slowly through the molapo far across the lagoon in front of camp.

"ELEPHANT!" I screamed, tossing my toast to the side. "ELEPHANT, ELEPHANT, ELEPHANT!"

Mom and Dad came running from their tent and Lucy from the kitchen where she'd been making a cup of tea. We stood silently for a while, watching the elephant slosh through the molapo, Dad's hand on my shoulder.

"Thanks for the alert," he said. "But that elephant is miles away. Let's only use the shrieking alarm if he's actually *in* camp, okay?"

Lucy giggled.

I watched the elephant reach the tree line and disappear, as silently as he'd appeared a few minutes earlier. *Fine*, I thought. *You stay right over there on your own island, but if you come over here, I'm going to know about it. This is my camp now, and I'm going to know everything that's going on here, spiders and all. Take that, Laura Ingalls Wilder.*

CHAPTER 5

SNAKES AND CAKES

Six months later

LONG BEFORE THE SUN rose over the rain trees behind the solar panels, the francolins began calling. These small birds were always the first to know when sunrise was coming, and in the darkness before the dawn they would crow like roosters, letting the still-sleeping world know that the sun was on its way. Since the francolins inevitably began calling right next to Lucy's and my tent, when they woke up, I did too.

At the first francolin call, my eyes snapped open. I lay completely still for a minute or two, sniffing the air to see if I smelled elephants or buffalo among the scents of dry dust and sage bushes outside the tent. Smelling only the earth and hearing only the birds scratching on the ground, I sat up slowly. Careful not to wake Lucy, I slid out from under the heavy blankets piled on my cot and pulled on shorts, a T-shirt, and my purple Patagonia jacket. I was supposed to wear shoes so I didn't track dirt into the tent, but I rarely followed this rule—I liked to feel the ground under my feet, the way the dust pooled between my toes and puffed up around my ankles. I could always sweep the tent out later if it got dirty. I slowly unzipped the canvas front flap to our tent, feeling each tooth of the zipper slither under my fingers one by one until the opening was just large enough for me to slip through and hop onto the tarp outside. Ignoring my flip-flops, I paused and looked around. Though my nose told me there were no dangerous animals nearby, it was always worth checking again, especially because I couldn't track lions or hyenas by smell as I could with other animals. When Dad was teaching me how to field a baseball, he used to say I had to stop, aim, and then throw. If I didn't take that one second to prepare for the throw, it wasn't going to be a good one. The same was true here; if I didn't stop and take a look around, I would never know what I was running into before it was too late.

My breath smoked from my mouth in the cold air and though I shivered in my shorts, I never wore pants. I knew the day would warm up quickly and I didn't want to waste even a second of my time changing clothes. Finally satisfied that there were no lions or elephants around, I took off down the soft, dusty path toward the kitchen, keeping one eye on the ground for animal tracks. Usually leopards came through camp at night, as well as hippos, impala, kudu, and sometimes lions. If the tracks looked fresh, I stopped and tried to figure out just how fresh they were, since it would tell me whether or not the animals were still close by and how careful I needed to be. Were the lines on the paw print crisp and clean or had they been muted by the wind? Was the grass underneath still bent? Which way had the animals come from and which way were they going? Had the hyenas eaten the soap from the shower again? Had a porcupine chewed up anyone's shoes?

The dust was cold under my feet, and I made no sound as I trotted along. The early morning was my favorite time of day, and the blood hummed through my veins with the anticipation of seeing an animal by myself before anyone else was awake. Approaching the kitchen, I slowed to a walk, peering through the chicken wire and hoping I would see my favorite nighttime animal, the genet cat. Genets are long, thin, and beautifully spotted, with gorgeous black eyes and a long tail that looks like a tiny snow leopard's. They live in trees and eat snakes, so we were glad that one decided to share camp with us. Every night after dinner, we left a few pieces of meat on the kitchen counter for the genet, hoping that keeping her around would encourage her to kill any snakes she might find on her nightly wanderings. Only the genet was small enough to slip through the cracks in the kitchen roof and make it inside. If I was lucky, she'd still be in the kitchen when I got there.

I pulled back the dead bolt on the kitchen door and shut it behind me, proud that I could move in what I believed to be complete silence. I filled two kettles from the water filter and put them on the stove, warming my hands on the heat from the burner and hopping from one bare foot to the other on the chilly cement floor. Outside, the cold air steamed off the lagoon as the sun rose above the trees and the jacana birds trotted across the lily pads, making barely a ripple in the water.

As the kettles began to boil, Dad appeared from his tent, rubbing his hands together and turning up the collar of his polo shirt against the morning cold. Even though the morning was still dim and dusky, he wore his sunglasses, just as ready as I was for the sun to come up and the day to get started.

"Anything interesting going on?" he asked quietly. I shook my head. He poured a cup of coffee from the pot I'd just made and joined me at the main table, where I sat with a cup of tea watching the crocodiles cruise through the misty lagoon and tracing the steam from my tea up into the fig tree where the songbirds were beginning to sing. I wrapped my hands around the warm mug, smelling bergamot and spices and watching the sun slowly creep across the melapo far in the distance.

We heard the sound of a male baboon's display bark (called a wahoo) and Dad cocked his head to the side. These were baboons in Mom and Dad's study group, though I thought of them as my monkeys too.

"What do you think?" Dad said. "Airstrip Island or C15?" Airstrip Island was the largest island in the baboons' home range and at one point in time had an airstrip on it. Most of the other islands in the baboons' home range were numbered. C15 was the closest island to the northwest of Camp Island, just across a deep molapo, with a swimming hole in the middle that we could sometimes splash around in if Mom said it was safe. I hesitated, listening to the birds and the wind and waiting for another wahoo.

"That sounds like Airstrip," I said, after another round of calling.

Dad nodded. "That's what I think too. That's where we left them yesterday, anyway. Makes sense they'd still be there."

The kitchen door creaked open and Mom emerged to get her own cup of coffee.

"The genet was here last night, Keena," she said. "There are little paw prints all over the counter and the chicken is gone."

I smiled. "I know," I said.

The sound of quiet voices interrupted our conversation and from the path to the car park, Mokupi and Mpitsang appeared. The men were brothers from a village about an hour downriver from us, next to a tourist lodge called Xaxaba. Both men were Wayeyi, born on the western side of the delta in a large village called Etsha, where their parents still lived and younger siblings went to school. Though they knew Shiyeyi, they usually spoke to each other in the more common language of Setswana. Mpitsang, the older and much larger of the two, rarely spoke, but Mokupi was an incredibly happy person who started every morning by shaking everyone's hands and smiling brightly. He taught me a bit of Setswana and I made sure to greet him just as enthusiastically as he greeted me. His perpetual good mood was infectious.

Mokupi had worked briefly for Bill Hamilton when he was in Baboon Camp, and was continuing his work with us as my parents' research assistant while studying to get his guide license. We kept Mpitsang on at Bill's recommendation, to help keep the camp in working order by doing things like chopping firewood, clearing reeds from the boat channel, and sweeping the paths with a tree branch to keep them clear of debris.

"Dumêla Mma," Mokupi said, shaking my hand.

"Dumêla rra," I said, and Mokupi laughed. He and Mpitsang began making their breakfast, which consisted solely of a large cup of tea with between six and eight tablespoons of sugar. I sliced bread from the loaves I'd made a day or two before and balanced the pieces on a wire rack suspended over the burners on the stove. If I tended them properly and didn't let them fall into the flames, I could make a passable piece of toast— though the slices never crisped up the way they were supposed to.

Shortly after breakfast, with Lucy still asleep, Mom, Dad, and Mokupi set off to find the baboons and begin their workday, listening to the male baboons' wahoos to guess where they were and whether they were on the move yet. Since my parents' work with baboons was in its very earliest stages, they were still working on collecting a library of every type of call from every individual so they could begin putting them together in different patterns to test the baboons' understanding of their own vocalizations. Mostly this meant following them around hoping they made the right noise so they could capture it on tape.

Mpitsang took the ax and wheelbarrow from the storage shed and headed off into the woods to cut firewood from dead trees. He never strayed far from camp because, though neither he nor my parents ever said anything about it, he considered himself Lucy's and my babysitter and wanted to be nearby in case we needed him.

Once I finished my tea and toast and Lucy had woken up and joined me in the kitchen, we turned our attention to a stack of papers Mom had brought from her tent and left on the kitchen counter. These were our school assignments for the day, which Mom and Dad had written up the afternoon before. Usually there were math problems for each of us, as well as either an essay composition or study questions from a discussion we'd had the day before or from a history book we'd brought with us as a reference guide.

KEENA'S WRITING ASSIGNMENT
NOVEMBER 27, 1992

Q: What was the Spanish Armada and why was it built?

A: *The Spanish Armada was a fleet of ships in 1588. The Spanish king, Philip II, decided to get back at the English for three reasons: one, that the English were Protestants; two, he wanted to take revenge on captains like Sir Francis Drake and Sir Walter Raleigh who had robbed his ships time after time when they were coming back from South America with cargoes of stolen Incan gold; and three, they both claimed the same land in North and South America.*

**Q: Write a one-page essay on the different types of insects and
how to tell them apart.**

A: *How to Tell Insects Apart. Hello my name is Keena and I'm going to
tell you about insects. The first thing you should know is that there
are very many types of insects. You are probably wondering how to
tell spiders apart from bugs. Well I'll tell you. Bugs have six legs
and spiders have eight, also bugs always see things multiplied like
looking through a kaleidoscope and spiders have eyes that see like
human eyes.*

KEENA'S MATH ASSIGNMENT
NOVEMBER 27, 1992

1. Robert, Dan Rawson, and Tico are drinking beers. Robert has three
   more beers than Tico, and if Tico drinks two of his beers he will
   have half the number of beers as Dan. How many beers do each of
   the men have? How many beers would Dorothy need to give them
   to make a complete case of twenty-four beers?
2. Two hippos are running toward each other down the road. The first
   hippo is running at two kilometers per hour and the other hippo is
   running at three kilometers per hour. If the hippos are one kilometer
   apart, how long will it take before they collide?
3. The average house in the United States in 1992 is roughly 2,095
   square feet. Take a tape measure and measure the square footage of
   the buildings and tents in Baboon Camp. Is Baboon Camp bigger
   or smaller than the average house in America?

As Lucy and I worked at the main table, the sun climbed higher in
the sky and the air grew warmer. Squacco herons and hadeda ibis flew
overhead, calling to each other, and hippos heaved themselves out of
the lagoon and onto the shore to lie in the sun and grunt amicably. The

sound of Mpitsang chopping wood echoed through the still woodlands, and the Okavango orioles and Kurrichane thrushes in the fig tree above chirped and sang as they hopped from branch to branch, eating figs and dropping discarded fruit onto our table and into our cups of tea. When I looked up from my problem set, I could see animals slowly moving onto the melapo in the distance to graze: herds of red lechwe, zebras swinging their tails back and forth to keep the flies away, and small groups of giraffes, splashing slowly through the water and bobbing their heads with every step. The sun was warm on my neck and as I worked I swirled my bare feet through the dust under the table, drawing patterns with my toes.

When our schoolwork was finished, I walked back to our tent to retrieve my book from the pile of blankets on my bed and discard my jacket. It was warm enough now that I didn't need it, and fairly hot in the direct sun. Carefully dodging around bush willow trees and jumping over patches of tiny paper thorns, I ran back to the kitchen, the path scorching the bottoms of my feet and making me hop.

I made sure the breakfast dishes were clean and swept out the kitchen, paying particular attention to the areas beneath the counters, which we made from pieces of old mokoro boats, and around the stove where pieces of our toast might have fallen. The kitchen had to be spotless. Messes attracted mice, and mice attracted snakes.

Lucy slapped a textbook shut and rolled her neck to loosen the stiff muscles. She leaned back in her white plastic chair and called out, "Hey, do you want to make a cake?"

I leaned the broom against the doorframe and opened the small fridge.

"Do you think we should?" I asked. "We only have four eggs left until next week's shipment from Maun."

"I only need two for the batter and I don't need any for the icing," Lucy said. "Might as well ask." She grabbed the small Motorola walkie-talkie from the kitchen counter where Mom and Dad left it for us to be able to reach them when they went out with the baboons. It had been silent for hours, which meant that Mom and Dad had found the baboons and were together with Mokupi. On days when they didn't find the baboons, the radio broadcasted constant chatter among the three of them, asking each other where they were and whether they'd heard anything, and maddening responses from Mokupi like, "Robert, I am here by the tree." Lucy held the radio up to her mouth.

"Dad, do you hear me?" We waited, but heard nothing but static. "Daddy, this is Lucy. Do you hear me?" Still nothing.

"We might need to get higher," I said. "Maybe they're farther away."

Lucy locked the kitchen door and the two of us walked out beyond the choo, where the car was parked under the shade of two leadwood trees, confined to Camp Island due to the flood. Lucy scrambled up the hood of the car, holding the radio antenna between her teeth. I took a deep breath and looked around. The air smelled different in the car park, probably because the bushes were a different species farther away from the water. I smelled mopane trees and more concentrated sagebrush, as well as ash from a fever-berry tree that had been hit by lightning the year before. Peering between the swaying bushes, I saw a herd of impala grazing in the woods to our right and three giraffes gliding slowly across the plain in the center of the island. Everything was calm and still, the cloudless sky a clear blue.

Lucy stood up gingerly on the roof of the car and lifted the radio.

"Dad, this is Lucy; do you hear me?" The radio crackled.

"Hello! We hear you loud and clear. But you're not calling properly."

Lucy looked down at me and rolled her eyes. I kicked my bare toes against the car tire and smiled.

"Okay, fine," Lucy said. "Base to Baboon One, do you read?"

"Baboon One to Base, reading you loud and clear, over," Dad replied.

"Can we use two eggs for a cake?"

"Try again, Lucy."

"Base to Baboon One, can we use two eggs for a cake please OVER."

"How many do we have left?"

"Keena says four."

"You girls know that means no eggs for Sunday breakfast then, right?"

"We know."

"Then go right ahead."

"Okay, we will. Thanks. Base out."

Lucy clambered down from the car and we set off back into camp, each walking in one of the tracks in the dirt road and picking paper thorns from our heels.

Mpitsang emerged from the woods behind the laundry area with his wheelbarrow of firewood.

"Keena," he said, "there is a snake in the laundry sink. I am getting the rake."

Lucy and I drew up short next to the shower. "What kind of snake?" I asked.

He shrugged. "I did not see. But the birds are upset."

I cocked my head to the side and immediately heard a chorus of harsh bird alarm calls from the laundry area, mostly arrow-marked babblers—the undisputed queens of snake detecting. Babblers moved about in family groups, grumbling to each other and foraging through the under-growth for seeds and insects. If there was a snake around, they were the first to find it. They would jump around the snake, screaming at it with their feathers puffed up until one of them built up the courage to dart at the snake, trying to peck its eyes out.

"Do you need help?" I asked. "Do you want the gun?" Again, he shrugged. Mpitsang never needed the gun, but I always offered it to him anyway, just so I could say that I did before taking it myself. Lucy said she was going back to the kitchen to get started on the cake but I followed Mpitsang to the storage hut, where he brought out an orange metal rake and a machete. I opened my parents' tin trunk and unwrapped their air rifle and a box of lead bullets. Since we lived in a game reserve we weren't allowed to have a real gun, but Mom and Dad said an air rifle was more than adequate for killing snakes. Technically, they said, we shouldn't kill anything in the park, but snakes are territorial and we couldn't have them living in camp, especially the black mambas. Black mambas are fast and aggressive and have a neurotoxic venom that can shut down a person's entire central nervous system in thirty minutes. When I offered it to him, though, Mpitsang shook his head with a smile. "You don't need a gun to kill a snake, Keena." He may have been right, but I wanted to participate anyway.

I braced the stock of the rifle between my feet and pulled back hard on the barrel to cock it. It had taken a lot of practice to learn how to use the gun since it was quite heavy and I was too small to manage it with my eight-year-old arms alone, but once I'd figured out how to brace it, I found it much easier. I often built pyramids of beer cans around camp and crawled through the bushes with the gun hung sniper-style across my back to assassinate the cans one by one for practice, always careful not to fire toward the kitchen. Mom hated that.

"Just promise not to hit a gas cylinder with the gun, please," she said. "The whole place will explode."

With the loaded rifle in my hands, I followed Mpitsang out to the laundry area. The babblers were hopping all around the faded pink

Snake-shooting practice never requires a shirt.

plastic sink, screaming and cackling and lunging at the sink from their perch on the soap dish just to the side.

"It needs to leave the sink," Mpitsang said. "I will kill it on the ground." I nodded. Mpitsang crept closer to the sink, the rake in one hand and the machete in the other. The babblers made room for him but kept up their relentless attack at whatever was in the sink.

"Can I shoot it?" I asked.

"If you want to," he said, smiling. "Here, let me give you a shot."

Mpitsang waited a minute or two and then reached out with the blade of the machete and slapped it hard against the bowl of the sink. There was an immediate explosion of calls from the babblers and a narrow, black head reared out of the sink. Mpitsang took an involuntary step back and gestured with his machete. This was no tree snake or harmless grass snake. This was a mamba. Even from where I was standing, I could see its distinctive coloring and eerily curved mouth. Shaking slightly, I closed my left eye and peered through the sight at the end of the gun barrel. I waited until the babblers were out of the way, took a slow, deep breath, and fired.

The body of the snake slammed against the side of the sink and Mpitsang quickly reached over and looped the blade of the machete under the snake. With a flick of his wrist he flipped the snake out of the sink and onto the ground, where it writhed in a heap as the babblers screamed and screamed on the soap dish. Mpitsang dropped the machete, gripped the rake with both hands, and beat the snake with the blade of the rake until it stopped moving.

The babblers quieted and I approached slowly, the gun still in my arms.

"Is it dead?" I whispered. Mpitsang nodded. He poked the snake with the rake to make sure and then flicked it into the woods behind the laundry area. He looked down at me.

"Breakfast for the fish eagle," he said.

"Did I hit it?"

Mpitsang smiled. "Not in the head. You hit it here." He pointed to his stomach. I frowned. I clearly needed more practice if I was going to be as good as my mother. She never missed the head.

The baboon watchers came back around 1:30 p.m., hot, sunburned, and exhausted. Their legs were torn and bleeding from walking through thornbushes and their feet were covered with layers of grime from walking through water, sand, and water again as they passed from island to island following the baboons. Dad took off his Red Sox hat and pushed the sweaty hair off his forehead.

"How was the day, girls? Everything okay?"

"Mpitsang killed a snake in the laundry area," I said. "And Lucy baked a cake."

"Fantastic!" he said. "Cake is exactly what I need right now."

"None for me please, Lucy," said Mom, peeling off her sandals and examining where the sandy straps had rubbed her feet raw underneath. "What I'd really like is some water. I'll save my cake for teatime if that's all right with you." Lucy nodded.

When Mokupi and Mpitsang went home after lunch, we completed various projects around camp until dinnertime. Sometimes there were things we had to do, like bake bread if we had run out, collect kindling for the evening fire, or clean and fill the water filters we used to purify the water from the river, but if our chores were done, Lucy and I were on our own. We explored the woods around camp, staged elaborate plays with our stuffed animals, and played endless card games of Spit and War in the kitchen. But most often, we read. Usually, around midafternoon, Dad would come find me wherever I was reading and hand me a frozen chicken in a plastic bowl.

"Guard this while you read," he would say. "It needs to defrost for dinner and I can't leave it alone because Dougie is around." Dougie was the old baboon who had left the group and decided to live in camp with us. We hadn't known about him until one day he grabbed a frozen chicken from where it was thawing on the solar panels and ate it in the shower. We only figured out what happened when we saw baboon tracks going into the shower and the chicken carnage on the inside, splattered all over our bottles of Pantene. Since then, no chicken defrosted without a guard.

When the sun passed over the top of the fig tree, I knew it was around 4:00 p.m., and I took a break from reading to light the fire under the hot water tank. We had a small barrel called a donkey boiler that heated up the water for our showers. It was gravity-fed from the water tank just like in the kitchen, but needed fire for the water to heat up. Every afternoon, I shoveled out the ashes from the fire the day before and built a new one using kindling from the wood and log piles Mpitsang collected. Once I got it going, I tended the fire while I read. Sometimes a gust of wind would stir up the fire and send ashes blowing all over me and my book. (This is why there are charcoal smears across page 47 of my copy of *Little Women*.)

I always took the first shower so that I had enough time to build the campfire for dinner. As my family trickled back to the kitchen in their evening clothes of pants and fleece jackets since it was getting cold again, we chatted about our day and helped cook—chopping vegetables, slicing bread, or escorting Dad with a flashlight while he carried chicken back and forth to the campfire down by the water. As the sun sank lower over the melapo, gigantic beetles cruised through the trees buzzing loudly, flocks of birds flew home to roost calling out to each other between the islands, and impala crept closer into camp, knowing that the smell of humans helped keep the lions away—most of the time.

Finally, we brushed our teeth in the kitchen sink and walked back through the darkness to our tents, flashlights bobbing through the bushes looking for eyeshine and headlamps tilted toward the path in front of us in case something came scuttling by. We sang at the top of our voices to keep the lions away—usually Christmas carols or the songs about Irish highwaymen and pirates that Mom taught us when we were small. I slid back into my cot and piled the blankets on top of me, my breath again rising in small clouds in the cold of the night. Every night Lucy and I argued over whose turn it was to climb out of our warm nests to turn off the light bulb overhead and every night I gave in, telling myself that I was older and it was my responsibility to take care of the things neither of us wanted to do. I hopped out from under the covers to turn off the light, flooding the tent and my bed in moonlight and the sounds of the night.

CHAPTER 6

STRANDED IN XAMASHURO

WHEN WE WERE FIRST preparing to go to Baboon Camp, my parents worried that Lucy and I might be bored. Not that living among the wild animals of the Okavango was in any way dull, but since Lucy and I weren't allowed to leave camp by ourselves and the camp smelled like humans, the animals stayed mostly to the outskirts. Though they passed by in the woods behind camp in the melapo to the north, often three or four days would go by without animals actually coming into camp. And without the stimulation of other children and organized activities, my parents thought we might become restless and unhappy.

We did not share their worry. Lucy fell immediately into a comfortable routine in Baboon Camp. She baked, she played with her stuffed animals, and though she never really let down her guard while in camp, she didn't seem to view the world beyond the borders of camp with the same trepidation and excitement that I did. I burned to know what was going on out there, on the islands and plains I could see from camp but couldn't reach. Every time an elephant passed through the woods, I willed him to stray just a bit closer, even just a tree or two, where I could get a better look at him, smell him, and listen to him snap branches and huff to himself as he ate, even if it was just a bit dangerous. Mom and Dad said it was stupid to wish for more danger when living in camp was dangerous enough, and I knew they were right, but I didn't care. While they and Lucy seemed content to let camp be camp and the wilderness be the wilderness, I wanted more. I was restless and unsettled, the peace and silence of camp doing nothing to calm me but instead reminding me that even though I was outside I still felt like I was inside.

Once, when we visited my grandmother in Chicago before we left for Botswana, a friend of hers said to Lucy, "You look like your father and have your mother's mannerisms," and to me, "You look like your mother and have your father's mannerisms."

To an extent, the woman was correct. Just like Dad, Lucy had grown into a gorgeous little blonde-haired, blue-eyed girl who could have inhabited the same Norman Rockwell painting as my father. But just like Mom, she had a buffalo glare that could stop me in my tracks and razor-sharp intelligence that was astonishing at times, even a little intimidating to people who weren't expecting it from such a small child.

But I thought the woman was wrong about me. I knew I looked a lot like Mom, so that wasn't news to me. When I looked in the mirror in the shower, I saw the same thick, dark hair and crooked grin that curved higher on the right, but that was where the physical similarities stopped. Mom was thin where I was stocky, elegant while I was clumsy, and had a sense of poise about her, even standing in a field surrounded by monkeys, that I wasn't able to emulate. I didn't think the woman was right about my father's mannerisms either—Dad was easygoing and relaxed, the kind of person who worked hard and had a good sense of humor and said things like "I've had an elegant sufficiency" instead of "I'm full." Dad didn't bubble with unease and restlessness under the surface, never wanted to scream and shout and run and run and run toward the sunset until his lungs burned and his legs collapsed.

"You know what it is?" Mom said one day. We were sitting in my tent on a hot afternoon and she was giving me a lecture on genetic variation. The seasons had begun changing, and as winter moved into summer, and though the mornings were still cool, by midday the temperature was easily in the mid-90s. Sweat dripped down the back of my T-shirt and my head buzzed from the heat, making me woozy and disoriented. I was tired of drawing grids about peas, and though Mom tried to engage me by talking about dominant and recessive characteristics using our family as an example, the only lesson I was learning was how different I was from the rest of my family. Mom put her hands on either side of my face and gazed at me thoughtfully. "It's your eyes," she said. "I've never seen eyes quite like them, and they certainly don't look like mine."

"They look like mud," I said petulantly.

She laughed. "No, not like mud! Let me see again." She was quiet for a while, just sitting and staring at me. I squirmed. The tent was too hot, and I was uncomfortable being stared at that closely. "Your eyes change color," she said finally. "Sometimes they're dark brown, sometimes hazel, and sometimes green with little gold flecks in them. Just like a cat."

"I have cat eyes?" I said.

"Yes," she said. "You really do."

I was glad my eyes were multicolored, and gladder still that even an evolutionary biologist like my mom couldn't explain why. I wanted to look different on the outside, because it might explain why I was beginning to feel so different on the inside.

I loved Baboon Camp. I loved the sounds of the birds, the dust beneath my feet, and the buzzing, electric sense of excitement that anything could happen at any time. I didn't want to know what my next week, day, or hour looked like; I wanted to feel all the time like I felt when I prowled around the outside edges of camp, like a coiled spring ready to jump at whatever terrifying or amazing thing the world threw my way next. I didn't particularly care whether it was an elephant at my tent or a pride of lions by the choo, I just wanted the opportunity to experience it. Dad used to say I was like a puppy that needed to be exercised every few hours or I'd start ripping apart the furniture, and he was right; I wanted to run, to jump, to find something dangerous and put myself right in front of it to see what I would do, how I would measure up, and if I could survive. I wanted lions to walk through camp, elephants to rip up the trees next to my tent, hippos to surface next to the boat and send my system into an overdrive of electric adrenaline that would leave me dizzy and panting with relief. I wanted Baboon Camp to be scarier than it was, but knew that it was foolish to wish for such a thing when it meant my family and I would be less safe. Confused and in a near-permanent state of alertness, I explored as far from camp as I was able to go by myself, and decided not to tell my parents what I was feeling. I knew they wouldn't understand.

Fortunately, I never needed to have this conversation with my parents because I could have it with the characters in my books. I knew these characters almost as well as I knew my family, and was sure they felt the same sense of restless anticipation that I did. Before we left for Botswana, Dad had gone to Barnes & Noble and said to one of the booksellers, "I need books about strong girls, dragons, and adventure, and the longer the better because my daughter already reads too fast." In a stroke of good luck for me, the bookseller Dad spoke to was a science fiction and fantasy enthusiast who led him straight to my second-favorite place in America after the farmers market: the science fiction/fantasy section in the bookstore.

Every afternoon in Baboon Camp, after Mpitsang and Mokupi had gone home and it was still too early to start the shower fire, I read. There were three trees I liked to read in, all within shouting distance of the kitchen in case someone was looking for me, and all rigged with rudimentary pulley systems so I could haul my book, water bottle, and the frozen chicken up to my reading spot once I'd climbed up. Though I read anything I could find in Maun (including a number of unbelievably filthy British romances we borrowed from the Longdens before Mom realized what they were about), I spent most of my time reading and rereading my fantasy books.

Through the Dragonlance series, I met the elf princess Laurana Kanan, who sacked castles, killed an evil dragon lord, and became the commander of a race of knights who, until her, had only been led by men. Through the Dragonriders of Pern, I met Lessa, who, as the sole descendant of a family killed by a ruthless dictator, recovered her family's throne, became bonded to a gold dragon, and went back in time two hundred years to gather a dragon army to save her planet. And through the Swallows and Amazons series, I met Captain Nancy Blackett.

Though Swallows and Amazons isn't a fantasy series, it was the first series I completed entirely on my own. Swallows and Amazons is about a group of British children who sailed around the lakes in the north of England and went on fantastic adventures, usually led by the eldest girl and captain of the boat *Amazon*, Nancy Blackett. Captain Nancy (she would be angry if I didn't include her title) was a tomboy, completely self-reliant, and independent, with a limitless imagination that turned fellow vacationers on the lake into pirates, caves in the countryside into bandit gold mines, and the hill above her family's house into the Himalayan mountain Kanchenjunga. The other children regarded Captain Nancy as their undisputed leader, and throughout their adventures looked to her for guidance and reassurance as well as a well-placed "Shiver me timbers!" if someone stepped out of line.

Captain Nancy was twelve in the first book, almost three years older than I was at the time. I fell in love with her immediately, when her first action upon meeting the other children was to fire a green-feathered arrow into their campsite and demand ransom for their youngest brother, whom she'd kidnapped and was sailing around with in her boat while she waited for her demands to be met. Though Captain Nancy was often the main character in the stories, it irritated me that she was never thoroughly described. I knew she was tall and had brown hair and wore a red hat when she was sailing, but I wanted more. Where did she get her imagination? What did she do when she was frustrated and felt trapped? Was she anything like me?

Captain Nancy, Laurana, and Lessa were my best friends. They were bold and unapologetic in their strength, role models before I knew to want such a thing. As I sat high in my marula tree, gazing across the melapo and thinking wild thoughts about elves, pirates, and dragons, I wished with my whole heart that I could live in a world like theirs, where I had a shiny sword and a bow and arrow and could go out and fight the monsters roaming the wilderness around me.

"I wish dragons were real," I said to Dad one evening as he tucked me into my cot and arranged the pile of blankets at the foot of my bed. Even the nights were hot now, and blankets were almost unnecessary as the temperature rarely dipped below eighty degrees. I kicked my feet free, needing to feel the cool night air on my skin. Dad looked down at me, his arms crossed across his chest.

"It would make the world a much more interesting place, that's for sure," he said. "But let me ask you something: Why do you need dragons when you have lions and elephants?" He didn't wait for a response, but kissed Lucy good night and zipped our tent closed behind him before clicking on his flashlight and walking through the darkness toward the glow from Mom's reading light in their tent.

I stared out the mesh window next to my cot. Dad was right. My heroines may live in worlds awash with mystical monsters where girls carried swords, but I supposed I did too, if I looked at it a little differently. My monsters were snakes and hippos, and even if I didn't have a sword, I did have a sharp pocketknife and an air gun, and really that was just as good when it came to adventuring. I wanted more out of Baboon Camp, and maybe my heroines were just the answer I needed—they didn't wait for adventure to come to them, they went out and found it themselves. Maybe I needed to do the same.

A soft gust of wind blew through the tent, causing the canvas walls to snap against the metal frame outside and sending a cloud of dust over my cot. I pulled the sheet up to my neck and grinned into the darkness as a hyena whooped in the distance. I wasn't waiting anymore; it was the beginning of a new day for Captain Keena, shiverer of timbers, Pirate Queen of the Okavango Delta.

By the beginning of September, the water in the melapo was starting to recede. The nights grew warmer, the days grew hotter, and the animals migrated closer to the river as water holes across the islands began to dry up. We packed our jackets away for the year and struggled to drink our tea, as the sun rose earlier and hotter with every passing day, the temperature already in the eighties by 7 a.m. By 10 a.m., it was in the high nineties, and by noon, usually above one hundred. Lucy and I began taking a second shower before bedtime, since we couldn't fall asleep unless our hair and pajamas were soaked in cold water.

Mpitsang had been busy clearing an area beneath some palm trees behind the water tank because another family was coming to join us in Baboon Camp for a few months. A colleague of my parents' from UC Davis, Joan Silk, was bringing her family to Botswana to work with my parents on a study they'd been collaborating on regarding baboon social relationships. I didn't know anything about Joan except that she was a small lady and brave, since she had worked with Jane Goodall for a while and wasn't afraid of chimpanzees.

Joan and her husband, Rob, were bringing their son, Sam, with them as well, who was six years old, just like Lucy. Lucy was excited to have another kid in camp, but I was skeptical. Captain Keena, Pirate Queen of the Delta, didn't tolerate intruders in her realm, and I prepared my imaginary animal armies to repel the invaders if they decided not to like Baboon Camp. But as it turned out, they were very nice, though I found Sam a bit sensitive when it came to the more unpleasant parts of living in Baboon Camp.

OCTOBER 29, 1992
KEENA'S JOURNAL

Today we had a scorpion experience. Joan and Sam were in their tent after Sam had a shower when Sam yelled, "Mom, Mom, something's biting me! Ahhhhhhh!" Then Joan said, "Oh, don't be silly, watch this." She put her hand down his shirt. "You're right! Ahhhhhhh!" she yelled. She pulled her hand out with a scorpion's stinger still stuck in it. She flung it on the tarpaulin outside and beat it with a metal tent peg until it was dead as a doornail. I went running over when I heard Sam screaming.

"What is it?" I yelled.

"A scorpion," said Rob. Sam cried for ten minutes. Then we went to dinner.

Joan and Rob fully embraced my parents' style of homeschooling and began leaving assignments for Sam in the same pile as Lucy's and mine. Though I felt the camp was noisier with three more people around, having more hands to help with the daily chores meant that we had more free time, which I had to admit I appreciated because I could spend more time reading.

By the end of October the water in the melapo was low enough to take the car off the island, so if Lucy, Sam, and I had behaved ourselves and could prove that we'd each done our homework and had a glass of the milk we got in our weekly grocery shipments ("for vitamins," Mom said), we were rewarded with a game drive in the afternoon. The drying floodplains drove the animals onto the islands closest to the river; the high concentration of animals on our island made these game drives a lot more exciting than our boat rides, and often meant that we got to see giant herds of animals moving along together like we used to in Amboseli. Dad said that the animals joined up in big herds when they needed protection against lions, which, according to my *Wildlife Fact-File*, is also one of the theories about why zebras developed their stripes—so that it would be harder for lions to pick out individuals when they were all running together.

One afternoon around Thanksgiving when it was easily 110 degrees in the sun, Joan and Rob took us three kids on a school game drive to Xamashuro looking for animals. Xamashuro was a spot about ten kilometers from camp down the main track to Maun, in the middle of a floodplain that had a deep channel running through it that we guessed was an offshoot from the main river. The determination of whether or not it was possible to drive to Maun was dependent on Xamashuro and whether it could be forded, and testing this always involved sending a child across before the car to see how deep it was. The tester child

Baboon Camp elementary school picture with Lucy and Sam

would wade across Xamashuro and then come back to stand next to the truck so the adults could see how the water level on our shorts matched up with the wheels.

On this particular day, Lucy, Sam, and I were tallying animals as part of Joan's school assignment. This was partly an exercise in averages (on average, how many zebras are on a molapo?) and partly about teaching us how to do a census so we could eventually help with the baboons if needed. The most memorable moment on the trip out to Xamashuro was when we asked Lucy what animal she was looking for, and she said, "I will count wild dogs!" We all responded with variations of, "Yeah right, Lucy; we never see them," only to round the corner and come upon a pack of forty-eight. Lucy smirked and clicked her pen, counting each tally mark aloud until she reached forty-eight. It was unbelievably hot, and the truck lurched along the sandy tracks, swaying from side to side and causing us to bump our heads against the doorframes at the back of the cab.

The road to Xamashuro involved going through a very sandy island that we called Elephant Sands, because we kids liked naming things. There was a way to navigate through the sand if you stuck to more solid ground, but it required lining the car up with a particular third tree to the right of another tree on the horizon that almost no one was able to do with any accuracy. Plus, a few days prior to this trip, an elephant at Elephant Sands had knocked the tree over, so there really was no way to find the right path. We had made it through Elephant Sands successfully on the drive out, but on the way back we got stuck.

We didn't have a radio so we couldn't let my parents know what had happened to us. We just had to hope we made it back to camp before it got dark, since we didn't have flashlights with us either, and we already knew from our exercise in averages that there were lions on Camp Island. Joan said my parents would probably guess that we'd gotten stuck and come looking for us, but there was no way of knowing.

There was an unofficial camp rule that whenever anyone went on a game drive they took at least two large water bottles with them, so we did have water, at least. But we also faced a ten-kilometer walk back to camp with three small children in flip-flops, one of whom (Lucy) was also wearing a sundress. We had a rough idea of the animal activity between the stranded car and camp thanks to our school assignment, but we also knew that in addition to the lions on Camp Island there were approximately two hundred buffalo on the molapo closest to it, and that the road ran right down the middle of where they would be grazing.

Even as I tried to remain calm for the sake of Lucy and Sam, I knew what a serious situation we were in—yet I was young enough, too, that the fear was leavened with a kind of thrill. Captain Keena, Pirate Queen of the Okavango Delta, was finally going on a real-life adventure. I grinned as Joan and Rob unloaded the car and eagerly offered to carry the water bottles. I was going to handle this situation better than any situation had ever been handled and no animal was going to get the best of me. We headed off down the road, stumbling behind Joan and Rob in the deep sand, the sun burning the skin on the back of my neck.

For the first three hours the walk was fine, though paralyzingly hot; Joan and Rob kept a sharp lookout for animals, and Lucy, Sam, and I waded dutifully through the sand in the tire tracks next to them, though it was hard going on short legs. We had half a sleeve of gingersnap cookies to share among us, and every time we crossed a molapo and reached another island closer to camp, Joan carefully doled out half a gingersnap to each of us as a reward. The skin on the back of my neck blistered and began to peel, and though I didn't want to admit it, I was enjoying myself immensely. As I said in my journal, "the heat, the dust, and the thirst made life almost unbearable, but I was full of energy." I didn't say anything out loud though, as Joan and Rob seemed to be taking the situation very seriously and I wanted to look like I was doing the same.

We'd been walking for almost four hours when we approached the last large molapo before Camp Island and, as we expected, found it full of buffalo. We crouched in the woods on the island on our side of the molapo and listened to the buffalo snort and grumble. Buffalo have a very distinct smell, kind of earthy and rich but with an undertone of cow poop, and it surrounded us like a cloud as we watched them through the trees and Joan and Rob quietly discussed what we were going to do.

Though buffalo usually travel in extremely large herds, these herds are often accompanied by lone-bull buffalo that skulk on the fringes of the herd, trying to gain access to the breeding females in the middle. Usually these males are old and partially deaf, which makes them especially good prey for lions (and the reason why lions follow herds of buffalo) but also very dangerous to anyone attempting to skirt around one of these herds on foot, since buffalo, more than any other animal, are likely to charge just because they feel like it. Joan was going to scout the woodland ahead, but when several bulls emerged from the trees in front of us, she insisted that we wait for her in a tree, where no buffalo could reach us even if they did charge. Sam, Lucy, and I found a good tree and clambered up, stabbing our flip-flops into the grooves in the bark to gain traction. Rob followed, and passed us the last of the water to share among us.

We didn't have to stay up there for more than a few minutes, but it was exhilarating being so close to so many buffalo, without the protection of a car in between. We could hear them mooing and crashing around in the woods as they moved closer, and the smell got stronger and stronger. Buffalo aren't the subtlest of animals. Joan soon returned from the opposite direction of the buffalo to say she'd found a safe route around the herd, and off we went, keeping our heads below the level of the grass and ready to jump up into the trees again if one of them charged. Mom always used to say you should never be out of range of a good climbing tree.

Sunburned, thirsty, and exhausted, we were just entering Camp Island, five hours after we'd set off on our game drive, when we ran into my parents, headed out to look for us with backpacks of rescue supplies consisting mostly of soda and chocolate.

"What an adventure!" Mom said as she sat with me and Lucy in our tent after I took a long shower. "You must have been terrified, going around all the buffalo."

I squirted aloe gel into my hand and smeared it over the back of my neck, clenching my teeth against the sting and determined not to show how much it hurt.

"I wasn't afraid," I said. "Everyone is home safe and we didn't do anything stupid. In fact, it was wonderful." Mom laughed but crinkled her forehead as if she didn't quite believe me.

CHAPTER 7

ONE HUNDRED CASES OF BEER AND A MAN-EATING CROCODILE

MANY MONTHS LATER, I was sitting at the kitchen table sipping my morning tea and reading *The Mists of Avalon* when I heard the low hum of a boat engine against the backdrop of early morning birdsong. This was unusual. Generally, the only boats that came by on weekdays were occasional tour boats from Xaxaba, the lodge far downriver, but those boats usually set out later in the morning when it was slightly warmer and the tourists were less likely to complain about the cold. (That always annoyed me because everyone knew dawn was the best time to see interesting animals—who cared if it was cold enough to freeze your water bottles?)

This engine sounded too choppy to be a Xaxaba boat though; Xaxaba's boat engines were expensive and ran quietly. So at this time of day and in this part of the delta, there was really only one other boat it could be.

As I expected, a large, flat-bottomed boat swung into the lagoon, scattering egrets and sending the redheaded jacanas scuttling across the lily pads on their long, spidery legs. I hopped off my white plastic chair and jogged down the path to my parents' tent, where they were getting their gear ready to go out with the baboons.

"Dad? Someone from Delta Camp is here," I called.

"Oh? Huh. Okay." Dad put down his recording equipment and followed me back to the kitchen, where Lucy was talking to Binky, the blonde South African manager of Delta Camp, a lodge more than two hours downriver and, aside from Xaxaba and its staff village, the only human settlement between us and Maun. I liked Binky. She sometimes stopped by on the weekends to tell us stories about her tourists, like the time when a baboon had stolen a kilo bag of sugar and sat in a tree above their dinner table eating sugar and sprinkling it down on the dinner guests like snow. But I knew that Binky wouldn't be visiting on a weekday morning just to tell stories.

"Robert. Howzit? We need your help." Binky explained that Delta Camp was due to receive a group of twenty guests that afternoon, executives from a beer company in South Africa. The company was sending them to Delta Camp for a corporate retreat that included a lecture from one of the guides about how termites cooperate to build termite mounds, the intention being, I supposed, that the executives learn to cooperate like termites. The executives, however, were less interested in team-building exercises and more interested in taking a vacation. Before their arrival, they called ahead to Delta's corporate offices in Maun to request that each executive be provided four six-packs of beer per person, per day, which Binky was determined to provide.

Dad's eyes went wide, and I tuned out of the conversation to do some quick math in my head. Twenty executives are staying at Delta Camp for five days. Each case of beer holds four six-packs, so that's twenty executives times five days which equals one hundred cases of beer...

This is where the problem began. Delta Camp had an airstrip and one plane, a six-seater that they used exclusively to take tourists back and forth to Maun. It would be impossible to get that quantity of beer up to Delta Camp on such short notice on their tiny plane; they wouldn't be able to take it out of rotation for that long because they had other guests to pick up, and even simply bringing the beer to the lodge would take several trips. So Binky had hired the Leopard-Spotted Lorry to bring up the beer from Maun instead.

The Leopard-Spotted Lorry was a gigantic truck painted army green with bright yellow spots, which was hired out by tourism companies for exactly this sort of purpose. When the road was passable and a lodge needed to bring up really heavy loads of cargo (or something flammable that couldn't be flown), it was the best way to transport it. However, the roads were tricky this time of year, as the floodplains had just begun to dry up and it was anyone's guess what state the tracks would be in after months of being underwater.

Nevertheless, a Delta Camp employee named Desmond had loaded up the beer in Maun the day before and set off in the Leopard-Spotted Lorry. But he had never shown up at Delta. When Desmond didn't arrive as expected, Binky radioed to town and confirmed that he had left Maun and must have disappeared somewhere on the road. At the time, she didn't know if the truck had broken down or gotten stuck, or if something worse may have happened and Desmond was hurt. The only way to look for him was to find a pilot willing to fly low over the road to Maun, trying to locate the Leopard-Spotted Lorry and hopefully drop Desmond a radio so he could communicate with Binky.

So Binky called Henny, a freelance bush pilot who lived in Maun and the only man for this job. Henny liked to fly as low as possible over the melapo, skimming the reeds with his windows open, tormenting the elephants and sending giraffes fleeing into the woods. He'd seen us fishing on the river once and skimmed so low over the boat that he sent my hat flying into the water.

Even before Binky came to visit us, Henny had been dispatched from Maun with a radio secured in Bubble Wrap, and he had soon found Desmond with the truck, stuck deep, deep in the mud between the islands a few kilometers away—not an unexpected or uncommon situation that early in the driving season. He was fine (aside from being out of cigarettes), but now they needed help getting the beer to Delta Camp before the executives arrived.

This was what brought Binky to Baboon Camp. The Leopard-Spotted Lorry and its one hundred cases of beer were on our side of the river, and Delta and Xaxaba were located on the other side. Their trucks couldn't reach Desmond from the opposite shore, so she needed our help to ferry the beer from the Lorry to a spot near Delta Camp, where an army of staff would use mokoros to transport the beer in batches across the river and to the lodge before the executives arrived that afternoon. It astonished me the lengths to which they would go just for some cases of beer, but if it was important to them, it was important to us; living as far away from civilization as we did, we all had to help each other when there was a crisis. My parents quickly agreed to help the cause.

Baboons and work abandoned for the day, Dad set off with Binky in our car to find Desmond. Binky left us with her radio so we could respond if anyone called from Delta Camp with an update, since she and Dad were driving farther away from the river and would be out of its range. After they drove off, Mom, Lucy, and I sat around the radio at the kitchen table, listening to the corporate office talk to Delta Camp and to Desmond, who was swearing colorfully as he tried to dig out the truck.

After an hour or so, I started to get bored of listening to the disembodied voices yell at each other and was thinking of returning to *The Mists of Avalon* when the radio crackled again: "Baboon Camp, Baboon Camp, do you read?" I knew the voice well; it belonged to Bob, Binky's assistant manager, an absolutely massive man from Zimbabwe and one of the kindest people I'd ever met. Mom had walked away to work in the laundry area, so I answered on our behalf as I ran the radio out to her.

"Baboon Camp is here!" I called back, hoping I sounded important.

"Hiya, is this Keena or Lucy?"

"This is Keena," I replied, slightly offended. How could he not know it was me from the sophistication of my voice? My voice was older.

"Ah, Keena, is your mother still in camp?"

"Yes, she's here, but my Dad went off with Binky to get your beer," I said, reaching the laundry area and handing the radio to Mom.

"Bob, what's going on?" Mom said.

"Dorothy, hey. Now two of our guides are sick. We need to fetch two replacements from the staff village at Xaxaba to take our guests out this afternoon, but we can't get them ourselves because our boat is up with you. So, we need one more favor. Any chance you can swing down to the village and fetch the guides for us?"

"Sure, no problem," Mom said. "We'll be down shortly." She balanced the radio on the side of the sink and wiped her hands on her shorts before looking at me. "Now our problem is figuring out how we're going to get both boats down to Delta Camp."

"Both boats?" I asked.

"Well yes, both boats. Otherwise how are we going to get home?"

"Oh. But Dad is out with Binky so who's going to drive our boat?"

Mom looked down at me and smiled. "Think you're up for it?"

This was huge. I had driven the boat before, but always with an adult, and I'd certainly never taken the boat so far on one trip. Delta Camp was almost two hours down the river.

Though it was getting on to lunchtime and the sun was high in the sky, I shivered as I waited in the boat for Lucy, who insisted on coming with me and not Mom, out of support, I hoped, for my mission. Mom said we couldn't leave my seven-year-old sister in camp by herself and Lucy said there was no way she was getting left behind while we went on an adventure anyway; she just needed a minute to get a stuffed animal. She came running back from our tent with her pink pig named Soogie tucked under her arm.

"You go first," Mom called from Delta's boat. "I'll follow you down to Xaxaba and then you can go on to Delta Camp. I'll stop by the staff village for the guys and meet you down there, okay?"

"Okay," I called. "I'll see you at Delta."

"You're all right?"

"I'm fine. I'll...see you in a little bit." I paused to take a deep lungful of air, then dropped the engine into the water. I checked to make sure the gas line was clear and the engine wasn't flooded, and pulled the rip cord. The engine roared to life, sending a cloud of smoke over Lucy and me. I sat down, shifted into forward, and flew out of the lagoon, turning left down the river toward Xaxaba. It was a beautiful day, clear and cool like most winter days in Botswana. I would have been warmer with a

Sometimes pirates need outboard motors.

jacket, but liked the way the wind ripped through my T-shirt and made it flutter across my chest.

The first part of the river was easy and familiar, with wide-open stretches of clear water—dark, deep, and free of hippos. I gave myself a few minutes to slow my heart rate, talking to myself as I drove. *I can do this, I can.* I'd driven the boat plenty of times. Not alone, never alone, but this was just the next step in becoming a real part of Baboon Camp—a real adult. It had always bothered me that people we knew both in America and in Maun made such a big deal about there being *children* at camp. I wasn't a child, or at least I never felt like one. Mom and Dad told me the whole reason we'd come to Baboon Camp was because they could trust us to act like adults, and they'd always treated me as if I was one. Why did people seem so surprised when I talked on the radio or made fires or changed the tires on our truck? My age had no reflection on my abilities. After three years, I knew this river better than anyone; Mokupi said so. I knew to take *this* turn extra wide where there was a sandbar under the weeds and not to fly around *this* turn or the boat would bounce sideways across the water and slam into the bank.

I can't get weeds, I can't get weeds, I told myself. If I steered poorly and the propeller clogged with weeds, I'd have to stop the boat, flip up the engine, and clean out the propeller while floating downstream. This was one of the most dangerous situations we could find ourselves in on the river, as I had been told time and time again. If the engine were disengaged, there would be no way to escape if a hippo popped up. I knew I was capable of lifting the engine (Mom hadn't let me learn to drive the boat until I was strong enough to do that by myself), but I wasn't going to need to, I insisted to myself. Only people who didn't know the river get stuck in the weeds. And I knew the river.

Lucy sat in the front with Soogie under her arm, her blonde hair flying in the wind. I knew she was singing to herself, as she often did on boat rides. Since the engine made it too loud to talk, we were left to our own thoughts. I usually used the time to tell myself stories or count birds, but Lucy always sang—usually Mary Chapin Carpenter songs she taught herself from Mom's cassette tapes. We entered a wide, clear straightaway and I used the extra space to waggle the tiller back and forth so the boat zigzagged from side to side. Lucy loved it when I did that, and she turned back and gave me a thumbs-up. I grinned and thought, *We are going to be fine.*

The riverbanks flew by and I kept my eyes open for reeds moving against the wind, a clear sign of animal activity. With the water high, it was unlikely there would be any animals close to the main channel other than elephants or hippos, but those were dangerous enough. The previous week, Dad and I had been driving down to Xaxaba in the early morning to borrow some tools from their mechanic when a hippo appeared on the bank above us, moving back into the water after a night of grazing on one of the islands. When he saw us, the hippo freaked out and leapt into the water, landing only inches from the side of our boat and completely soaking both Dad and me. It had happened so fast that we had no time to be scared, but as we made the rest of the trip in our dripping clothes, freezing in the wind, I realized again just how little control we had over our safety where the hippos were concerned. He'd come so close to landing on top of us.

I drove for an hour before slowing down at the entrance to the Xaxaba lagoon and bobbed on the side of the river, leaving Mom enough room to pass me. As she came around the corner about fifteen minutes later, the wake from her boat caused us to bounce up and down in the water. Mom didn't say anything, but opened up the throttle and roared off at top speed toward the staff village. I knew she was doing it because she was worried about running into hippos in the Xaxaba lagoon. They regularly showed up in the water near the lodge, often in very large groups. Though everyone in the family had their own fears and dislikes when it came to animals, Mom really, really hated hippos.

"Keena? You ready to go?" Lucy said.

"Yeah," I replied, gunning the engine and turning the nose of the boat back downriver toward Delta Camp.

I wasn't as relaxed on the river past Xaxaba. At that point, I had been in the boat for what felt like a very long time, though in reality it had only been just over an hour. The adrenaline had worn off, my arm ached from holding the tiller, and the enormity of the situation finally hit me. I watched Lucy's hair whip back and forth in the wind and wished she had gone with my mother. What would I do if something happened to her? Would I know what to do if we got stuck or there was an elephant in the river or something happened to the engine? If I screwed up, would my parents stop trusting me to handle myself? Would everyone else think I was just a kid after all? I'd never done anything like this alone before. I'd been so confident, but now I felt a hard knot of panic forming in my throat. *This boat is too small and too light*, I thought. *It's not safe. Just remember—if we're flipped by a crocodile, I should swim on the top of the water because it's harder for them to pull me down, but if we're flipped by a hippo, I have to swim underneath the water so it can't chomp me.* I swallowed hard. Well, it was too late to back out anyway. Nothing to do but keep going.

There were three main trouble spots on the river between Xaxaba and Delta Camp, a trip that should take forty-five minutes if there are no issues, accidents, or attacks. The first was a spot where the channel narrowed and went right alongside a bank where a gigantic crocodile lived. This crocodile had a scale missing on his back and had attacked two guides from Delta Camp who were poling a group of tourists in mokoros only a month before. The crocodile launched itself from the bank into one of the mokoros and grabbed hold of a guide named Kamanga around his waist. Kamanga tried to fight back by punching the crocodile and, to their credit, the tourists tried to help him by hitting the crocodile with whatever they had with them—water bottles, backpacks, and cameras. But it was no use. Kamanga was pulled into the river and never seen again. His death had shaken everyone pretty badly at Delta Camp, and was a harsh reminder that no matter how carefully we interacted with the animals, we were still very vulnerable. That was the one thing we all kept in the backs of our minds but never, ever spoke about; if we focused on all the bad things that could happen from moment to moment, we'd never get out of bed in the morning.

Delta Camp had since changed their mokoro route to avoid the area where Kamanga had been taken, but since this area was right along the main channel, I didn't have that option. We just had to drive right past the crocodile's lair and hope the beast was having lunch elsewhere. You couldn't go really fast in that section of the river either, since there was a sharp right-hand turn directly after the crocodile bank, and if you were being cocky about it, as Dad said, you'd slam sideways into the bank and have to stop and adjust the engine before moving on. I definitely didn't want that to happen.

The second trouble spot was the lagoon at the Game Scouts Camp, at about the halfway mark between Delta Camp and Xaxaba. This lagoon was small and full of hippos. The Game Scouts didn't drive their boats around enough to teach the hippos that boats were dangerous, and the hippos had developed a tendency to charge out of the lagoon into the main channel to attack passing boats. ("Like Hungry Hungry Hippos,"

I'd said to Dad, the first time we drove down to Delta Camp. "That's a frightening analogy," he said. "But yes, exactly like Hungry Hungry Hippos.") Hippos were easily capable of biting through a boat and sinking it on the spot, leaving the passengers to the mercy of the crocodiles in the deep water below. You couldn't do much about this situation either. Just go fast and hope the hippos weren't feeling aggressive that day.

The final trouble spot was a large, open stretch of river right in front of Delta Camp that was full of huge lily pads. If you didn't know exactly where to follow the main channel through the lily pads, you ran the risk of getting the propeller snarled up in the plants and causing the engine to stall out. There wasn't anything particularly dangerous about this since it wasn't an area where we usually saw hippos, but it would be embarrassing. Everyone in the Delta Camp lounge would be able to see me completely make a mess of driving the river, and that would never do. Not if I was going to show them I was an adult, capable of handling myself in the delta.

Though she couldn't possibly have sensed my growing unease as we set off from Xaxaba, Lucy picked that moment to turn around and raise her arms in the air, one hand still holding tight to Soogie the pig.

"GO KEENA!" she shouted, smiling. "GO KEENA GO!" I wanted to hug her, but that would mean abandoning the engine. Instead, I raised my free hand in response and shouted, "WOOHOO!"

Okay, we would be fine. We could do this. I just had to take it one turn at a time. I kept an inner monologue going in my head as a distraction. *This is just like a video game! Or a movie. I'm a pilot navigating down a narrow channel trying to get somewhere without my ship blowing up. This is just like* Star Wars! *I guess that makes Lucy R2-D2. What's scarier anyway, a TIE fighter or a hippo? Definitely a hippo.* The air was clear and clean, and kingfishers swooped overhead. I laughed to myself. We just had an hour more to go.

After about twenty minutes, we approached the turn where the man-eating crocodile lived. I knew I had only one shot to make this turn properly and was determined not to blow it. With my left hand,

I reached into my shorts pocket and pulled out my Swiss Army Knife, flicking the blade open with my index finger. Lucy turned around.

"Why are you slowing down? You know where we are, don't you? Don't mess this up," she said.

"I won't," I said. "Just hold on a second." I shifted the knife into my palm and squeezed the other tools shut, leaving the blade extended. I didn't know what exactly I was planning to do with my tiny knife if the crocodile was there, but I wasn't about to be caught unarmed if he jumped in our boat or went after my sister. Weapon secured, I fixed my grip on the tiller, opened up the engine, and roared toward the bank, trying not to think about poor Kamanga. We passed the bank (mercifully empty), and I yanked the tiller toward me, making the right turn at the perfect angle, if a little fast. *Just a bit too cocky on the turn there, kid*, I heard Dad say in my head. But, whatever! He wasn't there. Lucy turned around and gave me another thumbs-up. Knife still clutched tightly in my left hand, I pushed on, past reedbeds filled with weaverbirds and thick, overhanging trees sticking out from the banks over the river.

Next it was time to face the lagoon full of hippos. *What's your strategy here?* I asked myself. *There are usually more than a dozen hippos in there.* I looked up to the sky. The sun was high, just past noon, and the air was warm. If the hippos were behaving as hippos should in the middle of the day, they'd be sleeping—either deep underwater or lying in the sun in the reedbeds on the side of the bank. Though I knew from Dad's and my past experience that hippos on the bank weren't exactly an ideal situation for passing boats, if I was right about them being asleep they'd be too slow to get themselves up and back to the water in the time it would take me to drive by. We just had to gun it. I opened the throttle and we flew down the river, barely skimming the top of the water.

Again, Lucy and I got lucky. No hippos charged us as we flew past, either from underwater or from the bank, and by the time we entered the minefield stretch of lily pad–infested river in front of Delta Camp half an hour later, I was already taking my victory lap. I unclenched my hands and eased up on the tiller, zipping skillfully between the lily pads on my way to the boat landing area behind Delta Camp. As we approached the shore, I squeezed my knife closed and shoved it back in my pocket.

"You did it! I knew you could do it!" Lucy cheered as I shifted the boat into neutral and cut the engine. I grinned. I tried to lift the engine up to drag the boat closer to shore but found that my arms were shaking too much. So I got out of the boat and dragged it as close as I could and tied it to a clump of reeds. Lucy jumped over the side and waded through the shallow water to join me on the bank. In the warm afternoon sun, we walked down the path to Delta Camp.

What Bob saw, when he looked up from his desk in Delta Camp's office, were two tiny girls walking into camp completely alone. Both were sunburned and windblown, neither was wearing shoes, and the smaller one was carrying a pink stuffed pig. Utterly shocked, he came out to meet us.

"Girls? Where are your parents? Are you okay?" I nodded and explained that Mom was collecting the guides from the staff village and we'd brought the boat down ahead of her.

"You drove down here by yourself?" he asked. Again, I nodded. I was so proud of myself I thought I might explode, but was determined to act casual in front of other people. This was just what adults did, nothing to be surprised about. He stared at me. "And remind me how old you are?"

"Ten," I said.

"And I'm seven!" Lucy added.

"I see," said Bob. "Well, my girls, I think we better find you something to drink."

When Mom drove into Delta Camp half an hour later, she found Lucy drinking orange Fanta and me with a cold beer sitting in the guest lounge, doing what we always did when we visited Delta Camp: poring over the book of snakebites and discussing which looked the grossest. Though the beer wasn't my first, it was certainly the best-tasting beer I'd ever had, and definitely what an adult should be enjoying after a long day on the river.

Years later, Mom told me all she could think about on her drive to Delta Camp was the video game in which the frog hops across the freeway, trying not to get squashed by passing cars. Had she really sent her two young daughters down a hippo- and crocodile-infested river alone? In retrospect, she said, it was a terribly stupid thing to do. So stupid that sweet, mild-mannered Bob had actually admonished her when she came to pick us up. He hadn't realized that there wasn't anyone else to drive our boat when he asked us for the favor and was furious that she had taken such a risk with her children.

Mom drove us home as the sun dipped toward the horizon and the birds flew back to their nests to roost, through the lily pad minefield, past the lagoon at the Game Scouts Camp, and flying so fast past the man-eating crocodile lair that the insects whipped against my face and got trapped in my eyelashes. It was dark by the time we got to Baboon Camp and nearly midnight when Dad and Binky finally showed up, having successfully ferried all the beer to Delta Camp and gotten Desmond and the Leopard-Spotted Lorry unstuck. They were muddy and exhausted, but relieved that so many parties had pulled together to get the beer to Delta before the executives arrived.

"Well, I hope they enjoy their beer," I said. Binky laughed and pushed another log into the fire.

I couldn't stop smiling. Here I was, sitting around the campfire with the grown-ups, talking about all the things I'd done to help with trucks and planes and boats. If I could drive to Delta Camp on my own, I really could do anything.

JULY 29, 1994 (EXCERPT)
KEENA'S JOURNAL

Today was a very important day for me. And all because of beer!

CHAPTER 8

PEARL JAM AND OTHER THINGS
I DIDN'T KNOW

IT WAS A STIFLING evening in December a year after my boat ride to Delta Camp when my parents, Lucy, and I gathered at the dining table for a talk. The air was so thick and heavy it felt like I could hold it in my hands as we sat in puddles of sweat, swatting flies away from our food. We'd just finished a dinner of freshly caught fish and my thumb was throbbing from where I'd sliced it open with my pocketknife trying to remove a hook from an especially disagreeable pike. The water in the lagoon had diminished to a small stream, and upturned lily plants lay sprawled about in the dust like sunbathers on the beach. A group of giraffes drank from the river just to the north, and as they dipped their heads to the water they moved across the light from the setting sun, sending shadows slicing across the dinner table and my parents' tanned faces. Dad cleared his throat and reached for his beer.

"At the end of the month we are going back to America," Dad said. I stiffened. "We have a lot of work to do on the data we collected and we have to spend some time teaching at the university or we won't be able to renew our grant." He glanced at Mom, who was drumming her fingers on the table next to her tin plate. "No one *wants* to go back, obviously, but..." he trailed off. Mom stared ahead across the melapo. Lucy fidgeted in her chair and reached for her mug of milk. She'd put three heaping tablespoons of Nesquik in it, but the milk was still lumpy and sour. It had been ultra-heat treated in Zimbabwe to make it last longer, but that didn't make it taste any less disgusting. Mom and Dad still had a rule that we had to have one glass a day.

Mom shook her head to clear it and looked at Lucy and me.

"Well, it can't be helped, can it?" she said brightly. "We have to go, so we might as well enjoy it. Just think, you'll get to see all your friends again! That's at least something positive."

I scowled. I'd been planning to spend the next month building a tree house in my favorite reading tree, not packing to move back to America. I didn't even know if my school friends would remember me. It had been a year since I'd last seen them, when I spent a couple of weeks in fifth grade while my parents renewed our passports and got the solar power system fixed. I received an occasional letter from Meghan, but the only person who'd really kept in touch with me while I was gone was Nat, and he wasn't the most detailed correspondent.

10:05 a.m., June 12, 1995

Dear Keena,

I miss you a lot. But I disagree that Menolly is the best character in *Dragondrums*. We'll talk about it when you come home.

Today we're having our fifth-grade pool party. I wish you were here. Two more days and school's out. Could you please write soon? I'm getting anxious. I'm not sure if my first few letters have all reached you but if they haven't I hope they do soon. You are so far away! Why does the mail have to take so blasted long!?!? I really wish I could just teleport them there! Oh well. It's probably going to be a while before they figure out how to do that. Until they do it's just going to take some time for letters to get where they're supposed to go. Write soon!

Yours truly,
Nat

We left Baboon Camp on a hot and dusty day just before the new year. My parents had arranged for some graduate students to come from Penn to continue their work while we were in the States, so very little was going to change about the camp except who was living in it. Lucy and I packed some of our books and outdoor gear in duffel bags under our beds to await our return, and donated the rest to the children in Mpitsang and Mokupi's village. Though we were coming back the next summer, there was an element of finality in packing away our prized possessions that made me think of Amboseli and made my stomach lurch. I didn't want to be separated from my book best friends Captain Nancy Blackett and Laurana Kanan the elf princess for such a long time. How would I get to them if I needed them? Instead, I had to satisfy myself with my stuffed owl and my knife, both of which lay nestled against the small of my back inside my backpack as we flew to Maun, Paris, and then to Philadelphia, where we landed in an icy blast of December winter that felt like a physical assault after the Botswana heat.

Nat's mother, Cathy, picked us up at the airport and drove us home

The first leg of the trip back to the US

through the snowy streets, past houses still twinkling with Christmas lights and fields devoid of any movement except the swirling snow. Our empty house was dark and cold, and I could see my breath as I dragged our duffel bags into the laundry room. Mom said everything we had in camp had to be washed before it was put away—even our shoes and stuffed animals. This seemed like madness to me, since we never cared how dirty our clothes were in Baboon Camp. Why did it matter so much now that we were in America? Was there some kind of rule about having perfectly clean clothes that I didn't know about? There was too much change happening all at once, and I was tired. Dad drove out to find us something to eat and returned with microwavable dinner rolls and fried chicken, two things I hadn't eaten in almost three years. As I fell asleep under the icy sheets in my bed at the top of the stairs, I strained to hear the sounds of night animals but heard only the spitting and sputtering of the radiator in my bedroom welcoming me back to America, to a house with too many rooms and a second floor that still felt like it might tumble off at any minute.

I arrived at school for my first day of sixth grade a few short days later, on January 2. Mom and Dad dropped me off at a tall, modern-looking building far away from the familiar elementary school campus where I'd always gone before. They drove to work, leaving me standing in the tiled foyer, shivering in my school uniform of navy-blue pants and a white polo shirt, completely at a loss about where to go or what to do. My backpack was still covered with dust, and my sneakers were faded and tattered from years of nudging logs into place in our firepit and being ripped by thorns as I scavenged in the woods for kindling. I stared straight ahead, wanting nothing more than to turn around and run, as far and as fast as I could, until I got back to the heat and the sand and the birds.

A tall male teacher with blond hair and a trim blue suit emerged from the office in front of me and greeted me warmly.

"Welcome back!" he said cheerfully, shaking my hand. He handed me a clean white sheet of paper with my name at the top and a grid printed below it. "Here's your class schedule," he said, running his finger down the page. "Looks like your first class today is English with Mrs. Richards. Let me show you where that is. Do you have your books and a Trapper Keeper?"

"No," I said. What was a Trapper Keeper?

The hallways were full of kids I didn't recognize, milling about in small groups, talking with their heads close together or writing in brightly colored notebooks covered with stickers. A boy with blond hair threw a highlighter at another boy who shrieked and ducked, sending the high-lighter skidding across the polished laminate floor. I swallowed. I had hated laminate floor ever since my "Gorilla Man" debacle in second grade. My head buzzed under the fluorescent lights and immediately I was back on that gym mat, melting under the gaze of fifty other girls who were con-vinced I was a complete weirdo. I shifted the backpack on my shoulder as the tall teacher escorted me through the crowds, ignoring the stares from onlookers. It was a small school, and clearly the introduction of someone new halfway through the year wasn't going to go unnoticed.

Three floors up and down a long carpeted hallway, we finally came to Mrs. Richards's English class. Students trickled into the room in small groups, and I recognized some of them. One or two even waved to me or said hello. Mrs. Richards led me to a desk in the back row and handed me a copy of *The Giver*, a book her class was just beginning to read together and discuss.

"But I've already read it," I said quietly.

"Well, please don't ruin it for everyone else," she said kindly. "You'll just have to pretend you don't know the ending." She bustled away to the front of the class, motioning to the other kids to take their seats so she could begin the lecture. I stared at the floor, counting the crisscrosses in the blue carpet fibers. My stomach roiled with acid and the buzzing in my ears made it hard to hear the conversations going on around me.

This feels a lot like danger, I thought. *But it's not, not really. Nothing here is trying to kill me. Nothing here is going to make me sick or keep me from going home. So, okay then how bad can it really be?* I opened my eyes, not realizing I'd been squeezing them shut. Mrs. Richards was telling the class to open to some page or other but I hadn't been listening and my book sat unopened, spine unbroken and cover uncreased, on the desk in front of me. I saw the boy at the desk next to mine open his book to the title page and I reached for my book to do the same, horrified to see my hands shaking. *Stop that*, I told myself. *Stop being scared; this is not a scary place.* But my body didn't seem to believe me.

Since it was already halfway through the school year when I arrived, my classmates had already divided themselves into social groups and essential decisions had been made: who they were friends with, who they hated, and who they had crushes on—this last a completely new concept to me. Nat was still his old self, though he'd started wearing glasses, but Meghan had changed completely. No longer was she the little girl I knew from elementary school who liked stuffed animals and drawing. Seemingly overnight she'd become a poised and self-assured young adult, with a stylish new haircut and sweet smile that made some of the boys in my science class call her the Queen of Sixth Grade. Meghan also had our class's first real boyfriend, which conferred on her a degree of maturity that made her untouchably cool to the rest of us. I wasn't sure whether Meghan knew just how popular she was, but it was immediately obvious to me how far out of my league she now was as a friend. Though I'd missed Meghan and wanted to spend time with her in school, I wavered. I didn't look at all like the girls who hovered around her, and though I couldn't have said exactly why, I somehow felt unworthy of being in her presence—a thought that made me angry since I knew it didn't make any sense. Meghan and her new friends were another species entirely, and even though Meghan waved when she first saw me at school, I hesitated to go over and say hi. Her friends swirled around her like a flock of birds, and before I could gather the courage to talk to her, she was already gone—off in a crowd of smiles and giggles and faces I didn't know. It took me almost a week to finally say hello to her in person, but I quickly gave up trying to renew our friendship when I discovered I had much bigger problems to deal with.

There were some members of the class who had joined more recently and didn't know me at all. I heard some of them whispering, "Who's that?" and the classmates who did know me would sigh and say, "Oh, her? That's just Keena. Sometimes she comes to school and sometimes she lives with monkeys or something. She's weird." As much as I wanted to blend in, it was very hard to be inconspicuous, especially because of how I looked: My hair was short, bleached by the sun, and chopped in odd layers, since the last time it had been cut was by the firepit with a dull pair of scissors. I was deeply tan and covered in healing scratches, cuts, and mosquito bites, which made me stand out even more in a Philadelphia winter. Unlike the other girls in my class, I wore pants instead of skirts, and sneakers instead of dress shoes. I thought it was too cold for skirts, and dress shoes were impractical because it was impossible to run in them.

About a month after I joined the class, I arrived in homeroom early and sat down at a desk, not really sure what I should do with myself until class started. Nearby, two girls sat talking loudly, smacking their gum.

"Oh my God, I love Pearl Jam so much," one of them said.

"They're the best," the other girl said, nodding. "I'd, like, die for them."

"Excuse me," I said, feeling brave. "What's Pearl Jam?" The girls stared at me. "Because I know a little about animals, and no one makes jam from pearls. Not even in other places in the world. People farm oysters for pearls sometimes but no one eats those." The girl who loved Pearl Jam, like, so much, made a face.

"Do you even hear yourself talk?" she asked. "God. Just shut up if you don't know."

"I'm sorry," I said. "I was just trying to be helpful."

"Well, don't," she said. "Anyway, we're having a private conversation."

"Okay. Sorry." I shuffled my sneakers on the carpet and felt the heat rising behind my ears. What had I done wrong? I thought you were supposed to talk to people if you wanted to make friends, but that hadn't gone very well. And why was I reacting so strongly to these girls I didn't even know? I picked at a mosquito-bite scab on the back of my hand and sniffed. Why did I feel that scared feeling in my stomach when nothing scary was happening? I could always trust myself to know what to do if something scary happened in Botswana, but the sudden doubt that settled in the back of my mind like a headache made me feel even worse than what the girl had actually said. What if I couldn't trust myself here?

I started getting prank calls almost every night. One night in particular, I was doing homework in the dining room when the phone rang from the kitchen and Dad tentatively said, "Keena? I believe you have a phone call..."

"Hello?" I said.

Four or five giggly boy voices shushed each other on the other end and someone said, "So, like, do you wear a loincloth under your pants? Do you speak African and eat bugs? Do you have a monkey baby?"

And as I did every night, I squeezed the phone receiver and struggled to keep my voice measured and calm.

"Of course not," I would say. "That's ridiculous." The laughter continued on the other end of the phone and I flexed my free hand open and closed.

"You're so weird," the caller continued. "Will you be my girlfriend?" At this point the voices were howling in the background, and I'd moved on from being hurt to just plain angry.

"No," I said. "I don't want a boyfriend. Now go away and leave me alone." I slammed the receiver back in its cradle and stomped up the stairs to my room, my homework completely forgotten, like every other time this happened.

Every night, Dad would walk to the foot of the stairs from the kitchen and say quietly, "Keena? Are you all right?"

"I'm fine," I'd answer. "I just...nothing, yes, I'm fine."

"Okay," he'd say. "Dinner is in half an hour."

I would pace back and forth in my room, letting the anger burn through me until it faded away and I could think clearly. I wasn't hurt in any serious way by these calls. They were annoying and made me feel sad in the moment, but it wasn't what the boys said that irritated me, it was the fact that they took time out of their day to do something designed to cause me pain.

"Why do they do that?" I asked Mom one night. She and I had started a new tradition since we'd come back to America. Even though I was twelve and too old to be kissed good night, every night Mom brought me a glass of ice water at bedtime. I had made some remark about how novel it was to have a refrigerator that made its own ice and how much I liked the sound of ice cubes tinkling against a glass—a sound I'd heard only in restaurants and therefore equated with something luxurious and fancy. When Mom heard this, she started bringing one up to keep by my bed every night. On the way up the stairs, she shook the glass so the ice cubes tinkled extra loudly.

"I wish I could tell you," she said. "But there's no reason for it. Sometimes people are just mean to each other."

"Animals aren't mean to each other for no reason," I muttered from underneath my blanket.

"Sure they are," she said. "Or it could be something else. Remember that time you came out to the baboons with me and we saw Sylvia bite Balo for no reason?" I nodded. "Well, just before that happened, Selo jumped on Sylvia and bit her tail really hard. Sylvia attacked Balo because she was angry about being bitten, and Balo is lower ranking than she is so Sylvia can attack Balo. She couldn't do anything about Selo attacking her because Selo is the alpha and can do whatever she wants to anyone. Remember what we call that type of aggression?"

"Redirecting aggression," I mumbled.

"Exactly. So maybe these boys are being mean to you because someone else was mean to them." I rolled over in my bed and looked up at her.

"Well, it sucks," I said.

"I know. And I'm really sorry they keep doing it, but maybe if you just ignore them they'll stop. Now go to sleep; you have a big day ahead of you tomorrow."

I pulled the blanket up under my chin and stared at the wall. I didn't have a big day tomorrow. I knew exactly what kind of day I had tomorrow: wake up at 6:00 a.m., out the door by 7:30 a.m., at school by 8:30 a.m. in time for homeroom, and then class after class after class, all announced with bells that meant you had to get up and get moving if you didn't want to be late. Then home, homework, and bed, and getting ready to do it all over again the next day. No animals, no game drives, and no time for daydreaming, unless I wanted to do it between 11:43 a.m. and 12:17 p.m. when I was supposed to be eating lunch. I barely saw my parents anymore and never saw Lucy; the elementary school was nowhere near the middle school, and in the evenings, she had just as much homework as I did. As close as we were, my family wasn't the kind to talk about how they were feeling. For the first time in my life, I began to realize that I was surrounded by other people and yet completely alone in the world, just going through the motions of existing. Captain Keena of the Okavango, the reckless risk-taker who climbed trees and shot snakes, was my only companion— and she was pacing restlessly back and forth in my brain, begging to be let out but knowing that even if she could, there was nowhere in America she would have wanted to go.

It was a warm day in spring when I climbed the three floors to the sixth-grade locker room and headed for my locker, thinking half about

Me and Nat geeking out on a field trip

the day ahead of me and half about *Dune*, which I'd just started and which was waiting for me on my bed at home. I often let my mind wander while I went about my daily routine—I called it "the castle in my head," the place where I could think about anything and everything without anyone being able to judge me for it. I placed my brown-bag lunch on the top shelf in my locker and grabbed my copy of *The Giver*, the book we were *still* reading in English class, an unbelievable three and a half months later. I couldn't believe it had taken this long to read 208 pages. I read that much in a weekend.

I slipped to the back of the classroom to the same desk I'd been assigned on my first day, next to a boy named Jamie who I knew from elementary school and who used to invite me over to his house to play *Star Wars* computer games. He'd stopped talking to me years ago after I'd beaten him in *Star Wars: Rebel Assault*.

"So, class," Mrs. Richards said, "one of the most interesting themes of *The Giver* is that the author takes some concepts that are very familiar to us and presents them as if they are completely new and impossible to describe—like a sled or a sunburn. For our final assignment on *The Giver* I want you to take something that you think is ordinary and try to describe it as if it were extraordinary and you were seeing it or feeling it for the first time, just the way the author did in this book. What do you think you would choose? How about you, Keena?"

"Excuse me?" I said. As usual, I had only paid partial attention to what she'd been saying.

"What ordinary thing would you choose to describe?"

I thought for a minute.

"I'll probably write about the way the birds sing in the morning when the sun comes up," I said. Next to me, Jamie scoffed.

"That's what you'd pick?" he said. "Seriously? When you can write about anything else, like fire or hurricanes or airplanes?"

"Sure," I said. "The assignment is to pick something ordinary and describe it as something wonderful, right? Birds singing is something ordinary to me but something I also think is extraordinary."

"That's just stupid," Jamie said, shrugging.

"Why?" Captain Keena of the Okavango stopped pacing in the castle in my head and Jamie now had her full attention. "It's my essay. If *you* want to write about bombs or whatever, then go ahead."

"I guess I don't believe you," he went on.

"Jamie, focus, please," Mrs. Richards said from the front of the classroom. What was wrong with him? This didn't sound at all like the boy who cried when his mother accidentally vacuumed up his Boba Fett action figure.

"Sorry, Mrs. Richards," he said. "It just doesn't make sense that someone would find birds singing to be that great. It's just a random thing in nature."

"I really like it when birds are singing," I said. "It makes me happy."

"Well, whatever," Jamie said, shrugging again. "If that's true it just means you're an incredibly shallow person."

The bell rang to end the class period and students surged toward the door. I slid *The Giver* into my backpack and headed into the hallway, tension radiating through my shoulders. Who was Jamie to tell me something I liked was stupid? Wasn't it okay for people to just like what they like and have that be the end of it? I would never do that to him. I sighed. I realized that if I wanted to protect my birds, and everything else I loved, I needed to keep them safe in the castle in my head.

The fluorescent lights beat down like an alien sun as I shouldered my way between my classmates and their ever-present cloud of Cucumber Melon body wash from Bath & Body Works. Deep in the castle in my head, the elf princess Laurana Kanan touched me on the shoulder and said, "Be thankful you can feel pity for your enemy. The day we cease to care even for our enemies is the day we have lost this battle."

CHAPTER 9

CAN WE SWIM AWAY FROM THIS PARTY?

LUCY ARRIVED HOME FROM school one day angrier than I'd ever seen her. She dropped her backpack in the front hall next to a statue of a baboon carved out of the trunk of a palm tree and kicked off her sneakers, which thudded against the wall next to the baboon and left smudges on the wallpaper.

"Lucy, please," Mom said wearily, following her in from the car. Whatever was making Lucy upset had clearly been bothering her the whole way home from school. Dad and I paused fixing dinner as Lucy stormed into the kitchen and dropped into a chair, her hands in fists. Lucy had a temper, but I couldn't remember ever seeing her quite this upset.

"What happened?" I asked. I never saw Lucy in school anymore since the elementary school was several blocks from the middle school, but I still felt an obligation as the big sister to defend her against anything bad.

Lucy glared at me. "We had a substitute teacher today for social studies. He lied about Africa and sent me to the principal's office when I told him he was wrong."

Dad put down his knife and took off his glasses, something he only did when he was upset.

"He lied? What do you mean? What did he say?"

"He said that Africa is like America because it is one country made up of many different states."

"Bullshit," said Dad.

"I know," said Lucy. "I told him he was wrong, and that Africa was a continent made up of many different countries. Then he said that if that was really true, then why did everyone in Africa speak Swahili?"

I laughed. "What did you say to that?" I asked.

"I told him that they only speak Swahili in East Africa, and anyway it's called Kiswahili, not Swahili, and that there are thousands of different languages on the *continent* of Africa."

"Well, that's ridiculous," Dad said.

"But then," Lucy said, her blue eyes glittering with anger, "he said that people in Botswana are stupid because they build their huts out of mud and have to rebuild them every time it rains and the water washes them away."

My mouth dropped open, and Dad shot Mom a look with his eyebrows raised.

"I know," Mom said. "I already spoke to the principal. She said she would do something about it but that Lucy had already done her part to put the teacher in his place."

"What did you do?" I asked.

Lucy raised her chin and looked me in the eye. "I threw an eraser at him," she said.

Mom and Dad burst out laughing and hugged Lucy tightly. She immediately began to relax now that it was clear she wasn't in trouble.

"It's actually kind of funny," Lucy said. "Imagine people in Botswana not liking when it rains. That guy really didn't know anything."

Dad chuckled and went back to chopping beans with a smile on his face. Lucy kicked her bare feet against the legs of the chair and sipped the juice box Mom handed her from the fridge.

I knew Lucy would forget the incident completely now that it was resolved. Lucy never obsessed over her problems; she attacked them with the ferocity of a mongoose battling a snake and then immediately moved on. She was the best person I knew at putting the past solidly in the past and trotting off to do something more productive with her time than worrying about what others thought. I had always respected

Lucy's self-confidence but found myself admiring it more every day as she smoothly transitioned to life as an average American elementary school kid. Meanwhile I found myself still struggling with my own adjustment.

Though the prank calls had lasted several months and into the start of my seventh grade year, they had mercifully died down. Mom said it was because the boys got bored with bothering me when I wasn't responding, but I thought it was because their attention was occupied elsewhere. Over the summer, Meghan and her boyfriend quietly broke up and suddenly the most popular girl in seventh grade was back on the market. If Meghan noticed the sudden increase in male attention, she didn't show it. She calmly went to her classes, did her homework in study hall, and ate her lunch, either unaware of being the center of attention or choosing to ignore it.

Meghan's magnetism was felt by all members of the middle school, even those who weren't in our grade. A week after we learned about her breakup, the lunchroom watched in shock as one of the eighth-grade boys walked over to Meghan's table and asked her to go to the spring dance with him. To be asked out by an eighth grader was absolutely unheard of, and even the teachers paused their conversation to see what Meghan would do.

Smiling sweetly, Meghan politely declined the invitation and told the boy she already had plans to go to the dance with her friends, though she appreciated the thought. The boy slunk back to his friends, tail between his legs, while the rest of the room stared at Meghan, who was obliviously eating her turkey and cheese sandwich on a Kaiser roll. If she had been cool before, she was now untouchable.

I was mystified by Meghan's ascension to the status of middle-school goddess. Objectively, I couldn't see anything different about her that might explain the vast chasm in social status between her and the other girls, though it was clear there was one. She dressed like all the other girls, so it couldn't be how she looked—though I had to admit she was very pretty in a delicate sort of way. She was smart too, but that couldn't be it either. There were lots of smart kids at school, and they certainly weren't conferred godlike status by the rest of the class. This I knew for sure, since I spent most of my spare time reading with Nat, who was the smartest of all the smart kids but was often laughed at for cutting the crusts off his peanut butter and jelly sandwiches and not eating the fruit his mom packed for his lunch (he gave it to me instead).

No, it had to be something else that made Meghan so popular— something that was very important and that everyone else but me seemed to be able to see. Worse, it was something that I clearly didn't have and had no idea how I would get. In Botswana, it had been so easy to be the person I wanted to be: drive the boat to Delta Camp, do all the things adults did, and be treated like an adult. But I didn't know how I wanted to be treated in America, only that being myself got me laughed out of the room, as it did with my "Gorilla Man" dance, or prank called every night for months. One spring day near the end of a fairly quiet school year, as I watched Meghan and her friends eat lunch on the quad, the sun shining on their casually messy ponytails, I realized I knew one thing for sure: America was not a safe place for me to be me, and until I figured out what kind of person was safe here, I would just have to stay very quiet—just as I did when an elephant was nearby. I had to lie low and let the danger pass.

I shivered. It was cold where I sat, perched on the sill of one of the large windows on the bottom floor of the middle school. The windowsill wasn't as comfortable as the trees I liked to read in back in camp, but it was the closest I could find, so I had to make do. An early spring wind blew across the quad, made stronger by being forced to blow between two buildings rather than drift through the trees as it was supposed to. I knew it was probably too early in the year to wear shorts, but I'd been wearing them for more than a week already, assuming that the day would warm up the same way it did in Botswana and that by noon I'd be too hot in pants. I'd been wrong.

I repositioned myself in the windowsill to avoid the breeze and pulled my book out from my backpack. I was reading *The Golden Compass*, which Nat's father, Jonathan, had given me for my birthday. Jonathan told me that the main character, Lyra, reminded him of me because she was always climbing on roofs.

Suddenly a shadow fell across my book. I looked up and saw a tall boy standing in front of me with an armload of envelopes. He was one of the new kids, but I knew he hadn't been one of the ones who prank called me, since I would have recognized his lisp over the phone. He looked uncomfortable so I smiled and closed my book to show him I was paying attention.

"Here," he said, thrusting an envelope into my hands from the pile in his arms.

"What's this?" I said. The envelope was heavy and black and had my name written on it in loopy gold lettering. The only thing I could imagine arriving so mysteriously was a scroll written in runes that would unlock the door to a parallel universe where animals talked and people rode on broomsticks. As I contemplated this, I noticed he was staring at me, as if waiting for me to say something.

"I'm sorry, what did you say?" I asked. He shuffled his feet and cleared his throat.

"I said, you have to let me know if you're coming by Friday. My mom needs a final count for the caterers." I opened the envelope and pulled out a heavy piece of card stock with more gold designs on it as well as his name, Zach, and the words "Bar Mitzvah." I didn't know what those words meant but assumed it was a party of some kind.

"Thanks for inviting me," I said. "That's nice of you."

Zach shifted the pile of envelopes from one arm to the other and looked around the quad, presumably for the next person to deliver an invitation to.

"My mom said I had to invite everyone in the class," he said. He paused in his search and looked back at me, as if seeing me for the first time. He cleared his throat. "Ah...have you ever been to a bar mitzvah party before?" I shook my head. "It's...pretty fancy. You'll have to wear a dress."

"Okay," I said.

"Have you . . . ever worn a dress before?" he asked.

I curled my legs tighter against my body.

"Yes, I've worn a dress before," I retorted.

Zach seemed uncomfortable and cleared his throat again. "Okay. I'm sorry, I . . . had to ask. You never wear a skirt to school so I wasn't sure. Just please wear a dress this time."

"I'll wear a dress," I said, recovering my cool enough to remember my manners. "And thank you for the invitation." Zach turned away and started across the quad, to where Meghan and her friends sat in their pool of bright sunshine, all, I now noticed, wearing skirts.

I glared at Zach's retreating back and pressed my palms against the cold metal of the windowsill. *Of course I've worn a dress*, I said to myself. *I've worn a dress tons of times!* In fact, if I thought about it, I'd worn a dress as many as ten times before, and had only complained about it a little bit. I just didn't like to wear dresses; they slowed me down and made it harder to move. Dresses were what girls wore when they had to, like when it was their birthday or when their moms paid them to when their grandmothers visited.

"If you're nervous about the party, why don't you talk to your friends about it?" Mom said that evening after I showed her the invitation.

"I'm not nervous," I snapped. Mom looked at me over the top of her reading glasses, the invitation still in her hands. She'd been analyzing baboon grunts on the computer and had to turn the speakers down in order to hear me.

"You've never been to a party like this before," she said. "They've rented out a party boat that's going to take you all around the Philadelphia harbor. There's going to be a DJ, a live band, and the whole thing is going to be catered. Hell, *I've* never been to a party like this before. Do you know what you're going to wear?"

"I'm going to wear a dress," I said.

"Well, yes, of course you'll wear a dress. But which dress? And do you have shoes? And something to wear over the dress if it gets cold out there?"

"I...don't know," I said. There was more to wearing a dress than I thought. This was getting worse by the minute.

"Let's go take a look in your closet," Mom said. I followed her up the carpeted stairs to my bedroom, where the radiator clanged and hissed. Mom opened my closet and moved aside a Makishi ceremonial mask from Zambia and a San hunting kit from the Kalahari Desert in Botswana that I'd gotten for my tenth birthday. A stream of porcupine quill arrows spilled out of the hunting kit and I scrambled to pick them up off the floor while Mom pulled out the two dresses hanging in the back of the closet. One was from my uncle's wedding four years earlier, and the other was a floral monstrosity. Mom held the dresses up to the light and smoothed down the creases in the skirts. I obviously hadn't been very careful putting them away.

"Neither of these is going to work for an evening party on a boat," she said finally, laying the two dresses down on my bed. "You need something black. You should go shopping this weekend and find something that will work. Do you want to invite Meghan?"

My eyes went wide. Going shopping for dresses was already my idea of hell on earth, and inviting Meghan was terrifying. She would immediately see how little I knew about dresses, and what if she told everyone at school? After what Zach said I assumed they all thought I didn't know how to wear a dress, and what if I proved them right? I swallowed hard. *It's just a dress*, I told myself. *There is nothing scary here. Pull yourself together.*

"Sure," I said. "That's a great idea. But she's so busy with her other friends I don't know if she'll have time." At least, I hoped she didn't.

But as it turned out, Meghan did have time, and I was more than a little shocked to hear that she was looking forward to meeting me at the mall on Saturday to go shopping.

"Have fun!" Mom said as she pulled up to the curb in front of Lord & Taylor on Saturday morning.

"You're not coming with me?" I asked, surprised. I had assumed Mom would want to come shopping with me, since this was my first real party dress. And didn't she know I needed extra protection in the mall? I hated it there, with all those fluorescent lights and fake fountains that smelled like chlorine.

"No, I hate the mall," Mom said. "I'll just wait for you to call me to pick you up. At least there are no elephants in there!"

"I wish there were," I said, still feeling a little adrift as Mom drove away, leaving me standing stupidly on the sidewalk holding her credit card. *Okay, well, here we go*, I said to myself. *Nothing scary here. Just another adventure.*

To my utter astonishment, Meghan greeted me with a big hug in the entrance of Lord & Taylor and hurried me off to The Limited, a store I'd never heard of but that was full of black dresses like the kind Mom said I should get for the party. With Meghan's help, it didn't take us long to find a simple-looking black dress that fit me and that Meghan deemed appropriate for the party.

"Are you sure you don't want something fancier?" she asked, running her hand along a rack of dresses dusted with rhinestones and accented with silver chains linked together that looked to me like pieces of a horse bridle. I grimaced.

"I'm sure. That's...not really my style," I said, deciding then and there that "a style" was probably something a thirteen-year-old girl ought to have. The store's pulsing music thundered in my ears and the smell from the perfume samples was giving me a headache.

"Do you need anything else?" I asked, hoping fervently that she didn't. We'd been in the mall for almost half an hour and that was already twenty minutes too long for me. I missed the fresh air and being able to think clearly without the sounds of Real McCoy screeching in my ears. Meghan shrugged.

"Not really," she said. "But we can leave now if you want to. I'm going shopping with Sarah and Emily tomorrow anyway so I can always get something then if I need to."

I drew up short next to an artificial plant by the exit of The Limited. I'd been enjoying my time with Meghan and in my rush to get the dress and get out of the mall I'd forgotten about her other friends. Of course she was going shopping with them. She probably wished she was shopping with them now. Suddenly anxious, I shifted the shopping bag from one hand to the other and stared past Meghan to the window of a Williams Sonoma on the other side of the hallway.

"So, um," I said, still looking at the cookware in the window and not at Meghan. As uncomfortable as I was at the mall, I didn't want to lose this chance to spend time with one of my friends without the rest of her entourage. It happened so rarely. I decided to be brave. "Uh... do you need to go home, or do you want to come to my house for a while?"

"That would be fun!" she said, smiling again. "What do you want to do?"

I hadn't thought she would say yes and shifted from one foot to the other while I thought of what to say. I didn't have a Nintendo console and Dad had taken our computer to work to be fixed, so we couldn't play computer games. I didn't want to watch TV and it was too cold to take a walk, even if Meghan didn't mind the mud.

Realizing she was waiting for me to respond, I blurted out, "Do you want to make cookies?" It was something Meghan and I used to do when we were much younger and had playdates at her house, but something we hadn't done in years. Meghan laughed and punched me lightly on the shoulder.

"Yes, let's go make cookies," she said, starting in the direction of the parking lot. "That's a great idea; I never make cookies anymore." She laughed again. "That's the thing about you, Keena. You never grow up."

A few days later, I stood in my parents' bathroom while Mom ran mousse through my hair with her hands. I'd blown my hair dry but was having difficulty keeping it from sticking out behind my ears where it was still growing out from my last haircut by the firepit in Baboon Camp. Mom said no one would notice but I didn't believe her; my hair puffed out in some places and lay flat in others, an uneven patchwork of cowlicks and layers that even the fancy hairstylist Mom had taken me to hadn't been able to clean up. I stared at my reflection in the mirror.

Hair disaster aside, I didn't think I looked too bad; my face was clean, and I'd outlined my cat eyes with a thin line of mascara that made my long eyelashes look even darker against my skin. The dress was just as uncomfortable as any dress I'd ever worn but looked all right, I thought, all things considered. It was just another part of the costumes I had to wear here in America. Once she decided I looked acceptable, Mom and I got into our old Volvo and she drove me downtown to the Philadelphia harbor.

I stepped onto the boat for the bar mitzvah party with my spirits cautiously high. Most of the other girls were wearing black dresses that looked like mine, and I blended into the crowd seamlessly, wiggling my way through the sea of guests and waiters until I reached the bow of the boat, safely in front of the captain's cabin and set slightly away from the crush of people in the middle. Nat and I had agreed to meet there to make sure we both had someone to talk to at the party, since he had never been to a bar mitzvah party either.

"Hey, you *can* wear a dress!" a voice behind me said. I turned around slowly so as not to stumble in the low heels I was wearing and came face-to-face with a girl named Jessica. Jessica and Zach were friends from the same elementary school in the city. She'd always seemed nice enough, and I smiled gratefully. She had the curliest hair I'd ever seen and it shimmered around her head like a cloud.

"Yeah," I said. Jessica reached over and ran her hand down the side of my head.

"Did you do your hair yourself?" she said, and I smiled widely. Had I done something right? It had taken me hours to get my hair under control.

"Yeah!" I said again. "It wasn't so bad once I—"

Jessica tugged on a curl behind my ear and I felt it unravel and fall against my neck.

"This is such a mess," Jessica said, laughing as she yanked here and there on my hair and watching the arrangement fall apart at her touch. "It looks like you stuck your hair together with glue or something," she said. "It's all sticky and crunchy." I pulled back and gently pushed her hand away.

"Stop it," I said. "You're just making it worse."

She laughed again. "I don't think anything can make it look worse than it does already," she said. Taking a step back, she looked me up and down, from the heels I was cautiously balancing on to the mop of unruly hair on top of my head. "You really don't know how to dress, do you?" she said. "Just the same old jungle freak."

"Go away, Jessica," I said. She shrugged and turned away, walking casually in her heels much higher than mine. I watched her stalk down the aisle to the middle of the boat, where the DJ was beginning to whip up the crowd with some music that sounded like what they'd been playing in The Limited.

I flipped my hair over my head and ran my hands through it, breaking up the remaining pieces of mousse and pulling out the bobby pins. It was ruined anyway, so I might as well be comfortable. I straightened up and shook my head from side to side, feeling the wind rush against my scalp and burn my eyes. *At least there's a bit of nature out here on this boat*, I thought. *Though I'm sure I look like a dog shaking off after a rainstorm.*

"That looks much better," another voice said. Nat leaned against the side of the boat, wearing a dark blazer and a green tie with yellow spots on it. Most people assumed these were polka dots, but I knew they were actually tightly coiled Chinese dragons. Nat was holding two plastic cups of Sprite. He held one out to me. "I brought you some bubbles," he said.

"Thanks," I said.

"Sorry about your hair."

"That's okay. It probably wouldn't have held anyway."

"You look better now though," he said. "More like Keena."

I smiled wryly. "I think you might be the only person who thinks so," I said. Moving slowly on those damn heels, I crept away from the side of the boat and into the shade of the cabin to lean next to Nat. He sipped his Sprite slowly and looked across the harbor back to the shore.

"I don't think I like these kinds of parties," he said.

"Do you think we could swim to shore?" I asked. "You'll have to ditch your jacket but I bet we could make it."

"Mom's picking us up at ten," Nat said. "And I can't swim that far. You could, but you can't leave me here. I'd have no one to talk to for another four hours."

"Fine," I said. "We'll just be stuck here together." I turned my head to the side and watched my classmates dance, waving their arms and moving their hips in time with the music and circling around a small cluster of girls in the middle of the floor. I didn't need to look closer to know it was Meghan and her friends. I'd seen them arrive earlier and they looked impossibly gorgeous in their pastel-colored dresses and tall high heels. Why was Meghan wearing colors now when she told me black would be fine for me? I slid my feet out of my heels and rocked back and forth against the metal grid of the deck. None of this made any sense. How was it possible that I could act like an adult and be treated like one in Botswana but here in America I was stuck in some kind of frozen childhood where I couldn't grow up and spent my weekends making cookies while my friends wore pink and turned into women? I sighed. Maybe Meghan was right. Maybe in America I would never grow up.

CHAPTER 10

BABOON IDENTIFICATION AND OTHER HIDDEN TALENTS

MERCIFULLY, THE BAR MITZVAH party was my last commitment for the school year. Before I knew it, the time had finally come for my family to pack our dusty duffel bags and go back to Botswana. My parents had renewed their grant yet again, and now that the school year was over, their teaching commitments were done for another six months, which meant another six months of collecting data and conducting experiments with the baboons.

Most of my Baboon Camp gear was already safely under the cot in my tent awaiting our return, but Mom and I still made a trip to REI to pick up a few last-minute items we needed, an errand I always looked forward to. Shopping for camping gear was completely different and infinitely better than shopping for clothes.

Mom needed a new headlamp, since a baboon had grabbed hers from the hook by her tent and smashed it against a tree, and I needed to restock my emergency medical kit since I was out of sterile gauze dressings and oral rehydration solution. We had a book in camp called *Where There Is No Doctor* that had a recipe for homemade oral rehydration solution for cases of extreme dehydration, but the concoction tasted terrible and I always had a hard time choking it down since it was basically just water with sugar and salt in it. We all much preferred the flavored, powdered kind we could get in the US.

Mom also bought a stun gun, which surprised me almost as much as it surprised the clerk at REI.

"That's no good for bears, ma'am," he said, which I knew would piss her off. Mom hated being called "ma'am." Mom slid the stun gun out of its case and tossed it lightly from one hand to another.

"I'm not going to use it on bears," she said. "I'm going to use it on my kids." The clerk stared at her in shock but she merely buttoned the stun gun back up in its case and added it to the pile of medical supplies in our cart. In the chaos of packing and closing up the house before heading to the airport, I completely forgot about the stun gun until a week later, when we were back in Baboon Camp and Mom brought it to the kitchen from her tent and asked Lucy and me to join her at the table.

I was wrapped tightly in my purple Patagonia jacket, now faded almost colorless, and had been sitting in cozy warmth in my chair at the table. Mpitsang had given us the idea to carry shovelfuls of coal from the firepit and dump them under our chairs to keep us warm, and it was working beautifully. I was barefoot, slowly sipping a cold beer that had been chilled in the water by the boat, and deliriously happy to be back in Botswana. The winter wind whistled through the rain trees and shook the branches of the fig tree, dropping leaves and bits of figs into the waters of the lagoon below. A lone buffalo had been spotted by the water pump and there were three elephants feeding on palm trees by the car park, shuffling their feet in the sand and rumbling quietly to each other as they ate. I could smell them. The graduate students who'd been watching the camp had already gone home and we were once again alone, surrounded by nothing but miles after miles of floodplains.

Mom flexed the stun gun in her hand.

"I can't believe I bought this," she said. "But I want you girls to know why I did. One of our colleagues at Penn told us that a friend of his who works in Ecuador believes that if you shock someone who is bitten by a snake, you can neutralize the venom. I very much doubt that this is true, but I figured, why not? It's not like we have any other option if someone gets bitten by a mamba."

"So if someone gets bitten by a mamba you want us to shock them?" I asked.

"It's not supposed to be that painful, from what I hear," Mom said. She looked at me and then her lips curved into a slightly evil smile. "Want to try it?"

I looked across the melapo at the setting sun. I smelled dust on the wind, the smoke from the campfire, and the faintest hint of buffalo under the smell of the elephants. The heavy tension I'd been carrying in my shoulders for months drained away and everything in the world was right again: no more school, no more malls, and no more dresses. The relief was so acute I wanted to cry, but at the same time I knew that my time back in Baboon Camp was limited; as soon as I stepped off the boat, the seconds began ticking away until I would have to leave again. In an instant, I decided that every single one of those seconds had to count. I was game for anything. I looked at Mom.

"Sure," I said. "Lucy, hold my beer."

Mom turned the stun gun on to the lowest setting. She aimed it at me, and I nodded. There's a scene in *Return of the Jedi* when R2-D2 gets shot by a stormtrooper. When the blast hits him, he squeals and jerks. The electricity from the blast radiates across him in blue waves and makes all the pieces of his machinery blow up and start smoking.

That's what it felt like. My chair toppled over backward, sending me sprawling in the dust and staring up at the stars through the branches of the fig tree, gasping like a fish out of water. Mom was right; it didn't hurt exactly, but it sure knocked the wind out of me and made my fingers and toes twitch.

Mom helped me up and Lucy brought me a fresh beer from the river.

"That's what you want us to do if someone gets bitten by a snake?" Lucy asked. "That looks pretty bad."

"It was just an idea," Dad said from the other end of the table. "And probably not a very good one. But feel free to shock me if I get bitten by a mamba. With only half an hour left to live, I welcome any and all attempts to save my life, be they stun guns, limb amputation, or whatever you happen to find first." And with that he stood up and walked into the woods with a pile of chicken bones for the hyenas to eat.

I was surprised that Mom had even thought of buying the stun gun in the first place. We saw snakes in camp fairly regularly but had never had encounters that were close enough to really upset us. Usually the snakes we found were harmless and we let them go, or Mpitsang killed them with a machete. It seemed like we already had a good protocol in place.

But Mom said it wasn't the snakes in camp that really worried her, it was the snakes she and Dad ran into when they were with the baboons. The baboons walked on narrow game trails made by other animals like impala and kudu, and snakes often lay across these trails, searching for direct sun in the early mornings. The baboons also liked to sun themselves on the termite mounds that were scattered through the islands and looked like castles rising out of the grass. The sun heated the clay compound of the mounds and made them perfect places to warm up from the cold mornings. The problem was, the snakes thought so too. Almost every day in the cold months Mom and Dad saw snakes sunning on termite mounds and Mom said it was only a matter of time before they stepped on one by accident. She thought it might be a good idea to keep the stun gun in her backpack in case that did happen, but admitted it was a long shot since nothing had ever been proven to work against a mamba bite. Like all the animals we ran into, avoidance was still the best strategy to keep ourselves safe.

"Or maybe all these brushes with death are just too exciting for me," Dad said.

Too exciting? I thought. I never considered Baboon Camp itself to be *too exciting*. All the real adventures I'd had so far had taken place outside the camp, whether on the river to Xaxaba or when Mom and Dad took me out with the baboons. I wasn't allowed to go off on my own when we were with the monkeys, but even walking around with them was more exciting than doing laundry or reading in my tree. I wrinkled my nose. If there was something more exciting I could be doing, then that's where I wanted to be. I only had so much time in Baboon Camp and I wanted that time to be as exciting as possible.

I realized I wanted to participate in my parents' work. I envied how quickly Mokupi was able to identify all the baboons and how Mom and Dad gossiped with each other about which baboons were friends with other baboons and who had just had a baby. I knew who a few of the adult females were since we had a list of them in the kitchen, and I could identify them when they came into camp: Cordelia's left ear was folded over and Sierra's tail was bent from where it had been broken as a baby, but beyond that they all looked the same to me. Mokupi said, "Ah, Keena, how can you not see that is Balo and that is Nutmeg? Balo's face is like this and Nutmeg looks angry, angry, angry."

And Mokupi was right; she did. I tried to remember what he said when the baboons came into camp a day or two later. When I looked closer, Nutmeg's fur was darker than the other females' and wirier. Her face was more pinched than Balo's and her lower jaw jutted out like a barracuda, giving her a permanently unpleasant expression. Balo's face was rounder and softer than Nutmeg's and she walked faster than the other baboons, as if she were late to pick her kids up from soccer practice. And she might have been too; Balo had five daughters and one grandson by the time I met her and it seemed like one of her offspring was almost always in trouble.

I began a campaign to get my parents to agree to bring me with them into the field—to convince them I was old enough now. I loved their stories of dramatic fights between baboon families or the time when a young female tried swinging on the tail of a giraffe. Once Mom and Dad were convinced I was fast enough and strong enough to take care of myself if we ran into something dangerous, they agreed to start letting me go out with them every day, provided that I start helping them collect data as soon as I knew the baboons well enough.

As it turned out, this didn't take long. They say that everyone has a talent, they just have to discover what it is. I discovered mine the summer I was thirteen. What I am good at is recognizing baboons.

JUNE 16, 1997
KEENA'S JOURNAL

I went out with the baboons again today. They started out in the woods on Camp Island but moved through the melapo and across Airstrip Island. None of the animals enjoyed the water crossings and most either crossed with their tails in the air or on their hind legs, all the while making anguished grunting noises. The older infants like Amber and Akela got to ride their mothers across and watched the others struggling along beside them. Some of the very little ones like Jupiter and Lulu had to swim the whole way. The current was weak, but still swept them away from the rest of the group. When they got to Airstrip they were soggy and looked miserable.

I am getting a lot better with identifying the baboons. I like working on the medium-sized girls because they are cute and have more interesting personalities than the boys. The only problem is that there are about twenty of them and I confuse them all the time. After about two hours of staring at them they all start to look the same. Mokupi says that even he can't tell them apart some of the time, so at least I'm in good company.

In other news, there is a weaverbird in camp that is convinced that his archrival lives in the mirror in the shower. All day you can hear him hurling himself against the mirror and attacking it with his beak. I think we may have to start covering the mirror with a towel so he doesn't hurt himself. Dad also shot a spitting cobra near the shower today. We know it's hit, though we don't know where it crawled off to. I hate snakes.

(Later)

Lucy heard something shaking the tree above the dinner table and shone her flashlight up at it - it was the genet! We got a really good look at it. It was carrying a fat gray mouse in its mouth. We spent most of dinner talking about Mokupi and his way of helping me learn how to identify the baboons: "Is it dark?" "Yes, dark, but a little less light." Or, "It has a funny face" (to literally every single individual). He would look at baboons twenty feet away, deep in a bush with their backs turned, and expect me to know who it was. It reminds me of the dentist, when they fill your mouth to overflowing with tools and then ask you how your summer was. I don't know how he's so good at this.

I already knew a bit about baboon social structure since Mom taught it to me in one of our homeschool lectures, but it was much more interesting to see it played out in front of me as we walked through the islands and melapo. Every night, when I sat down after my shower to write my journal entry for the day, I found my pen flying across the paper, with so much to say from my day out with the baboons that I barely had enough space in my journal to cover everything. Whereas in the years before, my journal entries had shrunk to "and then we did this around camp," I filled page after page with my adventures out with the baboons, sitting by the fire as the sun sank and the impala trotted around in the woods behind the kitchen.

One morning, I got up as the sun rose to run laps around camp before it got too hot. Though in retrospect this perhaps wasn't the smartest thing to do, Mom and Dad agreed that if I walked all around the camp singing loudly and didn't see signs of any animals, it was probably safe for me to go running as long as I kept to the main paths.

I was circling back through the laundry area when the baboons, who had been sleeping in the palm grove behind camp, erupted in a wild clamor of screams, wahoo calls, and shrieks. At that time of day, that amount of noise could really mean only one thing: a leopard attack. I sprinted to the kitchen where Mom was getting a cup of coffee, shouting at Lucy's and my tent along the way, "GET UP, LUCY, THERE'S A LEOPARD ATTACK!"

Mom, Lucy, and I ran out toward the noise and found about twenty baboons sitting around the base of a termite mound with a small croton tree on it. Nothing seemed to be happening and we wondered whether the baboons had just freaked out over nothing, which they sometimes do. But then, just as we were about to leave, the baboons leaped at the base of the termite mound, screaming, jumping, whooping, and slapping at a hole in the bottom. Though several large adult males were leading the attack, even mothers with babies joined in, and a few of my favorite fluffy juveniles too. Immediately after this outburst, we heard a soft, low growl coming from inside the hole and knew the baboons had cornered a leopard.

Leopards kill more baboons than almost any other animal, but always at night when they creep into the baboons' sleeping sites to attack. During the day, their relationship is almost reversed; a fully grown adult male baboon weighs close to one hundred pounds, while an adult female leopard can be as small as just sixty pounds. And, since baboon troops often include more than twenty adult males, the baboons are at a huge advantage if they encounter a single leopard when they can actually see it. Baboon troops can (and do) easily rip leopards apart if they corner them during the day, though it's an incredibly rare thing to see.

As soon as it became clear that this is what was happening, Mom yelled, "I need my camera!" and for a split second, all the baboons looked at her. In that second, the leopard made a dash out from under the termite mound and ran straight at us, as we were the only break in the mob of baboons. Lucy turned around and ran back to camp as fast as she could but Mom and I just stood there stupidly as a small spotted torpedo cannoned toward us, followed by a wave of baboons.

The leopard missed my leg by inches and dashed off into the woods with all the baboons in pursuit. The crescendo of screams rose to such a fever pitch that Mom was sure the baboons had caught the leopard and were killing it. We sprinted as fast as we could through the woods toward the noise, and when we caught up to the baboons the small leopard was lying on its back under a thornbush surrounded by baboons screaming and swiping at it. The leopard's mouth was wide-open and I remember thinking she had some amazingly big canines for a leopard that small. The uproar continued until the leopard saw another opening and dashed away again, deeper into the woodland where the bushes are thicker and it's easier to split the baboons up. We didn't follow them this time.

Despite an extensive search with Mokupi when he arrived, we didn't find anything, so we assumed the leopard got away safely. The whole episode was difficult to watch and made it very hard for me to look at the baboons in the same way after I'd seen it.

AUGUST 2, 1997
KEENA'S JOURNAL

Yesterday I was sitting on a log in the middle of Airstrip Island when a gigantic red-and-black beetle flew into my face. I tried to slap it away but somehow it fell down my shirt and got stuck along the band of my sports bra. I shook it out as soon as I could, but it had been oozing something and now my chest is covered with huge, raised red welts. They ache terribly and are very itchy. I have to be careful which shirt I wear because it hurts to have any fabric touch my skin. I wrapped some gauze around my chest but I have to change it every few hours because of the ooze from the welts. It feels like I was kicked by a horse.

I was changing the bandages on my chest the next morning when I heard hyenas laughing on the plain behind camp. Hyenas only laugh when they're fighting over something to eat, so I assumed they'd made a kill.

I pulled on my T-shirt and flip-flops and jogged slowly down the road toward the plain. I knew the landscape well enough to know where I could get a good view of the plain without compromising my safety, and crossed over a small salt pan toward a leadwood tree that was my

favorite vantage point over the interior of the island. I thought I might
have heard buffalo in the woods nearby but didn't pay any attention to
them, distracted as I was by the hyenas and their kill.

I climbed into the tree and saw four or five hyenas loping around something on the ground just at the edge of the island where the molapo met
the shore. It didn't look very large, and I was about to climb down and go
back to camp when I heard lions roaring, followed by the outraged yelping
of hyenas. Six enormous lionesses had appeared seemingly from nowhere
and were running at the hyenas, trying to drive them away from what
remained of their kill. This, again, was a very rare sight to see; everyone
seems to think that lions are noble hunters and hyenas are lazy scavengers,
but more often than not the opposite is true, and when we did come
across lions with a kill, it was something they'd stolen from hyenas.

I watched for a few minutes until the hyenas trotted off and the lions
settled down to eat and then walked back to camp, thinking what an
amazing day I had just had—and the sun hadn't even fully come up yet.

When Mokupi and Mpitsang arrived an hour or so later, they said

Please don't sink our water pump!

they'd accidentally scared a big herd of buffalo onto Camp Island from the south. The moment we left camp, heading north in an effort to skirt around the buffalo, we ran smack into them feeding in the same clearing where the baboons had attacked the leopard. We circled around the herd very slowly, going through the molapo where the water was deeper and it's harder for the buffalo to run, and ended up on a small island near where I'd seen the hyena kill earlier.

I climbed up on a small termite mound to see if the lions or hyenas were still around and if it was safe to walk in that direction, since the baboons were on the island on the opposite side of the molapo. I didn't see anything, so I slipped out of my backpack and walked slowly over toward what remained of the kill, which looked now like a smallish wildebeest. I was about twenty feet away from the kill when three huge lionesses exploded out of a bush to my right and ran toward the shore of Camp Island, in the direction of the buffalo herd. They hadn't been that close to me, physically, but my hands shook like I'd been zapped with the stun gun and I immediately broke out in a cold sweat all over my body. I tried counting to ten, and then twenty, but it was only when I'd stood still, watching the lions run away, for more than ninety seconds that I felt steady enough on my legs to walk back to where Mom, Dad, and Mokupi stood. From their angle, they hadn't seen the lions at all and just thought I'd been standing in the molapo looking at the dead wildebeest. I thought about what Dad had said about "too much excitement" and decided not to tell them about the lions in case they said I wouldn't be allowed to go out with the baboons anymore.

But the baboons had seen the lions, and even though (as far as I and the baboons knew) the lions were still on Camp Island, the baboons decided that's where they wanted to be too, and made an extremely deepwater crossing back to the edge of Camp Island near Baboon Camp. No one liked making this crossing; it was too close to the river, and though the melapo were too weedy for crocodiles and hippos, the water was much deeper than the usual places where the baboons crossed, and everyone had to swim the distance—humans included. I swam with my backpack on my head and tried to keep pace with Domino, a juvenile born last year and my favorite of all the baboons. She gave me a funny look as we swam along together but didn't seem to mind the company.

As soon as we all reached the shore of Camp Island, we heard vervets alarm calling—and a lot of them too. I assumed they had seen the lions as well, and was about to suggest we go home a different way, when Mokupi, who was standing on a termite mound, shouted, "Leopard! Leopard! I see it!" I was up that damn termite mound so fast, but I didn't see the leopard.

My heart didn't stop pounding for the rest of the day, and it was only when I was lying in my bed under the stars that I allowed myself to replay the events with a critical eye. Though every time I started at the beginning and tried to make it to the baboons, I never got past the part with the lions exploding out of the bush before my eyes would begin to tear and my heart would thunder in my ears.

AUGUST 29, 1997
KEENA'S JOURNAL

We thought the baboons were on the peninsula of C5 Island, so we went there this morning. As we walked along the shore we found deep footprints from a lion running and giraffe footprints running in front of them. Midway through the mud area between palm groves, the footprints sprang claws and we started hearing the francolin birds alarm calling. Mokupi and I decided we wanted to find the lions immediately (predictable), so Mokupi left the path and led me into the deeper woods. We had circled about six feet from where we had originally been standing when we found the kill: a gigantic giraffe. It was barely eaten, and from all the tracks it was clear that the lions had momentarily left while we were in the area but were still very close by. They left huge bite marks on the giraffe's neck and for some reason had buried all the insides in a huge mound of dirt. We left pretty quickly, given how close the lions must have been, but we didn't see them.

Later in the afternoon, a tour group from some company we'd never

heard of (NOT Xaxaba or Delta, they know better) came up to us while
we were with the baboons (which they absolutely should not do).

> *Obnoxious Tourist: "I hear you are studying baboons."*
> *Me: "Yes."*
> *OT: "Haven't they been 'studied' to death already? I would assume*
> *that all monkeys have been studied to death by now."*
> *Me: "Well, there's still a lot to learn."*
> *OT: "I've seen monkeys before. Nasty little things aren't they? Like*
> *orangutans."*
> *Me: "Orangutans are apes, not monkeys. And they live in Asia."*
> *OT: "Whatever."*
> *Me: "What do YOU do?"*
> *OT: "I work of course! How do you think I could afford a vacation*
> *like this? Just keep their filthy little hands off my luggage."*

Right, asshole, because I really can control this group of monkeys. If I
could I'd tell them to steal your luggage and go through all your stuff.

SEPTEMBER 5, 1997
KEENA'S JOURNAL

We have a book about the flowers and plants of the delta and today I
read that there was a kind of acacia bush that has leaves that make a
local anesthetic if chewed and applied to a wound, like an insect bite.
I found the bush and chewed a bunch of the leaves but all they did
was make my tongue go numb. It was an interesting experience.

Lucy and I spent a lot of time poring over this book. There were
beautiful drawings of all the trees and shrubs but also a section describing the traditional Wayeyi uses for each plant, most of which were
confirmed by Mokupi. Lucy and I tested all of them.

In addition to discovering which plants could be used to make an anesthetic, we learned which tree had bark that could paralyze fish (we tried it, but it turned out to be a failure), which roots were used to weave bracelets to protect against witches (also a failure; not because we were attacked by a witch but because the roots didn't weave; they snapped in half), and about seeds called "lucky beans" that would bring you friends if you carried one in your left pocket (but don't eat them, because they are incredibly poisonous). We also read about a kind of squash that you could use as a symbolic representation of someone else's heart. If you left the squash in the sun, it would heat up and explode, making the heart of the corresponding person also explode. We didn't test this one.

We read that boiling a sausage fruit would yield a beautiful purple dye, but we boiled one for three and a half days and learned that it did not. We also discovered that palm wine is difficult to make if you can't figure out how to properly tap a palm tree. Marula liquor, on the other hand, is easy.

Thick and brown, with a taste like a fruity version of Kahlúa, Amarula is one of the exports Botswana is most known for. It is made from the fruit of the marula tree, which ferments easily after it ripens. As luck would have it, we had a marula tree right in camp—it was my favorite reading tree. Every fall, the tree would explode with fruit and the baboons would come into camp to fight over it, pooping all over the place and, once, running off into the woods with my copy of *My Ántonia*.

When Lucy and I read how easy it is to make marula liquor, we decided to make our own; we harvested a pile of the ripest fruits, washed and cleaned them, and put them in the storage hut in Tupperware containers full of water, at which point we promptly forgot about them.

Dad discovered the containers a few months later behind a case of beer, but insisted on tasting the liquid himself before letting us have some. He said it was a good thing he did, because the alcohol was so strong it would have likely killed us. As I carried the liquor into the woods to pour it out, I thought for the hundredth time since coming back to Baboon Camp how much more comfortable I felt in this land of beetles, baboons, and poisonous, homemade moonshine. I loved the baboons and the rush of running away from lions. Every cell of my body felt alive. This was the Keena I knew. And there was nothing she couldn't do now that she was back.

CHAPTER 11

THERE ARE NO DOCTORS HERE

LIVING SO CLOSE TO the river, it was easy to forget that Botswana is mostly a desert. Even as the seasonal flood receded and the melapo dried up, we could still smell the water and use the boat, though there were always a few weeks at the height of the dry season when we had to pull it out of what remained of the river and wait for the flood to return. Water controlled everything we did, just as it did for the animals. When the flood was high and we could boat, the animals moved farther inland and spread out, since the full melapo meant water was plentiful. But when the flood dried out and the water supply disappeared from everywhere except the river itself, our island quickly became crowded with all kinds of animals huddling closer to the last permanent water source. The baboons rarely left camp, and all around us herds of animals moved through the woods, either going to the river or waiting for others to pass by so they could ambush them to eat. All of a sudden, there were lions and elephants everywhere, big herds of buffalo, and zebras out on the melapo in front of camp, and we couldn't turn around without bumping into smaller herds of impala, kudu, and giraffes that kept close to the outskirts of camp.

As the temperature climbed higher and higher we became obsessed with the weather. How hot was it going to get today? What time would the sun finally set and give us some relief? And, most importantly of all, when was it going to rain?

People in the town of Maun called October "suicide month." It was still too early in the season for rain to arrive, but already so hot that just being outside was miserable. Cloudless day after cloudless day, the sun beat down for hour after hour of relentless, suffocating heat. Most of the tourist lodges closed for the season because it was too hot for tourists to visit, and even if they did, all they would see were animals lying around in the shade feeling just as miserable as the tourists.

The heat was so intense in camp that we had to completely change our daily routine in order to minimize our exposure to the weather. The sun rose, swelteringly hot, at 4:15 a.m. Soon it became too hot to stay in the tents, and even Lucy, who loves a good sleep-in, would be up and about by 6:00 a.m. Days like these were divided into two mini-days for my family: one from 4:00 a.m. to 9:00 a.m. when it was still cool enough to work and cook, and one between 5:00 p.m. and 10:00 p.m. after the sun had started to set. Between the hours of 9:00 a.m. and 5:00 p.m., though, it was too hot to function. We left the baboons and came back to camp, schoolwork stopped, and we sequestered ourselves in various shady spots around camp to sweat out the day. It was too hot to read. It was too hot to talk, too hot to eat, and too hot to sleep. We tried playing cards and darts, but the conversation inevitably turned to just how fucking hot it was. Lucy and I dunked our heads under the faucet at the laundry sink and lay around on plastic kitchen chairs, making stupid conversation about the weather. The pens we kept in the kitchen to record the temperature melted in our hands. All our electronics overheated and the freezer struggled to keep our food cold. Daily, we registered upward of 120 degrees in the sun and easily 110 in the shade (before the thermometer we were using also began to melt and we had to put it in the fridge).

Finally, as the sun started to set, we could muster enough energy to start doing camp maintenance and plug the computers in, though it never really cooled off. At night, Lucy and I woke each other up to walk to the shower and soak ourselves and our T-shirts before going back to lying on our cots, trying to sleep. We were lucky it wasn't humid heat, but it was dry enough to severely dehydrate us if we failed to drink enough water. I kept a bottle of water in my hands at all times and tried to stick to a drinking schedule of one full bottle an hour that I hoped would keep me from getting sick.

One afternoon, I was lying in the hammock behind my parents' tent reading a book I'd borrowed from Dad about the Napoleonic Wars. In the chapter I was reading, the British captain's ship had run into a calm off the coast of Martinique and the crew was slowly going mad from the heat and lack of water. The author described the crew baking in the sun on the exposed deck of the ship, getting sicker and sicker as they felt the boat rock side to side underneath them. As I read, I felt like I was falling into the book—I could feel the ship rocking beneath me, the blistering tropical sun beating down, and felt as though I'd become one of the crew members. *So this is what it feels like to die*, I thought to myself, *slowly wasting away off the shore of Martinique.*

I sat up, trying to clear my fuzzy head, and realized that I didn't just feel sick, I was sick. My head pounded, my hands were clammy, and everywhere I looked the trees vibrated in the thick air. Dizzily, I rolled out of the hammock and stumbled toward the kitchen, willing myself not to vomit. I realized I hadn't had my bottle of water with me for a couple of hours and I was now dangerously dehydrated.

Once inside the kitchen, I sat down on the cement floor and tried to figure out what to do next. We were already out of the oral rehydration solution I'd gotten at REI, so I had to think of something else. My brain wasn't working, but I knew I had to act quickly to keep myself from getting even sicker. No one was around and I didn't have the energy to shout. *Okay*, I thought, *you're going to have to figure this out by yourself.*

Hand over hand, I pulled myself over to the shelf where we kept our guidebooks. We had a book on emergency medicine and I knew somewhere in the middle was a section on dehydration. After a few minutes of paging through the book, I found the section that described how to make the at-home oral rehydration solution I hated. I remember thinking how horribly ironic it was that I'd let my dehydration get to this level, considering how often I badgered the rest of my family about the importance of drinking water.

Still moving very slowly, I mixed water, sugar, and salt together in the proportions specified by the book, and sat down on the cool concrete, determined not to move until I'd finished the whole bottle and mixed another. It tasted terrible, but I knew it would work if I gave it some time.

By the time Dad came to the kitchen an hour later, I'd managed to drink three bottles of my homemade rehydration drink, and was feeling much better. The trees had stopped vibrating, and my hands were no longer clammy, though I had a raging headache. When he asked me if I was okay, I told him I'd changed my mind about the Napoleonic Wars and he could have his book back.

The heat was all anyone could think or talk about. Our friends in Maun spent their days on the radio talking about who had seen a cloud and whether it meant rain might come someday. We waited for the smallest sign that the weather might change, from rumors of a cloud sighted upriver to a change in how the birds sang in the morning.

OCTOBER 19, 1997
KEENA'S JOURNAL

There is an enormous fire across the river. At night all you can see is a glow filling the whole sky and during the day, clouds of smoke billowing up all along the riverbank. I spent an hour sitting in the fig tree looking at it. I could almost see the flames. I was being very quiet and the squirrels forgot I was sitting there. One was eating a fig the size of his own head and it looked like he was wearing a helmet.

The fire is very close to us but we'll be safe as long as it doesn't cross the river. If it does, we would have to take everything important and put it in the boat and then set the boat loose out in what's left of the lagoon (this would include the computers and data from the baboons and all the recording equipment). Then we would have to roll the petrol and paraffin drums into the water by the boat dock so they wouldn't explode ... and then do our best to beat the fire back from camp so all the buildings don't burn down. They are all built with dry letlhaka so it wouldn't take much for them to be destroyed.

    (Later)

We can see the flames. They are exactly on the opposite side of the river. The fire is huge. It is sweeping across an area bigger than our island and the flames are rising high up into the sky. I can feel the heat from the flames and the roar from the fire is very loud. Little bits of ash are floating through the air and staining my hands and face black with soot. I hope it goes away.

OCTOBER 21, 1997
KEENA'S JOURNAL

We had only a tiny bit of rain yesterday, but it did enough to cool the dust and make the trees drip. The fire went out, as far as we can tell. No smoke, flames, or ash anywhere. Amazing that so small a rainstorm could put out so huge a fire. Or maybe it burned itself out? After my shower I got restless so I went running on the paths around camp. Mom said I was only allowed to run eight laps because she didn't know where the lions were, but I ran twelve. It was great, and I didn't get too hot because my hair was wet. I should do that more often.

NOVEMBER 3, 1997
KEENA'S JOURNAL

It is 130 degrees today. It is too hot to write.

NOVEMBER 5, 1997
KEENA'S JOURNAL

We were going to go for a game drive today, but, for the one billionth day in a row, the baboons came into camp to keep working on the huge crop of figs in the big tree. Even though Mom started screaming obscenities as soon as the first animals entered camp and settled in, still they came. She really, really hates it when they come into camp. It means we can't eat (because they can't see us with food) and have to spend all our time making sure they don't rip apart the tents or run off with any of our stuff. It's a full-time job.

Mom stormed into the storage hut and came out brandishing a huge jar of peri peri sauce. She marched into the baboons and started flinging the peri peri sauce all over the figs, hoping that they wouldn't like the hot pepper and would stop eating them. The baboons didn't notice. Still swearing, she went back to the storage hut and came out with a box of matches and started setting fire to the figs. They didn't really burn but started smoldering. Mom was still standing among the baboons and the spicy, smoking figs when an elephant ran out of the woods and bellowed at her, making her drop the matches and dash back into the kitchen. Lucy and I were dying laughing but were trying to hide it because Mom was so mad at the baboons.

NOVEMBER 6, 1997
KEENA'S JOURNAL

At about 11 a.m., guess who arrived: the baboons! My parents were PISSED. I think a large amount of their anger comes from how unbelievably, fucking miserably hot it is, but they took it all out on the baboons. Because her experiment with matches didn't work yesterday, today Mom decided to step it up a notch. Dad and I raked all the figs under the tree into a big pile (there were a LOT). The baboons ignored us the whole time and continued eating even while we raked. The final pile was more than two feet deep in the middle and covered most of the area under the tree. When we were finished, Mom came over and dumped a can full of petrol on the pile and set fire to it. She was in a terrible mood but I think hurling petrol on a flaming pile of figs made her feel a little better. It didn't really work so we threw water on it, but the muffled explosions from the middle of the pile and the smoke that billowed out of it seemed to be enough to scare most of the baboons away. I was very happy to take a shower after that, since I was covered with soot and ash from the burning fig pile.

Bart the baboon ignores my mother's rage.

NOVEMBER 7, 1997
KEENA'S JOURNAL

The baboons are BACK. They are still eating the burned pile of figs and I think Mom is going to lose her mind.

Instead of doing school this morning we started shoveling the charred figs into wheelbarrows and taking them out onto the plain behind camp to be dumped. Mom said if the baboons are going to insist on eating the figs, they could do so outside the camp. It took a long time and the wheelbarrow loads were very heavy, especially in this heat. I really wanted to wash my hair but we have no more shampoo. All the bottles melted in the heat and the shampoo dripped into the dust.

NOVEMBER 14, 1997
KEENA'S JOURNAL

It is HOT, HOT, HOT. It was so hot last night that I was awake, sweating, until midnight. I was trying to listen to animals but all I could think about was how hot I was. I finally fell asleep after I threw all my sheets on the floor, but I woke up again a few hours later when I felt an ant crawling across my face. I didn't think it was a big deal since this happens a lot, but after I flicked it off I felt two or three more on my forehead and then a LOT more on my legs and stomach. I turned on my flashlight and saw that I was COVERED with ants; they were all over me—the little worker ants, and the huge, pinchy soldier ants too. I screamed and jumped out of bed to turn on the light. Lucy woke up and threw some water from her water bottle on me to help get the ants off. We figured out that they had come through a small hole in the canvas (whyyyy!?) near my pillow. We smooshed them all with our textbooks and put some duct tape over the hole but I couldn't make sure they were all out of my sheets until morning.

Instead of going back to bed I piled my sheets on my cot and slept on the floor with my pillow. Yuck, I felt like they were crawling on me all night and I didn't sleep much. During dinner, lions killed something across the lagoon and we could hear the slurping, crunching, and growling echoing all around us. It was a bit scary.

Too hot to do schoolwork today. In the book I am reading the British are marching across Egypt to the Suez in 128-degree heat. I know how they feel!

NOVEMBER 17, 1997
KEENA'S JOURNAL

In the morning, Mokupi arrived to go to Maun with us. We started out all right and the road wasn't too bumpy. I thought, "Wow. We'll get there at 11 a.m.!" I was so wrong.

After about two and a half hours, the car skidded suspiciously. We got out and found that our back right tire was completely flat. No problem. We put on the spare and were about to get in the car when Mokupi shouted that the spare was flat too. For two hours Dad and Mokupi fought the rusty split rims of the spare tire, snapping one tire iron completely in half in the process. Mom, Lucy, and I tackled the other tire. Mom held a tire iron jammed in between the rim and the tire and Lucy and I jumped on the tire to get all the air out. The new tubes were put in, then the liners and hubs. Then we had to pump them both back up again, which takes a long time with only one tiny bicycle pump! But finally we got the spare on the car and the other tire in the back and started driving again. Getting close to Maun we heard a loud explosion. The back left was flat! Because we had spent so much time fixing the two tires, we luckily enough had another tire. From then on, the drive was fine, though we had to stop every half hour or so to cool the car off under a tree. The engine kept over-heating and making pinging sounds that Dad said were no good.

On that trip to Maun we stayed as we usually did with Tim and Bryony, our friends with the ostrich farm on the Boro River. In the early morning before the heat became too much to go outside, Bryony asked us if we wanted to go riding with her and her daughters, Maxie and Pia. Neither Lucy nor I were particularly good riders, but it sounded like a lot of fun so we said we'd love to.

The horses hadn't been fed yet and were a bit jumpy, particularly Bryony's new stallion, Kwebu, which she'd recently purchased from a San breeder near the Kalahari Desert in the middle of Botswana, near a town called Ghanzi. Bryony suspected the horse hadn't been treated well by his previous owners, and every time she tried to put the saddle on him he reared and snorted. Bryony showed me how to calm him down by rubbing his neck, which I did quietly while the rest of the horses got saddled and ready for our ride.

When the other girls were mounted, Bryony gave me a leg up and I jumped on Kwebu's back. Instantly, he took off. Since the paddock was gated and he couldn't get out, he raced toward the far side of the enclosure, which was connected to the saddling area by a small opening in the fence. As he ran through this opening, my left arm was wrenched backward by the fence post and I could feel one of the nails rip into my elbow. Kwebu wasn't slowing down, and I remember thinking, *He's going to jump the fence. He's going to jump the fence and I'm going to get swept off into that thorn tree.* I couldn't think of what else to do, and since my feet weren't in the stirrups anyway, I launched myself sideways off of his back, slamming into the paddock fence and landing in a pile of horse poop.

Bryony ran over and helped me sit up. My breath had been completely knocked out of me and there was a huge hole in my elbow—it looked like an animal had bitten a chunk out of it. There wasn't any blood, oddly, but I could see some kind of white stuff in the hole and something smooth that I thought might be the bone, before I leaned over and threw up in the sand. I don't remember how I got there, but I remember the cool tile of the Longdens' bathroom and something cool and sticky on my elbow. Bryony later told me that they didn't have any antiseptic so she'd cleaned the wound with the herbal salve they used on the ostriches when they got hurt. There was no doctor in town to take me to, and since the hole was too wide to stitch, Bryony covered the salve with a clean piece of cloth and duct-taped the whole thing closed. Later she winked and told me that a piece of the bone had indeed splintered off, but that she went back to the paddock and couldn't find it to put back in.

"Ha ha," I said, before throwing up again.

Mom and Dad had been running errands in town, and when they came back at sunset I was lying on a canvas chair by the firepit behind the Longdens' house, eating a piece of toast and talking with Lucy and Bryony's daughters, Maxie and Pia. My head had cleared and the throbbing in my arm had begun to fade into the background, though it still hurt quite a lot. I asked Mom and Dad whether I'd have to fly to Gaborone, the capital of Botswana and geographically the closest metropolitan area that might have a surgeon of some kind, but they said no, we'd just have to deal with it when we went back to the US in a month. Neither of them seemed particularly worried once they and Bryony discussed the situation, so I didn't think too much more about it.

NOVEMBER 22, 1997
KEENA'S JOURNAL

Last night the scene in front of camp was unbelievable. First a cow/ calf herd of elephants drank at the lagoon and grazed quietly while the sun went down behind them. Then, out of nowhere, two hyenas ran out of the woods, grabbed a female impala, and started fighting over her, laughing loudly the whole time. They wrestled and tackled each other all over the place. The elephants tried to ignore them but would trumpet and shake their heads whenever the hyenas got too close.

The elephants were nice to look at during dinner but at night they moved into camp and started tearing things down. They uprooted a tree near the choo and trampled all over our paths, which means we're going to have to resweep them tomorrow and clean off all the branches they've dumped on them. After a while Mom and Dad started to worry that the elephants would rip down something important like the radio antenna or the water tank, so they started running out from the tent to throw firecrackers at the elephants to "encourage them" to move out. No effect whatsoever. They just bellowed at us and continued ripping apart the trees. Lucy and I were up for most of the night listening to the elephants huff and puff next to our tent.

There isn't much I'm looking forward to about going back to America. It will be nice to have some cold weather, but why would I want to leave when so much is happening here? Mom and Dad keep trying to make it sound like going back to America is a good thing, but I know they're just doing it to make me feel better. It annoys me that they keep saying, "We're going home," like I'm not home already.

DECEMBER 5, 1997
KEENA'S JOURNAL

I'm going to miss the wide sky, the islands, and the beautiful views. Most of all I will miss the animals. All the babies are being born and they are so cute...also the early morning coolness and the way the birds sing after it rains. I ABSOLUTELY DO NOT WANT TO GO IT IS SO, SO, SO, SO SAD!!

CHAPTER 12

THE ELF PRINCESS PLAYS LACROSSE

WE RETURNED TO THE US in January so my parents could go through another round of teaching and grant renewal. The cycle was so familiar by this point it was just part of our lives: furiously working in the US in order to get the funds to go back to Baboon Camp and furiously collecting data before repeating it all over again. Again, Lucy and I packed away our Baboon Camp gear in duffel bags under our cots and braced ourselves for the freezing cold and the snow—both completely impossible to imagine in the searing heat of Botswana. Again, Nat's mother picked us up at the airport in the family minivan and drove us home to our cold and shuttered house to unpack. Again, Dad went out to find something for dinner and returned with frozen dinner rolls and fried chicken, claiming that nothing had ever tasted as delicious in his life. Again, I went to sleep wrapped in my cold sheets listening to the radiator clang and hiss while wishing that the noises I heard were elephants, lions, and hippos. The process of returning to America and settling in to such a different existence felt familiar by this point but never seemed to ease my sadness at leaving Botswana or the jarring sensory overload of life in Pennsylvania.

The next morning, my mother drove me to an appointment with a plastic surgeon. Though my arm was healing and didn't appear to be infected, Mom felt extremely guilty that we hadn't been able to get it stitched up by a professional. There were no doctors in Maun at the time, except for one ex-psychotherapist from South Africa who was sometimes able to obtain illegal antibiotics from Zimbabwe. He hadn't been available when I hurt my arm, however, since I was thrown off the horse at 10 a.m. and he was known to be blindingly drunk at any time after 9 a.m. So I was left with the beginnings of a half-dollar-sized mound of pink scar tissue surrounded by ropy, raised skin that itched and stretched around my elbow like dried glue.

Mom and I sat down in the waiting room and I flipped through the pages of a glossy magazine on the coffee table. It appeared that the world was still very upset about the death of Princess Diana a few months earlier. I'd heard about it from Bryony at the ostrich farm since she was British, and I knew that Princess Diana had been married to Prince Charles, who was next in line for the British throne. Bryony didn't have the details on what happened but knew it had involved someone named "Paparazzi," who I didn't recognize.

Finally, the plastic surgeon called us into his office. He sliced the dusty duct tape off my arm with a pair of surgical scissors and began poking the wound thoughtfully.

"Well," he said after a few minutes. "This is certainly a change from another breast enhancement consultation, that's for sure."

Mom looked uncomfortable.

"We did our best with what we had," she said. "I wish it could have been more..." I knew she was embarrassed and felt like a Bad Parent, something she seemed to be concerned about with increasing frequency. She'd said as much more than a hundred times on the way to the doctor. I didn't see why she should feel so guilty—it wasn't as though she could have done any more than what she did. This was just part of the risk that our family assumed in living where we did and I thought we had all made our peace with that. But maybe I had been wrong.

"It's actually fine," the doctor said, running a gloved finger along the edges of the raised patch. "Whatever you put on it seemed to clean it well enough and the duct tape was certainly effective in keeping out any infectious agents." He laughed. "It actually looks great. In fact, I don't think she needs surgery. Anything I would do would just leave her with a scar the same size as the one that she'll already have, so why bother?"

"That went better than expected," Mom said in the car on the way home. "At least, I don't feel quite so bad about it." I squirmed. The car was cold and my arm ached from being poked and prodded by the doctor. I was restless and had not seen the sun in nearly two days. The cold, still world smelled like salt.

"Can we just go back to the house?" I said. Nat's mother, Cathy, had lent me his copy of *The Subtle Knife*, the sequel to *The Golden Compass*, and all I wanted to do was make a cup of tea and curl up in a chair to read it. I had tried retreating into the castle in my head at the doctor's office but found it harder to get into than I remembered. I hoped a book would quiet the anxious pacing that my brain was doing instead. School started the next day, and I didn't want to go at all.

I entered school for the second half of eighth grade much the same way I'd started sixth and seventh: my hair bleached light brown by the sun and my skin deeply tanned and marked with mosquito bites and slashes from thorn branches. My backpack still puffed soft clouds of dust whenever I dropped it and now sported a brown stain on the side from where a baboon had pooped on it. (Mom made me promise not to tell anyone what caused the stain. Apparently, this would become another marker of a Bad Parent.) Armed with Nat's copy of *The Subtle Knife*, I walked through the doors of the middle school and searched the student lounge for him. I'd only made it halfway through the book but already had a lot of questions I wanted to discuss.

A group of blonde girls were chatting at the table closest to where I stood. I didn't pay much attention to them as I scanned the room for Nat's curly hair but thought fleetingly how odd it was that girls from the high school were hanging out in the middle school lounge. They were clearly too old to be where they were. I didn't see Nat and was getting ready to go to homeroom when one of the high school girls stood up and called my name.

"Hey, Keena!" she said. "Welcome back!" I stared in complete shock.

What had happened to Meghan while I was gone? Half a head taller than the last time I'd seen her and with a stylish-looking haircut that brushed blonde bangs casually across her forehead, she looked far older than fourteen. Did she magically become eighteen while I was gone? Didn't she know the rest of us only aged in one-year increments?

Meghan gave me a hug as the rest of the group looked on.

"Are you still fourteen?" I whispered over her shoulder. Her hair smelled like flowers and fresh grass and I pulled back. I didn't want to make her dirty.

"Yes, of course I'm still fourteen," she said, taking a step back to look at me. "But you look older."

"I do?" I said. "I don't feel any older."

One of the other girls came to stand next to Meghan and I realized that in giving me a hug in the middle of the student lounge, Meghan had bestowed upon me the blessing of the coolest girl in middle school. I was instantly accepted.

"Your tan looks really good," the other girl said. I vaguely recognized her and thought her name might be Sarah or Katie. "Where did you get it done? It looks so professional."

"Oh . . . um, thank you," I stammered and shifted my backpack on my shoulder. What should I say? I didn't know the names of any tanning salons and didn't want to lie to this girl. Should I tell her it's a real tan and I got it from spending two months baking in a heat so intense that it melted pens and shampoo bottles? Or should I just let it go?

"Come on," Meghan said, sparing me from responding to the other girl. "The bell just rang; it's time for homeroom."

I finally found Nat in my homeroom and slid into a desk next to him.

"You got tall," I hissed at him under the noise of the other students banging open the door and dropping books on their desks. "You're not supposed to get tall; you're supposed to be short like me." Nat shrugged.

"What do you want me to say?" he said. "Maybe I'll be faster than you now."

"Never," I said. "You're only good at math and losing when we play tennis." He reached over and punched me in the shoulder.

"I'm glad you're back," he said.

As they did the last time I returned from Baboon Camp, my teachers were insistent that they test me immediately to see if I'd learned all the things that I was supposed to have learned while I was away. They didn't believe that I could keep up with the curriculum while essentially teaching myself, and wanted to make sure I wasn't going to hold up the rest of the class. I understood why they wanted to do this but resented being assessed and tested more than the other students. Why didn't my teachers just believe me when I said I knew how to solve algebraic equations and that I'd actually read *Lord of the Flies*? I'd even had a whole discussion about it with my mom one day when we were out with the baboons. We'd decided that baboons could be called more civilized than humans because their social structure was more stable and they were less likely to devolve into chaos without leadership.

My new math teacher was a fierce old lady named Mrs. Graff (which no one seemed to think was funny except me) who made me stay after school to take an exam to see how far I'd gotten in that year's lesson plan. I scored a 92 percent, and after Mrs. Graff realized she'd mistakenly given me the final exam and not the midterm, called me into her office to apologize for not believing me.

"Well, you're just going to be bored for the rest of the year since you already know what we'll be covering," she said. Nat told me I had no right to call him a dork after that and said that if I wanted to be useful, I could do his homework for him so he would have more time for computer games.

I wanted so badly for eighth grade to be peaceful and calm. I'd figured that, as the oldest students in the middle school, we'd be mostly left on our own and could relax a little bit before starting to think about high school. I already felt uncomfortable around all the other students and wanted nothing more than quiet, though there seemed to be very little of that to spare in my American life. From the moment I got up to the moment I went to sleep, there was noise: cars honking at each other on the way to school while the reporters on the radio talked about wars and bombs in faraway places, lecturing from my teachers, gossiping and teasing from other students at lunch, and then more noise and honking on the way home. The beeps and rings and bells were jarring and artificial and nothing like the blowing wind and chirping birds in Baboon Camp. They made my ears ache.

I craved solitude and silence, but found it in only a few places. One of these places was lacrosse practice. Every day after my last class, I collected my textbooks and grabbed my lacrosse stick from the back of my locker, joining the steady stream of girls who walked down the sidewalk toward the fields at the elementary school. Everyone who wanted to play was on the team, so there was less pressure to be good, which I appreciated since I'd never played before. I usually walked by myself but sometimes followed Meghan and her crew, all of whom also played lacrosse because that's what the cool kids did. They carried their shiny aluminum lacrosse sticks in bags with their initials monogrammed on them in pink and blue thread and wore cleats to practice. When I told Mom about the special shoes other girls wore at lacrosse, she told me regular sneakers had always been good enough for her when she played lacrosse and they'd be good enough for me too. I did manage to persuade Mom to buy me an aluminum lacrosse stick like Meghan's when I reported that my coach said I shouldn't use Mom's old stick because I might "break an antique." My new lacrosse stick was shiny and had a yellow plastic head just like the other girls'. In my head I named her Laurana, after the elf princess from my Dragonlance books, but I knew enough not to say that out loud.

Laurana and I were a good team, as it turned out. We started each practice with two warm-up laps around the field and then a series of passing and shooting drills designed to teach us how to catch and throw quickly. While I carried us through the running drills, I had to give Laurana all the credit for the passing and shooting. The yellow rubber balls seemed magnetically attracted to her, and as we jogged down the field to where the goalie stood ready to fend off our attack, we snapped up every pass and tossed the balls back to our teammates with astonishing accuracy. So accurate, in fact, that after a week or so of practice my coach pulled me aside to ask if I wouldn't mind playing with some of the more experienced players because they needed another person for their practice game.

I was feeling extra chuffed (as Dad would have said) when I walked over to where the other girls were warming up on the field next to ours. I rested Laurana on my shoulder and tried to look casual. My God, these girls were all so tall and pretty. What was I doing here? I felt like the solitary wildebeest that mixed in with the herds of zebras and hoped the zebras wouldn't notice how hairy and ungraceful he was. The sweat on the back of my neck grew cold. What was I thinking? The zebras always knew. The field was muddy from a rainstorm the night before and my legs were already splattered with mud from my warm-up run. I tried wiping some of the mud off with the back of my sneaker but succeeded only in smearing it across my legs.

I was standing off to the side waiting for someone to say something to me, but the pack of girls turned and jogged away, leaving just one girl on the sidelines who was still tying her shoes. She looked up at me with piercing blue eyes. Her long, fine blonde hair had been whipped up into a messy bun with flyaway wisps framing her face. She was very tall and skinny but in a muscular kind of way that reminded me of an antelope. She was terrifying.

"I know you," she said. *You do?* I thought to myself. *Oh my God, how? I know we're in the same class but you've never spoken to me in your life.* "You're that girl from Africa."

"Yeah, hi," I said, amazed that I could even speak. "I'm Keena."

"I'm Brooke," she said. "What are you doing here?"

"Uh . . . my coach said you needed another player for your scrimmage game."

"Well, we don't." *Oh.*

"Okay," I said. "Sorry . . . I'll just wait here for your coach then.

I'm supposed to talk to her." Brooke cocked her head and narrowed her eyes.

"You really are new here," she said. My stomach flipped. What had I done wrong this time?

"I'm not new here," I said. "I've been going to this school for a long time."

"You so are," she said. "Those gym shorts look like they're your dad's"—they were actually my mom's—"and your hair . . ." Here, she paused for effect. "Is that a bowl cut?" I reached up and pushed a lock of hair behind my ear. I was actually pretty proud of how my hair was growing out after another disastrous cut by my mother in Baboon Camp. It was now long enough to cover my ears and if I tried really hard I could put it up in a ponytail. My hands started to shake and I swallowed hard.

"I'm sorry," I said, though I didn't know what I was apologizing for.

"I'll tell my coach you were here, monkey girl," Brooke said and picked up her lacrosse stick from where it was leaning against the aluminum bench. "Go make out with some monkeys."

I watched Brooke join the girls in the middle of the field and then turned around to walk back to my own team, scrubbing furiously at the trickle of sweat that ran down my forehead. My insides felt like they'd been scrambled in a blender. How was it possible I'd screwed up so badly just by introducing myself?

At the end of practice, I met Nat back at school. His mother was picking us up and I was going to have dinner at their house, since Mom and Dad would be working late and Lucy went to a friend's house. This happened often enough that none of the teachers on pickup duty bothered asking me for a note. I felt sad and tired but tried to smile as Nat's mom, Cathy, pulled up.

Nat climbed into the front seat of the minivan and I settled into the seat behind him, in what he called the "captain's chair." Cathy turned around in the driver's seat and said, "I'm glad you're coming over, Keena. I have a pound of grapes that need eating and my kids won't touch them."

I grinned. Grapes were my favorite fruit and we never got them in Botswana. They had been at the top of the list of foods I was looking forward to when we got back to America, right behind pizza. I loved it when Cathy unloaded all her family's fruit on me, though I never understood why Nat didn't eat it. As far as I knew, since first grade he had subsisted on the same diet of peanut butter and jelly sandwiches and chewy Chips Ahoy cookies.

"What do you want to do at my house?" Nat asked, and we laughed. Obviously, we were going to do exactly the same thing we always did— go down to the basement to play Battle Masters.

Battle Masters was a board game that pitted the forces of good (the Imperial Army) against the forces of evil (the Army of Chaos). Nat was always the Imperial Army because they had more complicated rules for attacking and defending, and I was always the Army of Chaos because they had wolf riders. Nat won every single game we ever played, but I didn't mind. I enjoyed the game, but even more so, I valued the hours of silence I knew I would get in Nat's company. As he quietly slid units of infantry soldiers and archers across the big vinyl mat toward the towers that I defended with my orcs and beastmen, I finally had the space to sit and think in a way I wasn't able to do anywhere else. Nat demanded nothing of me other than that I take my turn on time.

I didn't tell Nat about Brooke or how sad she made me feel. I had tried confiding in him once when I was getting the prank phone calls, but all he did was blink and tell me that sometimes people were mean and there wasn't anything we could do about it. He was right, of course, but I didn't sense that he really understood the nuances of girl drama. I didn't particularly want to talk about it anyway. There was already too much talking in my world, and if Nat could offer peace and quiet and wolf riders, I would gladly take all three.

I didn't tell Mom and Dad about Brooke either. In Baboon Camp they knew everything about my life. If something happened to me during my day, they were probably right next to me watching it happen (save that one lion encounter I still hadn't told them about). Except for reading in the afternoon or taking the boat down to Xaxaba, we were part of each other's lives in a way no one in America seemed to be with their families.

But in Pennsylvania, I only saw my parents and Lucy at dinner, and everyone was always in such a rush to get back to their work or homework that we never talked much beyond "How was your day?" and "What did you do in school?" I knew they cared how my day was and whether I was happy, but unless something really big happened, it didn't seem worth sharing. Would they care what we talked about in English class or whether Laurana and I had a particularly good day on the lacrosse field? Would they care about the mixed-up-blender feeling I got in my stomach whenever I saw the high school girls playing lacrosse on the field next to mine? Maybe, maybe not. It wasn't that interesting to me what a student had said to Dad after class or whether Lucy's friend had invited her to a sleepover on Saturday, so I assumed that the minutiae of my day weren't worth reporting either.

Whenever Mom asked me how my day was, I answered, "It was fine." And my days really were fine: school was fine, lacrosse was fine, and Nat was fine. Besides the occasional monkey-girl remark from Brooke when I practiced with the more experienced players (their coach had asked me to come back after all), nothing bad really happened to me. No large animals ambushed me outside math class and no baboons broke into my locker to steal my lunch. Latin class wasn't interrupted by the moans of a dying buffalo in the hallway and we didn't have to go without water because elephants ripped up the water pipes behind the girls' bathroom.

"Why don't you write in your journal?" Mom asked me. I had some free time in the evenings now that the school year was winding down and Mom was getting tired of me pacing back and forth in the hallway like a dog waiting to be let outside.

"What would I write about?" I said. "Nothing happens here."

I missed being outside and didn't understand why no one else seemed to crave sunshine like I did. When our English teacher said

Happier out with the baboons than basically anywhere else

we could have class outside, my classmates squealed and fussed about having to sit on the grass where there might be bugs and dirt. Like most Americans I knew, they acted like they were at war with nature. Instead of enjoying the seasons, even when they were unpleasant, they constantly complained about the weather and aggressively climate-controlled everything from their cars to their patios. Wild animals were always pests, even when they weren't doing anything wrong, and *that* I really didn't understand.

One morning in early May, a few weeks before school let out for the summer, I was walking into school after being dropped off in the morning when I saw a fat raccoon bumbling through the woods behind the gymnasium. Since I was early, I sat on a rock and watched him for a while before going inside. Seeing me smiling, my homeroom teacher asked me what made me so happy and I told him about the raccoon. I later found out that instead of letting the raccoon go about his business, the school called animal control and had the raccoon shot, claiming that since it was out during the day it "might have been rabid." I was heartbroken.

At the end of the school year, I received an academic prize—Mrs. Graff gave a speech about each kid who won, and in mine she pointed out my "strong sense of fairness," as well as my "childlike worldview." I was already uncomfortable standing in front of my class in a dress for the awards assembly, and this remark made me instantly defensive. The speech made me sound like a little kid (Meghan's words about not growing up still thundered through my head). Mom said later that Mrs. Graff was just trying to say I had a strong sense of how the world should work, particularly when it came to nature and animals. Though I allowed myself to be angry with Mrs. Graff for the "childlike worldview" part, I agreed that she might have been right about fairness, especially if she meant respect for other creatures. I already knew that was true, but it was yet another example of something I cared about that no one else around me seemed to. *Go ahead*, I thought angrily. *Tell the whole world how different I am. I am already out of place, so why not separate me even further?* I didn't care anyway. I already knew there was a place in the world where I did fit. I just had to wait a few more weeks to go back.

CHAPTER 13

FINDING THE MOON ON EARTH

WHEN WE FINALLY FLEW back to Botswana in early June, I knew I only had three months to absorb as much Baboon Camp as possible before going back to school. Mom and Dad decided that I was getting too old to homeschool and self-teach and that once I entered high school, it was time for me to be more serious about my academics. Even though I would only be a freshman, college was on the horizon and I couldn't afford to waste any opportunity to set myself up to go to a good school, or so I was told. Though I disagreed and said I was doing just fine teaching myself, I lost that argument almost immediately—which shouldn't have surprised me considering my parents were both college professors. Already apprehensive about high school and now feeling the additional pressure of this college thing, to which I'd never given any real thought, I decided my only escape would be to go out with the baboons as much as possible—to try and hide from the American responsibilities circling my head like a whining mosquito I couldn't slap away.

In a marked change from previous years, we weren't alone in Baboon Camp that summer. We were joined by my parents' new postdoctoral fellow, Dawn, and her husband, Jim. Dawn was from the Midwest and had been studying black howler monkeys in Belize, focusing on what the males could tell from each other's calls. The only thing I knew about black howler monkeys was that they yelled a lot. Dawn, it turned out, fit right in.

"Keena!" she shouted when we met her plane at Xaxaba. "Look where we are! Isn't this fantastic? Where are the monkeys? Are there buffalo? Oh my God, I'm dying to see an elephant!"

"This woman is going to kill us all," Dad muttered, unloading a box of vegetables from the rear of the tiny plane. Jim shook my hand and looked around cautiously. He was very tall and had long hair that he kept in a high ponytail next to two shiny, round earrings. He didn't speak much, but I guessed that it was rare for him to get a word in edgewise when Dawn was around. Jim worked for Big Brothers Big Sisters and had that aura of competence and calm about him that people who work with children often have.

On the boat ride back to camp from Xaxaba, Dawn screamed approximately twenty-four times: twice to elephants we saw sloshing through the melapo on the side of the river, three times to crocodiles basking on the bank, and the rest of the times to every bird, fish, or interesting tree we passed on our way. I couldn't tell if she was scared or tired from the trip, but somewhat to my surprise, I found I wasn't annoyed by her incessant shrieking. However she was feeling, it was clear that Dawn was incredibly happy to be in Botswana, as I was, and I found myself looking forward to introducing her to Baboon Camp and the baboons, whom I could already tell she would love too.

I began going out with the baboons every day, and since I could still recognize them all from the previous year, my parents immediately enlisted me again as their research assistant. Though Mokupi still went out with us, he had to spend most of his time teaching Dawn to recognize the baboons and wouldn't be able to help with the playback experiments.

Following up the research they did on the vervet alarm calls in Kenya, my parents did a series of experiments on the baboons' vocalizations to see if they had different types of calls for different social situations. We already knew that the baboons had different types of grunts for "Hey, let's move along here," and "Hey, that's a gorgeous new baby you have, mind if I grab its leg?" among many other varieties. Dad had already devoted an incredible amount of time to following the female baboons around and recording their vocalizations, and after many, many years he had finally amassed a database of every different kind of grunt from every individual female, as well as the distinctive grunts the baboons gave to threaten each other and their screams when they were attacked.

The idea behind the experiments was to put the calls together in different combinations that either could happen in real life or that couldn't and then see if the baboons recognized the manipulation. In one example, we would wait until Selo, Helen, and Balo were all sitting around and each of them had a baby about a year old—young enough to still need their mother's protection but old enough to go play by themselves for short periods of time. Dad would wait until the three females were out of sight of their babies and then play the scream of Balo's baby from a hidden loudspeaker a few meters away. Mom would videotape the three females' reactions. What they found was that when they played the scream of Balo's baby, both Selo and Helen would look at Balo, as if to say, "Hey, that's your kid screaming." These experiments proved that the baboons not only knew who their own offspring were but had the cognitive capacity to understand who everyone else was related to as well.

In a more complicated arrangement (and my personal favorite), my parents manipulated the females' social structure itself. We wanted to do another experiment on Balo, this time using the vocalizations from Selo (the alpha female) and Helen (a middle-ranking female), rather than their babies. Under normal circumstances, Balo shouldn't react at all to a playback of Selo's threat grunts followed by Helen's scream; Selo was higher ranking than Helen and could attack her if she wanted to, and Helen would always scream. That made sense. But if my parents played a recording of Helen's threat grunts followed by Selo's scream, Balo should sit up and look around as if to say, "That is NOT right. What's going on here?" In the hierarchy of the group, it would never be okay for Helen to attack Selo; my parents wanted to test if Balo understood that. As it turned out, she did.

My parents did a huge number of these social manipulation playback experiments, both between families, like the examples above, and within families, where younger sisters were supposed to rank higher than older sisters. It was fascinating to watch, but also very stressful waiting for the perfect moment when the baboons were sitting still, near the right individuals, and close enough to a bush to hide the playback speaker. Sometimes it took all day to get the setting just right, only to be interrupted by an elephant or a buffalo strolling by and ruining everything.

When we weren't doing experiments, I was assigned a number of focal animal follows to do. These "focals" were twenty-minute periods of time in which I followed an individual around and recorded everything she did and everyone she interacted with. The goal was to get a representative sample of how each female spent her time and who she spent it with, so that my parents had something to use as a control when they watched what a subject animal did after a playback experiment. I enjoyed doing the focals because of the challenge they presented in recognizing the females. The downside, though, was that spending so much time with my head bent over my notebook meant that I tripped and fell into every thornbush and warthog hole in my path. I ended every day with bruised and bleeding shins from stumbling through the bushes.

JUNE 22, 1998
KEENA'S JOURNAL

Jim decided to make a walking stick to help with some of the deeper, muddier water crossings and spent many days trying to find the right kind of buffalo thorn acacia from which to get the stick. This was a smart idea, since when we walk through the floodplains we're almost up to our waists in water and carrying a ton of very expensive electrical equipment that can't get wet: not that we haven't tried; I think my radio has been dunked several times and it still works.

Jim cut three potential sticks yesterday at great hazard to his hands. Buffalo thorn acacias are vicious and you can't get anywhere near the wood without sacrificing your hands and arms to a thousand and

one scratches. Buffalo thorn acacias are also known as "wait-a-bit"
trees because all their thorns are hooked and are hard to remove once
they've gotten stuck. Today he took me back to the tree he found on
the other side of the island to get a stick for me. I had to climb very
slowly to get through the thorns to the right branch, and another half
hour or so to saw it off the tree with the knife I had carried up in
my mouth. I was very, very cut up from the thorns when I got back to
the ground, but it's a fun project to have in the afternoon (though I
already cut myself pretty badly trying to get the bark off).

There were so many clouds out today that we barely saw the sun.
Mokupi says that clouds in June mean that a lion has been born. For
us it means that the solar panels don't get enough sun during the day
and we can't have lights at night.

When Mokupi arrived at work the day after Jim and I made the walking
sticks, he told us we'd chosen the wrong species of buffalo thorn and the
wood would never hold up to the water crossings. He took us out to the
other side of the island and identified the right kind of tree, but it turned
out to be much thicker and harder to climb. I was small enough to mostly
slither under the big branches but I had to hold my knife in my teeth and
getting all the thorns off the limbs was quite difficult. The toxins in the
thorns leeched into my hands and by dinnertime they were so swollen it
was hard to hold a fork. The walking stick was well worth it, though; it
was beautifully strong and smooth once I scraped the bark off. Mokupi
told me that the Zulu in South Africa believe that a buffalo thorn acacia
will protect you from lightning if you stand under it in a storm, so I carved
a big lightning bolt down the side of the stick as a reminder.

JULY 1, 1998
KEENA'S JOURNAL

Going out with the baboons was super entertaining yesterday. For a
long time they stayed on Camp Island, moping around in the woods.

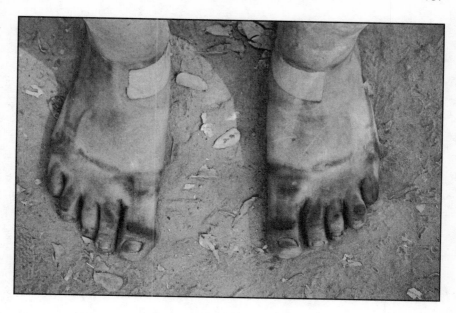

What my feet looked like after a day out with the baboons

Nutmeg, who is a crazy, irrational freak show of a monkey even on her best days, was acting extra weird. She was racing around twenty feet from Mokupi screaming with her tail in the air. Mokupi was wearing a ski mask because it was so cold and all you could see were his eyes. This was a problem because with baboons eye contact is a threat and the only part of Mokupi's face that was visible were his eyes. Anyway, Nutmeg sat in a bush yelling herself hoarse until the other baboons decided she might be onto something and started screaming at Mokupi too. He didn't wear the ski mask today and Nutmeg ignored him.

It wasn't always exciting going out with the baboons. Some days, the group wouldn't move at all—just sit in the trees and eat. These days were incredibly boring, since all we could do was sit on a log and wait for them to come down. It was impossible to track what an individual was doing that high up, so on slow days like these, I chatted with Mokupi.

Despite the many years I'd known Mokupi, we'd always had a relatively superficial relationship. When he and Mpitsang arrived in the morning, they only sat around long enough to have their breakfast before Mpitsang would start collecting firewood or cleaning the paths and Mokupi would leave with my parents to find the baboons. When they came back in the early afternoon, he and Mpitsang left to go home almost immediately. There was never really any time to sit and chat beyond pleasantries, and though I thought he was friendly and liked him well enough, it was only when I began going out with the baboons and spending more time with Mokupi that I realized I didn't know much about him at all.

I asked him about his family and learned that he had a wife named Rhombe and two children who lived back in his home village of Etsha. He saw them every time he took leave and at Christmas. He said he preferred working in the delta to working in Maun, though Mpitsang found Maun more exciting because there were more people. Beyond that, Mokupi didn't seem to want to talk about his life, and that was fine with me. I respected that it might be odd for him to share personal details with the young, white, female daughter of the American couple who employed him, and I was acutely aware of the differences that already existed between us. I remembered what Masaku had told me in Kenya about not being Maasai, and tried to continue to respectfully acknowledge those differences in Botswana as well. If we couldn't talk about our personal lives, I wanted to find some other area of common ground we could use instead and was relieved to see exactly what that was on the first day I went out with the baboons.

It was astonishing how comfortable Mokupi was in the delta. I knew the delta stretched as far as his village of Etsha to the west and that he'd grown up spending a lot of time poling mokoros and exploring the islands and melapo, but I didn't fully understand his skill and how advanced it was compared to my parents' until I saw it for myself. Mokupi moved easily and smoothly through floodplains and islands. He never seemed to get tired and, most astonishing of all, never got lost. We could be standing in a grove of some trees I didn't recognize, miles and miles away from camp, and he would turn to me and say with a big smile, "So Keena, where is home?" and I'd realize I had absolutely no idea where I was. Still, somehow, Mokupi knew and would lead us back to camp without a moment's hesitation. He knew the name of every plant and every bird, and the tracks of every animal. He put my *Fact-File* to shame, and when the full weight of his knowledge became clear to me, I wanted him to teach me everything.

I tried for a time to get Mokupi to teach me Setswana too, but I was terrible at the local language. Setswana is a complicated dialect that involves using a set of clicking noises on top of syllables. Xaxaba, which we all pronounced "ka-ka-ba," should really be said with a click on top of the "ka"s. I thought I could sort of say it correctly, but Mokupi would fall over himself laughing at me. It seemed to me that no one could really learn Setswana unless they grew up speaking it, and eventually I gave up. Instead, I asked him questions about everything we passed, saw, and smelled, and since he didn't seem to mind my constant questioning, I started bringing him flowers, berries, and feathers that I found as we walked along so he could tell me what they were.

One hot, slow afternoon I was sitting under a jackalberry tree with Mokupi watching the baboons pick through elephant poop. Elephants eat palm nuts, and as they digest them they soften the hard outer core, making it easier for the baboons to get to the white center of the palm nut. They pop these into their cheeks and suck on them for hours like jawbreakers. I was bored, so I picked up a smooth, red palm nut and began drawing on it with the Sharpie I kept in my backpack for DNA samples. Though Mokupi and my parents had a pretty good idea of who was related to whom in the baboon troop, they were always on the look-out for a stray tuft of hair, or sometimes a drop of blood on a leaf, that could be collected for later analysis to confirm these relationships. I carried sample bags and a Sharpie so I could collect a sample if I found one and write down which baboon it came from.

"What should I draw?" I said out loud, mostly to myself.

"What is an animal you have in America that I don't know?" Mokupi asked, sitting down on the log next to me. I grinned.

"We have bears," I said, but Mokupi shook his head.

"I know what a bear looks like! Try again."

"A wolf?"

"I know that one too! Try again." I tapped the cap of the Sharpie against my teeth.

"How about a beaver?" I said.

"Yes, draw that!" Mokupi said. "And tell me what it is and what it does." So I sat on the log and drew a beaver on the palm nut, complete with a dam and some half-eaten trees, and spent the next hour chatting with Mokupi about all the things I knew about beavers from my *Wildlife Fact-File*. And even though nothing technically "happened" that day, it was still the most enjoyable day I had spent out with the baboons.

As much as I loved these slow days, I craved the exciting ones like a drug. Though it didn't happen all the time, there was no greater feeling than staggering into camp after a six-hour walk with the baboons, sunburnt, bleeding, and exhausted, having dodged yet another elephant or snuck through the woods to avoid a pride of lions. Every night I

Mokupi watches a water crossing.

fell asleep listening to the sounds of the night world around me and every morning leapt out of bed, ready to start another day and have another adventure. I tried not to think about America, my friends, or the fact that high school was fast approaching. Instead, I savored each day like the first sip of a cold beer by the campfire and told myself to remember every moment so it could get me through another school year in the US.

One morning, we woke up to find the baboons already in camp, huddling in small groups in the early morning cold and looking very spooked. Balo and her daughters were actually sitting on the tarp outside my tent when I unzipped it, and my first reaction was to say, "Balo! Good morning. What are you all doing here? What happened?"

I walked slowly through the baboons toward the kitchen, trying to listen for whatever had them so scared. I was pouring my tea when I heard an animal scream from the direction of C5 Island, followed by a growl and a flurry of territorial lion roars. Several baboons squeaked and Balo alarm called from the tarp, even though I know she couldn't see the lions. They were clearly traumatized.

The baboons didn't leave camp for the rest of the day, and all morning we could hear the lions calling from C5. During lunch, which we ate sitting on the floor of the kitchen so the baboons wouldn't see us, we heard lions purring and growling from much closer, which made everyone freeze, sandwiches halfway to our mouths.

"How close do you think they are?" Dawn whispered.

"I don't know," I said. "Let's go see." Mom, Dad, Lucy, Dawn, Jim, and I walked slowly and silently out toward the car park. Mokupi and Mpitsang had gone home when we realized we wouldn't be leaving camp for the day and no work was going to get done. The rest of the group stopped at the car park, but I kept going, wanting to see exactly where the lions were and what they were doing.

"Are you going to be okay?" Dad called softly.

"Oh yeah, I'll be fine," I said, my blood racing. This is what I lived for.

I crept down the road, straining to listen for anything that might tell me where the lions were. When I got to my tree with the perfect view, I stepped out of my flip-flops and slid onto one of the lower branches, about ten feet off the ground and above a cluster of sage bushes on the edge of the plain. I hadn't been there more than thirty seconds when the lions emerged out of the woods to the left of my tree, no more than a stone's throw away. They were HUGE. There were two males, one of which had a black mane, meaning he was particularly healthy and well-fed. If possible, the four lionesses with them were even bigger. I don't think I had ever seen lions as big as these were, and when they began moving out of the woods and onto the plain, I could hear their paws slap against the hard dust as they walked. I watched them cross the plain and disappear into the woods on the far side of the island before climbing back down and going back to camp.

Even though they were well-fed and didn't appear to be hunting, the lions didn't seem sleepy either. The baboons had moved into the jackalberry trees behind camp, which put them between the lions and us, and in clear view of the lions as they moved through the woods. Every so often we'd hear an eruption of baboon alarm calls and then the lions roaring to each other. No one really wanted to take the car and drive out to see what was going on, since it sounded like the lions were just being territorial and the baboons were reacting to it, but by late afternoon, the yelling was so incessant that we piled into the car to figure out what the hell was going on.

What we found was a standoff: half of the baboon troop was still on Camp Island while the other half had crossed to Airstrip Island. It looked as though the whole troop had been moving to Airstrip but found the lions camped out on a small island in the middle of the molapo that the baboons usually used as a bridge. Every time one of the lions moved into view among the bushes, the baboons would shake the tree branches and alarm call. Someone from our car shouted, and when the lions realized there was a car nearby, they stood up and ran toward Air-strip Island, scattering the baboons that remained on the shoreline. We saw one male lion make it to the tree line, followed quickly by one of the females who was carrying a baboon in her mouth. We couldn't see who it was, but by the size it was probably a subadult male or female. I hoped it was Heloise, that little bitch. She scratched me once and we'd been enemies ever since.

AUGUST 23, 1998
KEENA'S JOURNAL

We came down to Maun yesterday and had a great night with Tim and Bryony at the ostrich farm. As a special surprise before we fly back to America we're going to Jack's Camp for the night and I am so excited! Jack's Camp is a lodge in the Makgadikgadi Pans to the south of Maun. It's the off-season for tourists and Tim has been given a free night's stay there since he once lent them his plane. I can't wait to see the pans!

Tim and Bryony's house was always filled with random stragglers passing through town, and since there were no spare bedrooms on this particular visit, I ended up unrolling my sleeping bag on one of the living room couches—the same one I'd recovered on after my horse injury. In the morning, the four of us and the four Longdens set off for Jack's Camp. I was in a car with my mom and Bryony; we kept falling behind the other car in our convoy because we had oil problems, and then part of one of the wheels came off, but after five or six hours, we made it to the salt pans. Bryony told me that the three pans that make up the Makgadikgadi Pans—Sua, Nwetwe, and Nxai—used to be one ancient lake called Lake Makgadikgadi, but as the lake dried up, all the minerals became concentrated in a smaller and smaller area until it created the salt pans. Now they are mostly empty salt flats in the dry season, but in the rainy season they fill up with water, and lots of tiny shrimp are born from eggs laid in the salt the previous year.

Jack's Camp was closed for the season, but Tim was owed a favor by the camp manager and had been given access to the camp for a night. Once we'd parked the cars and set up our tents, Chris, the manager, led us out to a row of ATVs on the edge of Nwetwe Pan. This was the real deal, and what we (at least Lucy and I) had been waiting for ever since we heard we were going to Jack's Camp. We wrapped kikoi cloths around our heads to keep out the dust, and after Chris showed us how to operate the ATVs, drove off into absolute nothingness. Chris instructed us to leave eighty-meter gaps between each ATV and not to leave the tracks or we'd squash the shrimp eggs. The salt flaked off the pan in white slices that looked like shaved coconut and the air smelled crisp and tangy. It was impossible to imagine that in a few months the pans would be full of water, shrimp, and flamingoes. The salty expanse stretched to every horizon and though I tried to describe it to myself as I drove along, I couldn't find the words. I felt like I was on the moon.

Chris drove us to a row of chairs randomly placed in the middle of the pan and made us drinks from a cooler strapped to the back of his ATV. As the sun went down over the white, bare nothingness, I sat on my ATV drinking a gin and tonic and smelling salt, dry grass, and the wind. One by one, the stars popped out of the purple-black sky and the sun burned the salt all shades of red and orange and yellow. It was the happiest moment of my life.

Only a week later we were, somehow, back in America again. After I dragged my duffel bag into the laundry room and kicked off my sneakers, I sat down heavily on the floor of my room and tried to center myself in where I was and what I was doing. How was it possible that only a few days after sitting on my ATV in the salt pans I was back in the steamy August heat of Pennsylvania, getting ready to start my freshman year of high school? Planets weren't supposed to shift this quickly, and the whiplash in my brain stopped it from processing properly. I tensed every muscle in my body and tried relaxing them one by one, just to check in with myself. Feet. Knees. Stomach (churning but okay). Elbows (partially functioning; the damaged one was never really the same again). Shoulders. Head. I opened my eyes. What did I hear? A lawn mower. Cars on the road. Mom and Dad talking downstairs. Someone was on the phone. I sighed. *Well, I guess I'm here again*, I thought.

CHAPTER 14

HIGH SCHOOL WATER HOLE

DAD ALWAYS TOLD ME that I wake up as if I've been shot. I've read that this is how doctors and military personnel operate since they have to learn to sleep when and where they can and be ready to go immediately if there's an emergency. I'm no doctor or soldier, but years of sleeping in my tent did train me to wake up to every rustle and snapping twig nearby. What if it was a lion? A hyena? I had to be ready.

But when we returned to the US in 1998, I started having a terrible time waking up in the morning. When Dad would stand at the bottom of the stairs and call, "Girls? It's time to get up," I'd roll over and scoot backward under my covers to the bottom of my bed, like warthogs do when they enter their holes. I didn't see the point in getting up. Gone was my excitement, that adrenaline rush I got in Baboon Camp from knowing that the sun was rising on a day filled with adventure and possibility. Well, it wasn't completely gone, I had to remind myself. It was still there, just on the other side of the world, where I wasn't. I was stuck in the Philadelphia suburbs, and I had to get up and go to high school.

The Upper School, as Shipley called its high school, was housed in an old manor house with brick walls and large white windows that never opened. The manor house hadn't been renovated before it became a school, so classes were held in what used to be bedrooms, down tiny, cramped corridors that could only be reached by twisty staircases in the building's corners.

Going to high school was both familiar and completely foreign. I knew the drive to Shipley by heart, since I'd been going there since first grade, but I had never set foot in the high school before my first day of freshman year, even though it was right next to the middle school and shared the same open-air quad space between the two buildings.

I'd seen the Upper School students eating on the quad during their lunch period, but had never given them much thought since I had so many other things to worry about. They were older, taller, and cooler, but didn't really stand out to me as individuals in any way. I didn't know any of them personally. But they all knew who I was.

A few days before the school year started, the *Philadelphia Inquirer* published an article about my parents' work titled "Eavesdropping on the Apes" (even the headline was factually inaccurate because baboons aren't apes). In it, the reporter described my parents as "radiating a brisk cordiality" and said that they could just as easily be "planning a run up to a friend's house for dinner and drinks rather than another trip down a flooded delta to a tented encampment on the Okavango." The reporter went on in dramatic fashion to exclaim how brave my parents must be to do this unusual and dangerous work while "homeschooling their two daughters until the girls got old enough to require the socializing experience of the Main Line's Shipley School."

Mom said the article was poorly written and the reporter was an idiot, and Dad promised he'd never said anything like that about me and Lucy, but the damage was done. *"Require the socializing experience."* We all agreed it was ridiculous and untrue and I laughed at the article along with my parents. Lucy and I were fine; we didn't need to be socialized! Family friends called to congratulate my parents on the article and share how wonderful it was that they were being recognized for their work. *But wasn't it awful*, they'd say, *what that woman wrote about Keena and Lucy?* How unkind and untrue it was. *By the way*, they'd add casually, *is Keena free this weekend? So-and-so would just love to have her over; maybe they could go bowling or out for ice cream or do something else generic and American.* I scowled, imagining the conversations between the kids I knew and their parents: *Wouldn't Keena like that? A big ice cream sundae and a trip to the movies? Wouldn't that be an extra special treat for her, the untamed, feral child of the jungle? I bet she's never been to the movies before. Does she comb her hair? Can she speak in complete sentences? Does she even know what a Fruit Roll-Up is?*

The imaginary conversations echoed through my head, and I declined every playdate that was suggested. Were they even called playdates now that we were fourteen years old? I knew the parents meant well and that I would have a fine time if I did go spend time with their kids, but it felt forced. They weren't inviting me over because they wanted my company; they were doing it because they felt an obligation to civilize me.

Even after school began, I kept fixating on that article and wondering what the other kids would think of me. I let the imaginary conversations continue, thinking about them in my classrooms, the cafeteria, and on the quad. *See her, that girl sitting with Meghan at the cool girls' table? She's made such progress since she came back from Africa—did you know she can tie her shoes all by herself now?*

Every day, Mom and Dad drove us to school on their way into the city. Every day, I sat in the back, always on the left-hand side, and drifted, mentally preparing myself for the day. With every turn, my shoulders and neck tightened like they were being wound by a screw, and I knew they wouldn't unlock again until I got home in the evening. It didn't matter how familiar Shipley itself was, everything about high school made me tense and jittery.

"Am I weird?" I asked Nat at lunch one day. We were sitting by ourselves in the corner of the cafeteria. Nat was reading a gigantic book and, in classic Nat fashion, was completely oblivious to the comings and goings around him. He looked up.

"You seem all right to me," he said and went back to reading. I scowled.

"No, seriously," I said. "Look at me; am I weird? Do you think that article was right that I need to be socialized?" He looked up again.

"The article was stupid. You're fine. Now be quiet so I can read."

Nat made me feel better, but I didn't think he was being completely honest with me. My friends' parents clearly thought something was missing in my socialization experience given all the invitations I was getting, so I had to consider the possibility that they were right. I certainly didn't feel integrated—after all, here I was sitting in a corner of the cafeteria hiding from the rest of the world behind a book about dragons. I had no idea what to wear, how to act, or what being in high school was all about, except for getting good grades. Every time I came back to school, it felt like everyone had moved light-years ahead of me in maturity, as Meghan seemed to. The minute I'd get comfortable with what we were supposed to be wearing and who was dating whom, I'd go back to Botswana and the world would shift into a new social dimension with new styles, new crushes, and new rules. Every year I was completely left behind and had to relearn how to live on whatever new planet we'd landed on in my absence.

I looked across the cafeteria to where a group of junior girls were eating lunch by the bright windows in the "cool" part of the cafeteria. I recognized most of the girls from the field hockey team I'd joined as my mandatory fall sport, and a few of the girls were also in my advanced European history class. *What would happen*, I asked myself, *if I got up and went over to where they're sitting and said hi?* I knew they were all nice people and would probably say hello back to me, but still, the idea of even attempting such a social feat made my neck sweat. What if they laughed at me? What if talking to cool older girls wasn't allowed on this new planet and would just prove to everyone how little I knew about other people? Lost in my own imaginary humiliation, I was distracted by something bright pink moving across my field of vision and looked up to find Brooke standing over my table with two of her friends. It seemed like Brooke had become even taller and blonder in Shipley's latest dimensional shift. She looked down on me with that pair of sparkling blue eyes that reminded me of a snake about to strike.

"I guess you're back," she said. "And here I was hoping you'd stay in Africa and leave us all alone. But I guess you missed your boyfriend here."

I stared back at her. "You knew I was back," I said. "We've been playing on the same field hockey team for a week."

She rolled her eyes. "No, I play field hockey with a weird, hairy little monkey, not a girl. We should just call you Abu." She laughed and her friends whooped. "Abu the monkey! Abu the monkey!" they chanted as they walked away. I glared after them.

Brooke passed through the cool part of the cafeteria and out onto the lawn, where the rest of her friends had reserved a picnic table. Though Brooke nodded to the junior girls from my history class as she walked past them, I noticed that none of them nodded back. Maybe they didn't like her either. They'd been nice to me so far, and they were all beautiful and popular and cool. I didn't care what Brooke thought about me, since it was pretty clear she'd made up her mind that I was Abu the monkey, but I realized that I did care a great deal about what these other girls thought. I wanted them to like me, and I wanted to be like them: successful and cool without being mean. Their approval mattered. *They*, I decided, were what it meant to be socialized.

"Nat." He looked up again. I pointed to one of the girls, the quietest of the popular group who sat to my right in my European history class. Her hair was light brown and straight, and she walked in a delicate way that made me think about impala in the forest. "Christine lives near you, doesn't she?"

He squinted across the room. "Yeah. She used to come trick-or-treating at my house. Our moms are friends."

"She's nice, right?"

"Super nice. Doesn't really talk to me though." He paused and put his book down. "You don't, you know," he said.

"Don't what?"

"Look like Abu the monkey. After all, he wears a hat." I grinned but looked down at my hands, clasped on the table next to my lunch bag and book—tanned, scarred, and without a hint of nail polish on them. Not monkey hands, maybe, but definitely not the hands of a cool high school girl. I didn't know what I was, but at least now I had an idea of what I wanted to be.

Mom used to tell me to lead through strength up to weakness. She meant it in the context of playing a hand of bridge, but I always thought it was a lesson that could be more widely applied. If you want to win, she used to say, you should always start with the things you know you're good at, and end with the things you aren't so good at. So what was I good at? I could drive boats and cars, run from animals, and was handy with a pocketknife, but Mom used to tell me that my greatest talent was observation. In Baboon Camp, I was always the first person to see animals, the first to spot the snakes in the trees, and the only one who could read the way the wind blew across the water and know whether there was a sandbank underneath. I could spot lions from miles away and blended in to the forest as seamlessly as any of the baboons.

I rested my chin on my hands and stared across the cafeteria. *Pretend it's a water hole in Botswana*, I told myself. *Those kids over there are the giraffes: tall and quiet and not really doing anything. Those other kids are the baboons: loud and messy, and probably a lot of fun. And those kids—* I looked out the window to where Brooke and her friends sat—*are the buffalo: unpredictable, grouchy, and really very stupid.* I smiled. *All you have to do is learn how to blend in here*, I thought. *Just the way you would in Botswana.* My eyes settled back on the cool girls and zeroed in on Christine. I had a plan now. I just had to set it in motion.

I decided that if I was going to fit in at high school, I first had to put the Botswana pieces of me away. People rarely asked me about Botswana anyway, and if I never spoke about it, there would be fewer chances for me to stick out. A new year meant a chance to reinvent myself, in a way. The newspaper article had been a blow, but as it turned out, fewer high school students read the newspaper than I'd feared, and aside from Brooke's posse, no one really thought of me as having anything to do with monkeys or Africa. They didn't seem to think much of me at all. If I was going to fit in, I had to keep it that way, as much as I might hate being invisible.

I started with my bedroom. We had recently moved to a new house a few miles away from our first house with the growling radiator and the pirate bannister. Mom and Dad wanted a bigger lawn and said we didn't need the playroom anymore since Lucy and I weren't as obsessed with Legos as we used to be. Our new house was a renovated farmhouse that stood at the end of a long driveway among tall pine trees devoid of monkeys. I liked the house well enough but didn't love it. It had doors and walls just like the old house and didn't really seem that different, if I was honest. The new house just flooded a lot more and I often spent my evenings mopping the basement as water seeped up through the cracks in the concrete.

I had a small room at the top of the stairs and across the hall from Lucy's. It had a creaky wooden floor, two big bookcases, a desk, and my bed, which I'd positioned under a window that looked out onto our front lawn and across the street to a beautiful field—my favorite feature of the new house. I kept this window open always, even when it was freezing outside. I was used to sleeping outdoors even on the coldest nights, and I liked the way the wind smelled when there was frost in the air. Sometimes I could even hear owls.

The rest of my room was pretty tidy. I'd had enough dust in Baboon Camp, so naturally I kept things orderly to avoid having to clean them. Yet despite the cleanliness, items that reminded me of Baboon Camp were everywhere: a San hunting knife hung off my bedpost, a spear was propped in the corner next to a bow and arrow I made from porcupine quills, the walking stick I'd carved from the buffalo thorn acacia lay next to my bed, and hundreds of souvenirs from the gift shop in the Maun airport lined the shelves of my bookcases. There were dolls from Swaziland, owl feathers, ostrich shell bracelets, whistles I'd carved from palm nuts, and jars full of dried beans and berries that I probably shouldn't have brought into the US in the first place. All of this, I decided, had to go.

I brought up empty boxes from the basement and packed up all the stuff that reminded me of Baboon Camp and Botswana. I handled everything carefully and wrapped each item in newspaper like the precious possession it was. It made my heart hurt to put my things away, but this was what I had to do. *No one will see your room*, part of me screamed in my head. *They won't know it's full of spears and lucky beans! But no*, I told myself. *American Keena doesn't have those things in her room. No more spears and lucky beans.* I packed away my tapes of South African pop music, including "Gorilla Man." *You have to listen to new things now*, I told myself: *Third Eye Blind, Usher, and what's that other guy called? Puff Daddy. That's what Americans listen to. That's what those cool girls from your history class listen to. And you want to be like them, don't you?* I did. Finally, I had only one box left. This one I'd reserved for my books. My eyes burned and I bit down hard on my lip.

"I'm not throwing you away," I whispered to my bookshelf. "Just...putting you away for a while. I'm so sorry. I'm so, so sorry." I felt insane, talking to my books, but it felt like I was betraying them. The characters in these books taught me to be strong and brave and now I had the audacity to put them away? How dare I?

Into the box went Captain Nancy Blackett from Swallows and Amazons. Into the box went Lessa the dragonrider of Pern, and the elf princess Laurana Kanan. I didn't have time for dragons and swords and beastmen. Now it was time for things like *Friends* and *Frasier* and *ER*. I didn't much like TV, but I could maybe learn to like it if I tried. I had to do this right or not at all, I thought. I knew very well how long I would pay for even the smallest social slipup, and I didn't want to give Brooke or her friends any more ammunition.

Once the boxes had been carefully stacked in the back of my closet, I looked around. My room felt empty. Normal, but uncluttered and sterile. There was nothing bright or interesting, no weapons, and nothing that would be out of place in any other fourteen-year-old's room in any home in America. It felt dead. Part of me felt dead too. What living part of me there was left lived only in Baboon Camp, where she was safe. American Keena was just a shell of her.

Next, I needed to work on my appearance. I asked Mom to take me to the mall. I had to have new clothes if I was going to dress like the history class girls. After a week, I had studied them long enough that I thought I could duplicate their style.

"You shouldn't feel like you need to be like everyone else," she said as we drove. "What you wear has nothing to do with the person you are on the inside." Did she think I was stupid?

"I know," I said.

"I'm not saying you can't get some new clothes, but please don't think you need to change."

"I *know*," I said. She obviously didn't understand what I was trying to do.

"I love you just the way you are," she went on, "my brave little bush kid who likes trees and birds and books."

"Stop it, Mom," I snapped. "I *know* that already. I just want to get some new clothes." And I stared stonily out the window as we drove the rest of the way in silence. Why didn't she understand that everything I was doing was about *protecting* Botswana Keena, not getting rid of her? This is just what I had to do to survive.

At the mall, we had a predictably unpleasant time. The stores were bright and loud and smelled like cheap cologne. Squealing teenage girls crowded around stacks of distressed hoodies, and shirtless male models pressured shoppers to buy tiny tank tops and jeans with holes in them. Mom found the models to be "a bit over the top" and told me she'd wait in the car. I tried to move quickly, since the music was hurting my ears, and managed to make it out of the store in one piece, my purchases clutched tightly in a big bag that smelled like the same cheap cologne.

I tried out my new look at school the next day: a distressed, fitted plaid button-down shirt with three-quarter-length sleeves, and flared khaki cargo pants. Shoes I hadn't figured out yet, but I needed my sneakers for field hockey practice anyway, so I just wore those to save time. The pants felt too tight in the thighs and too loose everywhere else, though the shirt was soft. *It's so flimsy!* I thought while adjusting the buttons. *This wouldn't last a second out with the baboons.* I supposed it worked though. I looked just like everyone else. The same shirt, same pants, same cookie-cutter teenage person, if a little shorter than the other girls and with a big scar on my arm. World, meet American Keena.

"You look cute," Christine said as I settled into my seat in history class that afternoon.

"Oh . . . thank you," I said, blushing a little. *Really, thank you,* I thought. *You wore this exact same thing last week and I copied it.* She smiled.

"You ready for the timed run in field hockey practice today?"

"No," I said, still not quite sure I was having an actual, real-life conversation with one of the cool girls. My head felt fuzzy. "I really hate anything that's timed. I can't seem to relax."

"I know what you mean," she said. "I have to do math problems in my head to distract myself." I laughed.

"You do? I should try that," I said. *I would do literally anything the same as you*, I thought. *American Keena needs all the help she can get.*

That afternoon after school, the whole field hockey team lined up on the edge of the field, nervously pacing in the dry, crunchy grass. Compared to the flooding in the Okavango, it felt like the US was in a constant state of drought. The grass was always dry in the summer, never green and lush the way it was in Botswana. I reminded myself it was still alive, underneath. I took a deep breath and looked up to the sky. I didn't want to be timed, but I wasn't afraid of the run, despite what I'd said to Christine earlier. I was just happy to be outside, free from my fancy new clothes and back in a T-shirt and shorts. I'd been sitting still all day and it was time to move.

Our coach settled onto a bench and took out her stopwatch, motioning us into a line in the corner of the field. *Eight laps*, I said to myself. *This'll be fun.* I heard the sound of a revving throttle in my head. Christine looked a little sick, so I smiled at her. At the sound of our coach's whistle, we were off. I began to run, immediately passing Christine and settling into a quick pace directly behind Brooke, who, as one of the tallest girls, was also one of the fastest. I knew I couldn't beat her—she was too fast for me—but if I pushed myself hard I could stay right behind her. Legs pumping, I watched Brooke's blonde ponytail bounce against her back ahead of me. *Don't look back, Brooke*, I thought. *There's a monkey on your tail.*

I finished the run in second place, trailing Brooke by ten seconds or so. She collapsed in a heap on the grass, gasping for air and glaring at me, clearly somehow offended that I had kept up with her.

"You really are a freak," she panted. The other runners began to trickle in, flopping on the grass next to Brooke. I stood to the side, looking up at the sky and feeling the sweat drip down my back. My legs ached but my head felt calm and clear, more peaceful than it had all day. I closed my eyes, blocking out the sounds of cars on the road and airplanes passing high above and focusing instead on the smell of the dead grass and the feeling of the warm sun on my face. When I opened my eyes, Brooke was still looking at me. The rest of the team was quiet, recovering from their run. All told, probably twenty girls surrounded Brooke and me at the end of the field.

"Why aren't you on the cross-country team?" Brooke asked nastily. "You're a fast runner and a terrible field hockey player."

"Of course I'm terrible," I said, seeing no reason to lie with so many people looking at me. It was true; I could move quickly but I was horrible at actually playing field hockey. We'd always been in Botswana during the fall and I never had the chance to learn the sports kids played in that season. "What do you expect? I only learned the rules this week." Someone laughed.

"So why exactly are you here?" Brooke said. Why couldn't she leave me alone? I hated having the rest of the team stare at me. I sought Christine out in the crowd and she smiled at me, giving me just enough confidence to respond.

"You read the article, didn't you?" I said casually. "I'm here for socialization."

CHAPTER 15

THE HIPPO SITUATION IS GRIM

MY FIRST YEAR IN high school ended up being fine, just like my eighth-grade year had been. I kept my head down and worked hard. By following Christine's example of how to fit in, I settled into high school like a human chameleon, blending into the crowds of students as seamlessly as one of the striped kudu in the woods behind our camp. I moved silently through the halls, keeping to myself and trying to stay off the social radar. I was not popular (and did not want to be), so my ability to become invisible was the biggest indicator of my successful transformation into American Keena: if no one saw me, I was doing something right.

The year went by slowly but eventually the spring semester started to wrap up. Summer was coming and our return to Baboon Camp was getting close. We would all be going back until school began again in September, though as usual my parents planned to keep us away until the last possible second. I was feeling good and thought it might be time to be just a little brave and relax my new rule about not reading fantasy in school, a rule I'd created because reading fantasy was more a Botswana Keena thing and not at all something my new school role models would do.

It was a warm day in May when I mustered enough courage to walk down the hallway in school carrying my book. Though I'd sworn off all fantasy fiction with dragons and elves, I thought *Watership Down* might be more acceptable to bring to school; the cover was plain enough and no one could immediately tell that it was also fantasy fiction, not just about rabbits. I felt a great affinity to animals on a mission.

I was just at the part where General Woundwort began his attack on the rabbit colony of Watership Down when my book went missing. I'd left it lying on the top of my backpack in the cafeteria while I went to the bathroom, and when I returned it was gone.

At first I thought Nat might have swiped it but thought that unlikely when I remembered how angry he'd been when I borrowed his copy of *Dune* without asking. I couldn't figure out why anyone else would take it. No one else read those kinds of books, and it had been sitting on top of a backpack that was very clearly mine, since no one else's backpack was faded and dusty and had a brown stain on the side that was definitely *not* from baboon poop.

I had three classes left in my day before lacrosse practice and found it harder than usual to focus on my schoolwork. Where was my book? I looked for it everywhere. I didn't really expect to find it just lying on a bench in a hallway somewhere, but I couldn't stop myself from scanning the halls just in case. Half of me thought that if someone had taken it accidentally they might have left it in an obvious place when they realized their mistake. That's what I would have done, anyway. Taking someone's book was a cardinal sin in my world, second only to giving someone a book you'd already read as a present. Mom told me that when she was little she used to believe that if you read a book before you gave it to someone else it "weakened the words."

When the bell rang to end the school day, *Watership Down* was still nowhere to be found, and I walked to practice in a foul mood with Laurana the lacrosse stick slung over my shoulder. I was thinking that at least now I could work out some of my frustration by running when I heard someone call my name behind me. I turned around and saw Meghan's friend Sarah come jogging toward me, the one who had remarked on my fake professional tan the year before.

"Hey," she said. "I found this in the seniors' lounge. I think it's yours." She reached into her backpack and pulled out *Watership Down*, the spine broken and the front cover bent in half. Most of the pages had been ripped out. My head swam and I felt hot, angry tears building behind my eyes.

"Thanks," I managed to say.

"I'm really sorry," Sarah said. "I don't know what happened to it. I...uh...it was behind a trash can and I figured it was yours. No one else reads books about rabbits." I wiped my eyes on the backs of my hands and harshly told myself to pull it together. It wasn't Sarah's fault my book was wrecked, and she had been nice enough to bring it back to me.

"That's okay," I said.

"Are you all right?" she asked. *No*, I wanted to say. *No, I'm not all right. It's not fair that I can't even read a book without people harassing me. I am sad and angry and embarrassed that everyone knows I like rabbits and I am terribly lonely and want you to walk to practice with me but don't know how to ask.*

"Yeah, I'm fine," I said. "Thanks a lot for finding my book. I'll talk to you later." I turned away and continued walking toward the practice fields, my heart racing and my hand clenched so tightly around Laurana that the aluminum ridges cut into my palm. *Well, I guess that's that*, I told myself. *No more books at school. Ever.*

All the way back to Baboon Camp, as we flew through New York, Paris, Johannesburg, and Maun, I fumed. I'd been trying so hard to fit in, and it had been working fairly well, but nothing had really changed. It didn't matter that I dressed the way everyone else did or kept to myself or helped other people with their homework when they asked. No one was interested in liking me for me, and even the tiniest, slightest deviation from the norm had such dramatic consequences. The most frustrating thing was that there wasn't any reason behind it, at least none that made sense.

When animals attacked each other in Botswana, they always had a reason for doing it, like their baby was threatened or someone was trying to steal their food. Animals were violent and dangerous, but never without reason. That was why I had never been as scared of the animals as I maybe should have been. Lions didn't attack people for no reason. If I respected them and left them alone, they would do the same to me. Same with elephants, and same with leopards, though I couldn't count buffalo and hippos in the same category because I knew they were much, much stupider. I couldn't understand why people didn't operate the same way. *But if that's the way it's going to be,* I said to myself, *I will give them nothing. Botswana Keena will stay completely in Botswana, and not even the tiniest bit of her will go back to America.*

The second I dropped my bags on the tarp outside my tent, I took a deep breath. My lungs filled with the smells of the river, dust, and the sage bushes that grew by the laundry area. A fish eagle called to its mate from the fig tree, throwing its head back and forth in the bright blue sky and echoing through the quiet woodland beyond the shower. The wind blew softly through the trees and if I closed my eyes, I could hear all the other noises from the forest—the snap of twigs as squirrels raced each other up and down the sausage tree, the liquid burble from the Okavango oriole in the rain tree, and the babbler birds muttering to each other as they foraged through the dry leaves on the forest floor, looking for insects, seeds, and snakes to attack.

Everything is just the same, I said to myself. *Everything is right, and good, and the way it should be.* I ripped off my sneakers and went racing down the road toward the open plains behind camp. My feet had lost their calluses after a year of wearing shoes and the thorns tore into my feet as I ran across the dust. *That's it,* I thought. *Start with my feet. Turn me back into the person I'm supposed to be.*

JUNE 10, 1999
KEENA'S JOURNAL

Everything was very chaotic yesterday, but we are HERE! The flood hasn't arrived yet in full, but the floodplains are at their highest that I've ever seen, or even that the Maun old-timers have seen. The water is almost up to the kitchen table in camp and it's virtually impossible to walk to C5. Flying up we could really see how the water was taking over the islands.

And the hippo situation is grim. At Delta Camp a hippo bit through a mokoro that a tourist was taking a ride in and the tourist lost her leg and bled to death. I have never heard of that happening before. And another hippo bit through one of the fancy Xaxaba boats and sank it (though luckily no one got hurt).

Dawn and Jim left to go visit their family in the US and left a note that there's a group of seven buffalo that pretty much live in camp, as well as a giant crocodile that has taken up living near the water pump. All this, combined with the fact that all the plains are filled with tall, tall grass due to all the rain, makes me a little nervous. Tall grass is where lions like to hide. I don't know what I'm going to do about going running. Maybe I'll start running with a machete? Ha ha.

Mokupi seems happy to see us, but that may be only because he has

Hello, ladies.

"business" to discuss with Dad. He and Mpitsang are not speaking to each other. It started, as far as we know from Dawn, when Mokupi had a swollen leg. He said he had been cursed and spent almost three months' worth of his salary going to see a traditional healer in Etsha for a cure. The healer gave him a mirror that was supposed to show him the face of the person who cursed him—and Mokupi saw Mpitsang (though this is not that hard to believe since they are brothers and look alike).

This discovery led to a series of really scary physical fights between the two of them in camp and two months in which only one of them would show up for work. Then, the climax: they got attacked by a hippo on the way to work and barely escaped with their lives. The hippo came up under their mokoro and bit it in half, just like the one at Delta Camp had done. Being intelligent bush guys, they swam underwater to get away from the hippo and Mokupi actually kicked the hippo a couple of times.

We got more of the story later when Mom and Dad sat down to talk with Dawn and Jim after they arrived back at camp in September. According to Dawn, Mpitsang reported that the hippo attack had been staged—that Mokupi had hired the hippo to kill Mpitsang because of the mirror and the curse described by the healer. Mpitsang said that the hippo must not have understood Mokupi's instructions properly because Mpitsang was still alive, but he refused to work with Mokupi anymore because Mokupi had tried to have him killed. Mokupi also said he refused to work with Mpitsang because of the curse that originally resulted in his swollen leg.

Dawn hadn't known what to do, but ended up letting Mpitsang go because she couldn't really do her research without Mokupi, and even though Mpitsang had been employed longer, he was, in the end, only a day laborer. She asked Mokupi to recommend someone from the Xaxaba staff village who might want to take over Mpitsang's job, and the next day Mokupi showed up with a new guy named Press. Press was a cousin of Mokupi's and Mpitsang's, and looked almost identical to Mpitsang: tall and quiet, but with a lighter personality that was much more reminiscent of Mokupi's.

It was sad to think that I might not see Mpitsang again. Though I didn't know him as well as Mokupi at this point, I had known him for seven years and worried about him. Mokupi assured me that it would be easy for Mpitsang to find another job, but in the meantime, he was traveling back to Etsha to spend some time with his children and, though Mokupi didn't want to see him again, promised me that he would be okay.

JUNE 13, 1999
KEENA'S JOURNAL

I stayed in camp today to take care of Lucy who has a fever and a bad sinus infection. We can't get her medicine so I'm boiling chicken to make her some broth. Mom is worried that the raft holding the water pump is sinking, so we need to figure that out ASAP. Last night I was woken up by enormous crashing next to the tent; turns out it was a hippo that left deep footprints all over the area by the kitchen table and sprayed poop all over our firepit. I had a dream that an elephant ate one of the kitchen walls, and Mokupi told me he has been having a dream that a hippo is standing over him with a knife.

The camp was very quiet. Dawn and Jim had left a few days before we arrived to visit family back in the US and wouldn't be returning until September. They left the camp fully provisioned for us, but as per usual, the supplies they had been able to find in Maun were mismatched and somewhat challenging to work with. A week or so after we arrived, I showered and bundled up against the freezing winter evening, then went to help make dinner. Dawn had left us a note saying that the butcher wasn't selling whole chickens and she'd been forced to buy individual breasts that had been frozen together into a block that she and Jim had labeled "Block o' Chick." Dad pulled the gigantic hunk of meat out of the deep freeze and attempted to slice it into pieces using a hacksaw from the storage shed while I held one side up and tried to help.

I braced my shoulder against the Block o' Chick and used my free hand to pop open a can of Hansa, my favorite Botswana beer. Dad sawed back and forth with the hacksaw and slowly carved away a chunk of chicken to grill on the campfire for dinner. His face looked grim in the glow of his headlamp and I realized he hadn't said anything for several minutes.

"Dad?" I asked.

"Hmm?"

"What's wrong? Aren't you happy to be back?" A chunk of chicken detached itself from the Block o' Chick and landed on the cutting board with a satisfying thunk.

"I'm very happy to be back," Dad said, leaning the hacksaw against the doorframe. "I'm just a bit anxious, to be honest with you." This was new. Dad never talked about his feelings. None of us did. I'd never once heard him say anything about his emotions other than that he was hungry or tired. And Dad was never anxious—or at least never told me before that he was. The only thing I'd ever suspected of making him anxious was going through customs.

"Why are you anxious?" I asked. Dad sighed.

"Maybe anxious isn't the right word," he said. He leaned against the kitchen counter and took a sip of his Hansa. "I'm nervous. Remember last year when I said going out with the baboons was getting too exciting for me?" I nodded. "Well, I meant it. When we first came to Baboon Camp in 1992, do you remember how often we saw elephants and lions?"

"Not that often," I said. "It was something like a week before we saw an elephant and it must have been a couple months before we saw lions."

"And how often do we see them now?"

"Last year it was...more or less every day, I think. At least with the elephants, we saw them so often I stopped paying attention." I remembered talking to the guides at Xaxaba about it at one point. They told us that the population of elephants and lions was increasing so quickly because the animals were all moving into Botswana from Zimbabwe because it was safer and there were fewer poachers. While that was a good thing from a conservation standpoint, it also meant that the elephants were more likely to charge people because they'd been exposed to poachers and knew that humans were dangerous.

"That's not a good thing for us," Dad went on. "Having more elephants and lions around means there's a greater chance that we could get attacked by them. Maybe not you," he added quickly, seeing me instantly bristle at the insinuation that I couldn't handle myself out in the bush. "But we have postdocs here that we're responsible for, and Mom and I aren't always here when they are. We can't guarantee their protection. What if one of them just has a bad day? The project would end immediately if that happened, besides the fact that someone could be seriously injured or killed." I took a sip of my beer. Dad had never talked to me like this before.

"Do you think something really bad will happen?" I asked.

"That's the thing," Dad said. "We have no way of knowing. I just don't like the odds." I looked past Dad and out through the chicken-wire window of the kitchen. Lucy was on her way from our tent and her headlamp bobbed down the path in the fading light. I'd always understood that there was a chance something might leap out of the bushes and grab her, I just never truly believed it would ever happen. It hadn't so far.

"Besides," Dad said, poking the chunk of frozen chicken with a spatula, "I'm going to be fifty-two next year and Mom will be fifty. Who knows how long we'll even be able to run away from animals? We're not as fast as we used to be and lions always pick off the weakest in the herd."

"That's true," I said thoughtfully. The kitchen door creaked open and Lucy came in, carrying a copy of *Harry Potter and the Chamber of Secrets*.

She was taking her sweet time reading it and I was desperate for her to finish so I could have my turn. "You really think you and Mom are in more danger than you used to be?"

"I don't know," Dad said. "But I don't want to find out."

He was right, of course. I understood what he said about the researchers who worked in Baboon Camp. After all, it had sometimes been my job to walk around with Dawn and point out animals that she had not yet noticed. I could see how bad it would be if someone got charged or trampled by something. But Mom and Dad? In danger, or killed? I couldn't picture it. They'd been working in various countries in Africa for more than twenty years, and when they went out with the baboons they had me and Mokupi with them; between the two of us we saw everything. What could possibly go wrong for them? I knew that every time we got on the plane in Maun to go back to the US, Mom buried her head in her hands and said, "Thank God we did it again and no one got hurt," but I always thought she was just being dramatic to make us laugh when we were sad to leave. I never thought it was serious.

I took a long, hard look at Dad, who was rubbing the chicken with some spices and dried herbs before grilling it. Still the same glasses and polo shirt he'd worn all his life, but as I looked closer I noticed that the hair on his temples was thinner than it used to be and that his shoulders had lost some of their solidity. Could this person still outrun a lion if he needed to? I had to admit I wasn't so sure anymore.

When Mokupi arrived the next morning and we headed out to find the baboons, I felt an uneasiness about the familiar woods that I'd never felt before. And I didn't like it.

JULY 10, 1999
KEENA'S JOURNAL

Yesterday Lucy was reading in our tent while I was having a shower. According to Lucy, while I was in the shower a pack of wild dogs ran through camp, around the shower, and down the path to the laundry area while she watched. As Mom stepped out of her tent, she was almost run over by an impala barreling down the path pursued by one of the dogs. When I stepped out of the shower one of the dogs was sitting on the path between me and my tent. I didn't know what to do so I stood there dripping in my towel for a few minutes until he got up and trotted away. I can't believe how habituated these dogs are, and it would be so cool if they had a den nearby.

JULY 12, 1999
KEENA'S JOURNAL

Out of consideration for the wild dog puppies I have decided live nearby, my running route has been changed to loop out behind camp onto the plain and then back into the woods by the storage hut. It's a much, much more dangerous route though since we don't know what could be in the tall grass on either side of the path, or in the woods for that matter. Today Mom stood on one part of the trail with a walkie-talkie and Dad stood out on the road with our air rifle and a walkie-talkie while I ran. I'm not sure why he needed the gun, it would be useless if a lion showed up. Every time I passed one of them they'd radio to the other, "Okay, here she comes," in a security guard–type voice.

Dad also thinks I read too fast, since I finished all the books we brought with us weeks ago. He bought me War and Peace *in Maun and told me to come back to him when I've finished it. I'm on page 250 today, with 1,200 pages to go! It's really heavy, but at least I can use it to kill mosquitoes while I read.*

Mom and Dad did seem much more anxious this summer than they had in previous years. It wasn't just that they watched me while I ran. When we were out with the baboons, they insisted that we had our radios on all the time and that I didn't stray too far from the monkeys when I was by myself. The constant attention was stifling, and a huge departure from how we usually operated in Baboon Camp or how little they watched what I was doing in America. I understood that the animals were more a presence than they had been before; after all, I was standing next to them whenever we saw elephants or lions, and I looked for snakes even more carefully than they did. But aside from the snakes, I couldn't understand why my parents' attitude had shifted so much. Animals were predictable, and therefore easy to be safe around. If there was an elephant, we just had to move upwind of him so he didn't smell us. If we saw lions, we left the area or climbed up a tree. If we saw buffalo, we did the same. If we all followed the rules, no one would get hurt. It made so much more sense than in America, where no one followed the rules and whether I got bullied or teased had nothing to do with my own behavior. So what was there to be afraid of?

JULY 31, 1999
KEENA'S JOURNAL

This morning the baboons moved out onto the plains behind camp pretty early. It was cold, and as Dad and I walked past a sunny spot on a termite mound he yelled, "Jesus Christ, Keena, GET BACK!" I jumped backward and a HUGE snake slithered away from my feet across the sunny spot. Its tail went over my sandals and I could feel it on the top of my foot. Oh my God, I hate snakes. The scariest part was I got that feeling that I almost just died. For a second I honestly thought that could have been it. I don't usually get that feeling when I am happily looking at baboons in the sun, but it really scared me. With lions, I constantly think, "I could die, I could die," but I'm never really in any danger. I can get away from lions. With snakes it's totally different; a small movement in the grass is far deadlier than claws and teeth. Yeah, so enough snakes for me.

AUGUST 2, 1999
KEENA'S JOURNAL

Today everything was quiet and slow out with the baboons. Mokupi, Mom, and I had just crossed to a small island on the way to Airstrip in the morning when Mokupi said, "Oh! Many buffalo!" A huge herd, maybe one hundred or so, were quietly feeding on the molapo between us and Airstrip. Since we couldn't pass them to get to the baboons, we left them feeding and mooing and came back to camp. Last night a hyena came through camp and ate all the soap from every sink. So . . . now we have no soap.

AUGUST 16, 1999
KEENA'S JOURNAL

Today was our last day. When Mokupi and Press arrived, the whole family decided to go out with the baboons one more time. After a lot of searching we found them eating palm nuts on C5, which they then proceeded to do for six mind-numbingly boring hours. And Dad says it's dangerous out here. Ha! I don't know why he's so worried. Nothing bad is ever going to happen to us.

CHAPTER 16

ONE UNHAPPY CAT

A BOAT RIDE, A flight in a propeller plane, three flights, and four days later, I was back in America. Back in the stifling heat, sitting in the high school cafeteria in my distressed polo shirt and completely impractical flared khaki pants. Back to American Keena, who was just trying to survive.

It was a Tuesday, and I was trying to come up with an answer to Sarah's question. Who did I have a crush on: Dawson or Pacey? My answer seemed very important to the group of girls sitting across from me in the lunchroom, and I knew I couldn't give them my real opinion, which was that both Dawson and Pacey were ridiculously boring and I didn't have crushes on boys anyway. I didn't actually like anyone on *Dawson's Creek*, girls included, though I had watched a whole season on video to try and catch up before season two started. Was this supposed to be entertaining? I didn't get it. Sarah looked at me expectantly.

"Uh...I guess I like Pacey better," I said. Sarah poked a finger in Meghan's direction.

"See? Even Keena thinks Pacey is hotter than Dawson." Meghan shrugged and took a sip of her Diet Snapple.

"Keena doesn't even like *Dawson's Creek*," Meghan said, and I felt the hairs rise on the back of my neck. *Oh no. How did she know? We're all supposed to like Dawson's Creek. Did I slip up and say that I didn't? Or was it the "I don't like boys, I like girls" thing? I've only been back from Botswana for a week; how could I have screwed up already? Can she see through my shields like some kind of wizard?* I cleared my throat and waved my hand in what I hoped was a casual but dismissive gesture.

"Yeah, not really," I said. "*ER* is more my thing. More action." At least that was true. Of all the shows on TV that we were expected to care about, I did like *ER* the best; everything happened very quickly and if you weren't paying attention, people could die. Just like in Baboon Camp. It made it a lot easier to relate to the characters.

"I bet you like Abby the best," Meghan said, twisting an Oreo cookie in half and taking a bite out of the side with the cream. *How does she do that? I always end up snapping them in half.*

"I do, yeah," I said.

"You look a lot like her," Meghan said. "Who plays her again? Maura Tierney?"

"Really?"

"Totally." The bell rang and the group of girls surged to their feet, reaching for backpacks and books and Diet Snapple bottles before heading off to their next period. I sat in my seat, stunned. Had Meghan really just told me that I look like an actress on a TV show? And a good-looking one? No one had ever told me I looked like a celebrity before, unless you counted Abu the monkey. Could it be possible that I was finally getting this America thing right?

Somewhat dazed, I wandered down the hall toward class. The backpack slung over my shoulder was lighter these days since I no longer brought my books to school. Recently I had settled for using my free periods to read ahead in *Jane Eyre* for English. I felt oddly light as I walked along, like I'd just cracked some kind of code. Thinking about nothing in particular, I smiled, enjoying the sunshine.

In class, I plopped down in a chair next to Nat as I usually did. I was just beginning to pull out my notebook and pen when I realized Nat was sitting completely still, staring at the desk in front of him with a vacant look on his face. On the other side of him, Brooke sat sideways in her chair, casually spinning a purple gel pen in her hand. I stared at that purple pen, which had fascinated me for weeks; I had been secretly hoping that she'd forget it in class someday so I could take a closer look.

"So what's she like?" Brooke hissed. Nat said nothing, and I realized Brooke had been talking to him. I frowned. That was odd. I didn't think Brooke even knew his name. She poked him in the arm with the gel pen. "Come oooon, you can tell me. I bet she's wild."

"You bet who's wild?" I asked. Nat didn't say anything and continued to stare at the desk in front of him. Brooke ignored me.

"I bet it's wild and sloppy and she'll let you do anything. Am I right?" Nat's neck turned bright red and he clutched his hands in his lap.

"Hey, leave him alone," I said. Nat hated being teased, and I knew he had a bad habit of blushing the second someone made him uncomfortable. He was a terrible poker player. Brooke kept ignoring me and leaned across the space to tap Nat on the head with the gel pen. I knew he'd hate that too.

"What base have you gotten to yet? Second? Third?" Nat's blush deepened to maroon and he broke his stare to look up at me with an expression of near panic.

"I said leave him alone." Brooke moved back into her seat and the classroom door slammed, breaking the tension. Brooke began talking to someone else and Nat smoothed his hands down his khaki pants, erasing imaginary wrinkles. Now that I had a moment to think about the conversation, a wave of nausea hit me and stars danced across my vision.

"Was that about me?" I whispered, aware that the room was filling up and we could easily be overheard. He cleared his throat.

"Don't worry about it," he said thickly. "I keep telling her we're not dating, we're just friends. She just doesn't listen to me." Dating? Of course we weren't dating. I didn't like Nat that way. I didn't like any boys that way. I thought Nat knew that already.

I stared at Brooke over Nat's head and seethed. Why was she even bothering him? Everyone knew we were friends. We'd been friends since we were six years old! Nat had his first sleepover at my house. He wore blue footie pajamas and brought his stuffed bear named Bergie. We read books and kept each other company, and didn't she know that Nat couldn't take care of himself and if she wanted to go after anyone she should go after me since I wasn't afraid of her anyway or her stupid purple gel pen that I never wanted in the first place? Bully.

I stole another glance at Nat, who was paging to the middle of *Jane Eyre* along with the rest of the class. He looked calm, but I knew he was hurting. His glasses were smudged and he hadn't polished them yet, which was a sure sign of trouble. I looked back up at Brooke and felt my shoulders tighten like a lion's, ready to spring. *Who do you think you are, anyway?* I thought. *If you want to mess with someone, pick someone who can at least fight back. And leave Nat alone. If you want to tease him about me, there's a pretty easy way to fix that. I'm hurting plenty already. And unlike him, I can take it.*

When the bell signaled the end of class, I didn't wait for Nat as I usually did. I grabbed my dusty, poop-stained backpack and headed for the door. *Don't follow me*, I thought, as I headed to the library. I didn't sit in our usual study spot either. I found a spot in a distant corner of the library where no one ever visited, sat down in the windowsill, my back propped against the wall, and stared out the window into the gathering darkness. *Figures it gets dark in the middle of the afternoon here. What a stupid place.* I closed my eyes and leaned my head back. Botswana Keena paced back and forth in the castle in my head, angry, sad, frustrated, and fucking pissed off (a new term I'd learned from watching *ER*).

It wasn't that Brooke thought Nat and I were dating or that she made nasty insinuations about what we did when we were alone. What made me mad was that she went after Nat in order to get to me. And that was low. Baboons did that sometimes—when they couldn't attack who they wanted to attack because they were higher ranking, they instead went after someone smaller and weaker who couldn't fight back. *At least in that scenario I would be higher ranking than Brooke*, I thought with a wry smile. *Well, fine. But you can't tease Nat about us dating anymore if you don't ever see us together. That just means I can't hang out with him anymore at school. I'm alone almost all the time anyway; what does it matter if I have one less person to talk to?* I sighed again. My legs twitched and I felt a headache building behind my eyes as it did every afternoon in school. Stupid fluorescent lights. At least by now I'd learned how to fix it.

When the final bell of the day rang, I shoved my backpack into the bottom of my locker and trotted down the hallway, past the seniors' lounge where *Watership Down* had been destroyed, and down a steep concrete staircase to the gym underneath the basketball courts. I pushed open the heavy doors to the weight room and bounced up and down on the balls of my feet, breathing in the scent of old sweat and metal. Everyone thought the weight room was gross, but it's where I had to report every afternoon for my chosen winter sport of "gym." It's what the nonathletic kids did if they didn't want to play basketball or volleyball, but something I discovered was perfect for me. My gym coach had said I was sadistic and crazy for taking gym, but I loved it because it allowed me to use my time to run.

As she did every afternoon, my coach, Katie, helped get the other students started on their lifting machines before turning to me, still bouncing on the balls of my feet in the doorway.

"Where to today?" she asked. I grinned.

"The usual loop. Should take me forty-five minutes, I think." She raised an eyebrow.

"You sure? It's pretty cold out there. It's supposed to snow."

"Yeah, I'm sure," I said.

"You could always run up and down the stairs for an hour instead. You did that the last time it snowed."

"I only did that because you told me I couldn't run on the ice. I'm not afraid of the cold." She gave me a long look.

"Fine. Have fun. If you're not back in an hour I'm sending someone after you."

"Okaybye!" I said, already halfway out the door.

I ran up the concrete steps, across the basketball courts, and out the doors of the gymnasium, the icy winter wind hitting me like a wall as the door slammed behind me, leaving me alone on the tarmac in the darkness and swirling snowflakes. The cold burned the bare skin on my legs as I started running down the road, beginning the loop that would take me through the neighborhood around school and end up back at the gym just as Dad would be pulling up to take me home.

I ran faster and faster, keeping one eye on the sidewalk looking for ice and the other glued to the road ahead of me, filtering out the lights from the cars that blew past me on the road and giving me the room I needed to think again.

Brooke sucks, Brooke sucks, Brooke sucks, I chanted to myself as my sneakers pounded the pavement.

As I made the last turn of the loop and jogged up the school's driveway to the gym, I saw Katie standing outside with her arms crossed, glowering at me, just as she did every day.

"It's been fifty minutes," she said.

"Sorry," I panted, leaning over and rubbing my legs that were bright red from the cold.

"You getting slower?"

I coughed out a laugh. "No, the damn traffic lights wouldn't give me greens today." She patted me lightly on the shoulder, backlit against the bright lights of the gymnasium and the roar of the crowd watching the boys' basketball game unfolding inside.

"Good. I can't have our top goal-scorer getting slower." I grinned. Katie was also the assistant coach of the varsity lacrosse team. "Now go put on some sweatpants before you freeze to death."

We repeated this pattern every day as the winter months stretched on and on, darker and colder than the darkest and coldest day in Botswana and with no animals in sight. Every day, I avoided Nat and was relieved to see Brooke start leaving him alone and go in search of weaker prey. Every day, I sat alone in my corner of the library, looking out the window and watching the branches of the bare trees dance in the wind against a perpetually slate-gray sky. And every day, I met Katie in the weight room and went running down suburban streets sparkling with Christmas lights, knowing that no matter how little attention I paid to where I was going, there was zero chance that a lion would jump out and attack me. It felt wrong, somehow, to let my guard down that completely after years of living on high alert for danger. *But there's nothing here*, I told myself. *Nothing here is scary. Nothing here can get you. It's all safe, and gray, and fine.*

Finally, spring arrived. Crocuses and snowdrops pushed through the melting snow and I was surprised to find myself smiling as I saw them blooming on the sides of the lacrosse field. *Maybe there is something in America that is nice.*

The months of running under Katie's guidance paid off. I was proud to find I was still one of the fastest girls on the varsity lacrosse team that spring, always vying for second fastest behind Brooke with one of the nice girls from my European history class named Maggie. I didn't mind battling Maggie for second place, especially since every day we silently pushed each other to be faster. We both ended up passing Brooke on one glorious spring day, which was made even sunnier by the fact that Brooke looked as if she'd swallowed a bug. *That one's for Nat*, I thought as Dad drove me home. *Told you the monkey would get you one of these days.*

Dad slowed the car at the bottom of the long driveway that led up to our house.

"Would you mind getting the mail?" he asked. I climbed stiffly out of the car. Dad continued up to the house. The legs that had finally carried me to victory over Brooke appeared to be rebelling against the extra effort I put in that afternoon and were refusing to work properly. Every muscle ached as I hobbled over to the mailbox, and I absently wondered how I was ever going to run tomorrow if it hurt this much today. Something soft grazed my shins and I looked down to see a big black cat weaving back and forth between my feet. I smiled and reached down to pat her.

The same cat had shown up at our house a few weeks earlier, filthy and hungry and with no collar to indicate where she'd come from. Lucy and I fell in love with her immediately but knew we couldn't keep her on account of Dad's terrible cat allergies. He loved cats but said that ever since he spent a week in a tiny apartment in Nairobi with a friend and her six cats, he wasn't able to be around a cat without sneezing. We didn't officially adopt her, but we fed her every day on the porch and gave her a bath in warm water we carried out to the garage. She liked to follow me around when I was outside and sometimes let me pick her up.

The cat had jumped up on the mailbox and was rubbing against my hand when I heard a car slow on the road behind me. I turned around and saw a middle-aged man with brown hair lean over and open the door of a rusty red car. A few empty fast-food boxes fell to the ground and the stench of body odor and old food poured out. The cat and I wrinkled our noses.

"Hey, come here," the guy called. I glanced down at my legs and thought it was unlikely they'd ever move again.

"Can I help you?" I answered.

"Yeah, come here," he said again. I took a few wobbly steps forward, the cat behind me. The guy's eyes were unhealthily bright and I noticed he wasn't wearing a seat belt. "Is that your cat?"

"Um...not really," I said, stopping a couple of feet from the open passenger-side door. "She just showed up a couple of weeks ago and we've been feeding her." He leaned farther across the passenger seat.

"That's my cat," he said. "I've been looking for her." *Really?* I thought. *But she's so clean and friendly and you're kind of gross.*

"Oh, she is? Sorry, we didn't know."

"Yeah," he said. "Come here and give her to me." I picked up the cat and placed her gently on the passenger seat, where the guy grabbed her and tried to move her to the back. She hissed and wriggled out of his hands.

"Guess I'm glad you found her then," I said, not feeling glad at all. The guy made no move to close the passenger door.

"That your house up there?" he asked, gesturing up the driveway with his chin.

"Yeah."

"Your parents home?"

"Yeah."

"Get in. Let me drive you up there so I can thank them for looking after my cat."

For a split second, I considered taking him up on it. My legs ached horribly and I really did want a ride up to the house. Though it was spring, the wind was chilly and I was shivering.

"Come on," the guy said. "Just get in." From the back seat, the cat looked out the window and hissed.

"No thanks," I said.

"Come on," he said again. "Just get in and I'll take care of you."

"No," I said again and took a few steps backward. I didn't like the way his eyes glittered or the way the cat's ears were plastered back against her head. I'd seen enough fucking pissed-off lions to know that was one unhappy cat.

"Bitch," he said. He slammed the passenger door closed and tore away, leaving me standing in the cold.

"The weirdest thing just happened," I said after I finally made my way up the driveway and into the house with the mail. Mom and Dad were unpacking groceries in the kitchen and Lucy was doing homework at the dining table.

After I told them what had happened with the guy in the red car and the cat, Mom dropped the broccoli she was holding and immediately pulled me into a tight hug.

"Oh, Keena," she whispered, hugging me even tighter. This was unusual. Mom wasn't a very physically affectionate person and I could never remember her hugging me like this. She seemed deeply upset, which scared me too.

"What?" I said. "It was just some creepy old guy who thought we had his cat."

"No. No, it wasn't," Mom said. "Not when you're a sixteen-year-old girl in a lacrosse skirt."

"I don't get it," I said again, failing to see why what I was wearing had anything to do with it. "I wasn't in any danger, if that's what you're thinking." Mom's hands were shaking.

"Keena, let me just tell you this," she said, holding me at arm's length. "In all the years in Baboon Camp when I've sent you down the river in the boat by yourself, or out with the baboons with the lions and elephants and buffalo, you have never been closer to being killed than you just were this afternoon in our driveway." I made a face.

"What?" I said. "No way." How could that possibly be true? How could this gray, monotonous world of "fine" ever be more dangerous than Botswana?

My mom was very quiet for the rest of the evening. After dinner, we heard meowing outside and saw the cat pawing at the screen door on the porch. Without a word, Mom let the cat into the house and presented her with a bowl of leftover chicken pieces from our dinner.

"Thanks for your help out there," I said to the cat as I ran a hand down her back while she ate. "Guess I really don't know how to take care of myself as well as I thought I did." She purred.

At the time, it hadn't occurred to me that the guy could be a predator, but something about him had warned me off immediately. I just hadn't had my guard up since I didn't think I needed to be careful in America. What danger could a dude in an old car possibly pose to someone who was used to lions and elephants? A lot, as it turned out. America was turning out to be more dangerous than I had always assumed it to be. Could it be that Botswana Keena was needed here too?

CHAPTER 17

WE'RE JUST GOING TO
MAKE A RUN FOR IT

MY JUNIOR YEAR OF high school passed in a blur. All I did was work. Nat and Meghan effortlessly set the standard for academic achievement with A after A in every class they took, and I was determined not to be left behind. Though it took many late nights and early mornings frantically reviewing flash cards before tests, I managed to keep pace with them until at last the year was almost over. We wanted to get back to Botswana as quickly as possible that summer since my parents said they had "more work to do than ever," but because of my final exams, we weren't able to leave in May as we often had in the past. I was bored and tired and so desperate to get back to Botswana that I decided to ask my teachers if I could leave early. All my teachers and the headmaster were very much opposed to this plan, since it meant missing out on three weeks of studying before the exams.

"Are you sure you want to risk it?" the headmaster asked. He had called me into his office to discuss my proposal before deciding whether or not he'd let me go through with it. I was pretty sure he would be on my side—he was a nice guy, as far as I knew, and I thought my proposal was more than fair. And why should I waste any more time in the US than I absolutely had to?

"You know that the final grades from your junior year are pretty important when it comes to applying to college," he went on. I said I understood but pointed out that the Advanced Placement tests for college credit were given a month before classes at Shipley ended. For those students that took them, these tests also served as their final exams. Since I was taking five AP courses that year out of six total subjects and would take the AP tests before I went to Botswana, there was really only one class exam to take early.

"I'm sure that this is what I want to do," I said. I felt a little guilty for causing such a fuss over something that didn't seem like a big deal to me, but honestly, I wasn't all that concerned about my final grades. Yes, I wanted to do well, but my heart wasn't in my schoolwork, and I had a secret plan brewing that would make all of that college stuff irrelevant anyway.

My parents were having a hard time finding research assistants to work in Baboon Camp—a critically important issue because we needed other researchers to run the camp while we were in the US. Every two years, they looked for a new postdoc (sometimes two) to work with them, and every time they posted the job announcement, weeks would go by without a single application from a viable candidate. It wasn't that students didn't want to work with my parents—many of them did, especially since my parents were very well-known in their field by this point. But the list of job requirements for working in Baboon Camp was long and very difficult to meet by anyone who was just coming out of school. My parents wanted someone who already had their PhD, had experience doing fieldwork somewhere in Africa, came with a spouse or partner who could keep them company, knew enough wilderness skills to keep the camp running, was cool enough under pressure to handle lions and hippos, *and* who met my parents' rigorous standards for scientific aptitude. Mom and Dad were incredibly meticulous when it came to conducting their experiments, and they weren't comfortable leaving their study site in the hands of anyone who didn't operate to the same degree of maniacal precision that they did. Even when they included candidates from Europe and South Africa, it was an incredibly small pool of people to pull from. I never remembered a time when there had been more than two or three people in serious consideration for the post, and I'd been involved in choosing almost every one.

But this year, their advertisement had received only two applicants, mostly due to the fact that all the postdocs they knew who might have been a good fit were either already in a teaching job or abroad doing fieldwork somewhere else. By the end of April, they had lined up a couple who was available to come to Botswana in six to eight months, but no one who could be there on time to take over when we left in August. That was when I came up with my new plan: if my parents couldn't find anyone to take care of Baboon Camp in between postdocs, I would ask to do it.

I knew college was important, and I knew that I would eventually end up going since Mom and Dad would force me to, but I didn't see why that had to happen so soon. Plenty of British kids I knew took time off between high school and college, and plenty of them worked in remote locations doing something unusual and exciting. How lucky was I that I already had such a place ready and waiting for me? And I wasn't worried about the science part of it either. I knew I could keep my parents' data collection going. I could recognize the baboons better than anyone except Mokupi, wasn't afraid of the other wildlife, and didn't mind being alone either, so they wouldn't have to worry about anyone keeping me company. The camp would be taken care of, their data collection would continue, and I would get to put off college. Everything would be perfect, and best of all, I would be happy. I just had to convince my parents.

Eventually the headmaster agreed to let me go. I took my final exams in early May and my family prepared for another four-month-long stay in Baboon Camp. All through the flights to Europe and South Africa and finally to Maun, I doodled in my journal, planning boat trips I would take up into the north of the delta and the running trail I would clear around the border of Camp Island, and calculating how long my books would last before I had to start rereading them. I drew detailed columns of how I would ration out my food and medicine and decided that this would be a great opportunity to begin harvesting fruits and mushrooms from the forest the way that Mokupi did, if he would show me how.

I stepped off the boat in Baboon Camp full of renewed determination: I wasn't going to let even the slightest thing faze me this summer.
Snakes? Lions? No problem. My parents may have already known I
could take care of myself in the wilderness, but I was going to show
them just how capable I was before asking them if I could stay. No
anxiety here. Captain Keena, Pirate Queen of the Delta, was back, just
a little older and just a little taller.

MAY 10, 2001
KEENA'S JOURNAL

*Dad is sick with some kind of "achy" sickness and Mom's feet are red
and swollen after a bad tsetse fly attack, so no one went out with the
baboons today. Lucy and I drove the boat down to Xaxaba to get all
the supplies we couldn't fit on the plane on the way up here. Most of
the stuff is clothes and boots we brought from the US for Mokupi and
Press, but the managers at Xaxaba asked if we were starting a colony.
It is so windy that the tent sides are buckling in on themselves and
there are leaves and dirt everywhere. My eyes are filled with dust all
the time and we can't keep it out of our food.*

JUNE 13, 2001
KEENA'S JOURNAL

*Lucy and I tried to play Frisbee golf this afternoon in the woods behind
the laundry area. We made a course all around camp and designated
various places we had to hit with our Frisbees as the "holes." I was walking out to the Land Rover (we have a new fancy Land Rover in camp
now and the Hilux stays in town as our town car because it's too beat-
up to handle the roads up here) when I stepped on a thorn. A mean,
nasty, evil little (well, BIG) thorn. Lucy helped me peel off my flip-flop
since the thorn had pinned it to my foot and we saw that the thorn had*

gone really far into my heel. I could feel the pain from the toxins all the way up to my knee and I couldn't put any weight on my leg.

We tried to pull out the thorn but it snapped in half and left a big piece of itself inside my foot. It was so deep I couldn't reach in to pull it out with my fingers. This is bad because puncture wounds get infected easily if you can't get in there to clean them out. Mom gave me the bottle of rubbing alcohol and her set of sewing needles to try and tweeze out the thorn, but I had to eventually switch to my knife to cut a hole deep enough to get to it. It was so horrible. My foot was bleeding so much I couldn't see what I was doing and digging deeper and deeper into my heel with my knife hurt a lot. I just sat there on the tarp outside my tent trying to keep everything clean and wiping the knife with rubbing alcohol. I sweat through my T-shirt and got blood all over the tarp. I actually feel a bit sick. But the thorn is out and everything is clean so that's really all I can do.

I was just back on my feet one early morning in August when Mokupi and Press arrived at work and said that a very large herd of buffalo was moving onto the island from the melapo to the south by C5 Island. Mom took the car out to investigate and saw more than 150 buffalo (she guessed) crossing into the woods from the melapo on the far side of the island. We decided to go out with the baboons anyway, and Dad gave me his usual list of baboons he needed focals done on for the day, the twenty-minute follows where I wrote down everything the baboon did and everyone they interacted with to get an idea of how they spent their day and with whom.

We took the long way to the other side of Camp Island, moving through the woods along the shore by camp and toward the water hole crossing to the north, to a smaller island named C15. We were hoping that the buffalo hadn't gone that far onto the island yet and that we'd manage to cross to C15 just ahead of them.

Eventually we ran into the baboons on the far side of C15 and they were not happy. Since it was still pretty early in the morning, that level of jumpiness meant that there had probably been a leopard hanging around their sleeping site the night before, and it usually took them a while to calm down after a scare like that. It was freezing cold and they usually would have been sunning themselves on termite mounds or snuggling together to stay warm, but not today. They were all grunting nervously and milling around in the bushes. Even the adult females looked anxious, which is unusual considering they were usually the calmest of all the baboons.

Dad and Mokupi went off with one group to practice a playback experiment and I started doing a focal follow on my old friend Balo, who was sitting in the sun with her daughters Barbara and Domino, my favorite baboon of all time. Domino had an adorable hair flip at the back of her head and walked with a saunter you could pick out miles away. She seemed to like me too, and would sometimes sit on my feet if she was feeling brave. Even though I knew it was ridiculous, I often wished she could talk. I think we would have been buddies. Maybe I could have confided in her about this whole high school and college situation.

Out with my baboon friends

Balo didn't do much for the first ten minutes, but then she, Barbara, and Domino seemed to relax and began to forage with another small group of baboons. The sun rose higher and it got warmer, and I began to relax along with the monkeys. After I finished with Balo I did a follow on Jeanette, who was nearby, and then on Comet. We weren't technically supposed to do follows back-to-back like that because it overrepresented the amount of time the baboons spent with each other, but I was being lazy.

After I did the follow on Comet, I finally looked up from my notebook and realized we were completely alone. My little group had wandered far, far off toward the north and I couldn't see or hear any other baboons. It seemed like my little group realized this at the same time too, and they began lost calling and running around trying to find the rest of the group. I was a little scared being all alone, but I decided the best thing to do was start tracking the group and listen, as Mokupi taught me, for birds, branches, monkey coughs, and all the other things that could tell me where the baboons had gone and where they were headed next.

In the end it took us more than three hours to find the rest of the group, tracking them slowly, slowly across the molapo to Airstrip Island, and then all along the island through leadwood trees and palm groves to a clump of jackalberry trees almost three miles from where we'd lost them. It was getting close to noon when I finally found Dad untangling his recording equipment from a bush and talking to Mokupi about something having to do with acoustics. They hadn't even noticed I'd been gone, and I didn't say anything about it. If they hadn't noticed, then what did it matter?

Even though that was plenty of excitement for one day, it wasn't over yet. After my group of baboons rejoined the rest of the troop, they all decided to take off running west toward White Island. I hated when they did this because I couldn't do any work at all; I just had to tighten my backpack straps and run along with them until they decided to stop. I also didn't really like White Island because there were fewer trees and less shade. The sand was also deeper there for some reason, and soft, as if it had been mixed with ash. It coated our feet in white, clumpy dust that inspired the island's name.

I had just started a follow on Cleo when I saw a honey badger appear out of some thorny scrub about ten feet away. It obviously hadn't seen me or Dad, who was standing nearby, and was rubbing its head against a tree stump. It started trotting toward Dad, who dropped his microphone and yelled, "OH SHIT!" really loudly. Honey badgers can be very dangerous because they're so strong and often attack animals more than ten times their size. When Dad yelled, the honey badger stopped, realized it was standing pretty much at Dad's feet, and then hissed, screeched, and bared its teeth. I was trying to think of something to do when out of nowhere the alpha male baboon, Power, came barreling through the troop, headed right for the honey badger. The honey badger hissed and screeched again and took off into the scrub with Power on his tail. I asked Dad if he thought Power was protecting him, but Dad said that, while it's a nice thought, he doubted the baboons thought about him that way.

Finally, around 2 p.m., it was time to begin the long trek back to camp, swatting a never-ending swarm of tsetse flies. It was the end of the dry season and the temperature was just beginning to be uncomfortable, reaching probably the high eighties in the afternoon with not a cloud in the sky. My back was sweating and white foam appeared under the straps of my backpack. When we were in radio range of camp, Mom called to say two things: first, that she scared up a pair of male lions near the swimming-hole crossing when she took the car out to check on the buffalo, and second, that the buffalo herd had split, half moving north toward the swimming hole and the C15 crossing and the other half feeding in the molapo between Camp Island and Airstrip Island, where we were. This presented a major problem for the three of us; from where we stood on the shore of Airstrip Island, we could see not only the herd of buffalo between us and home but also several elephants moving into the molapo from the south.

There were only two ways onto Camp Island by foot: the crossing from the north by C15 Island and the swimming hole (lions and buffalo), or the molapo between Camp Island and Airstrip Island (elephants and buffalo). And Mom couldn't drive the car out to get us because the water was too deep. Dad and I had different ideas about what we should do at this point; I said we should go to the swimming hole because there might be fewer buffalo there, but Dad said there was no way in hell he was knowingly walking into a group of lions—he'd rather die.

"You WILL die," I said, but he didn't think it was funny. Eventually we decided the best option was for Mom to take the Land Rover out to the edge of Camp Island, drive back and forth along the shore, doing what she could to scatter the buffalo, and then drive out into the molapo as deep as the car could go to pick us up. As Lucy was listening to the radio Mom had left at camp, the last thing she heard from any of us was me saying, "Okay, we're just going to make a run for it!" and then silence. She was sure we'd all been trampled by buffalo or killed by lions, but it actually worked out fine—Dad, Mokupi, and I did our best to run through the deep water, holding the recording equipment above our heads and trying to stay out of sight from the buffalo until we reached the car and could jump in the back to be driven to camp. We were soaked and covered with mud but made it home safely, if a little dazed and beat-up by the whole experience.

By the middle of August, my parents were preparing the camp for the arrival of their new postdocs, who were actually going to be there sooner than expected. It was very clear that their intentions for me were solidly fixed on college and nothing else. I was deeply disappointed, though not particularly surprised. As much as I wanted my secret plan of living alone in Baboon Camp to work, I knew deep down that my parents would never have allowed it. They took their work, and academia in general, extremely seriously and college application time was not a time to play around with adventures.

"It's about *choice*," Mom said for the thousandth time. We were in the laundry area on a hot Sunday morning, only a few days before leaving to go back to the States. Mom was washing clothes and I was using a bullwhip to beat the dust out of the small rugs we kept in our tents.

Beating rugs was by far the worst chore in Baboon Camp, but today I was frustrated and grouchy and taking out all my pent-up anger on the rugs. "You need to go to the best college you can so you have more choice over what you do after that. Better colleges equal more choices, whether we like it or not." I'd heard this argument before and it was doing nothing to cheer me up. It pissed me off that I had no choice over something that was supposed to give me choices.

"So I can't just stay here with Thore and Jacinta?" I asked finally, referring to the new postdocs, a husband-and-wife team who were coming from the Ethiopian Highlands, where they'd been studying gelada baboons for several years. I was covered with dust, panting and sweating, and even the thought of going to college was making my throat close up. Absently, I wondered how long I'd been clenching my teeth.

"No, you can't," Mom said, leaning an elbow on the faded pink sink. "I know you want to, but you can't. You aren't on our research grant, so you would be living here illegally. Without a work permit, the government could kick you out and refuse to let us come back at all. When your dad and I go, you have to go too. That's just how it has to be." She turned back to the sink and began wringing out a pair of jeans. "Just think of it this way; your dad and I have to leave so we can come back."

But that has nothing to do with ME, I wanted to scream. *You can come back here whenever you want but I don't know what MY future here is going to be if it's all tied up in what YOU'RE doing. College may have a summer vacation but that is SO FAR AWAY and I can't wait that long. I'll suffocate.*

But Mom couldn't hear my silent screams. As far as she was concerned, the question of college was now settled. She began making me practice writing college application essays after I came home from the baboons. I already had decent grades, she told me, but the essay was where I could really "let my personality shine through." She had printed out a few sample essay questions from the admissions office at Penn for me to practice with—because of course she had—and finally, during our last week at camp, managed to make me sit down to talk about them.

"Write about what you love!" she said. "Make yourself seem as witty and complex as possible."

"You want me to be witty and complex in 850 words?" I had plenty of time once we got back to the US to think about college, and I deeply resented tarnishing my last few perfect days in Baboon Camp thinking about school. School made my stomach flop and acid rise in the back of my throat, and that had no place in Baboon Camp among the birds and sunshine.

"Just try, okay?" she said. "You have to do this anyway. Might as well do it while you're here and your inspiration is all around you. Why don't you write about that day when you and Dad had all those crazy animal encounters?"

"That wasn't witty or complex," I said. "We saw a lot of animals. Just like most days." She was pissing me off, and I wanted nothing to do with this new project of hers.

"Okay," she said, pushing. "But didn't you get separated from the group for a while? What happened when you were out there alone?" I sighed. There was a jacana building a nest on a lily pad in the lagoon and I wanted to watch him work, not think about this.

"Um...I ran into some lions."

Mom started. "You did? Why didn't you say so?"

"Well, nothing really *happened* to me. I ran into some lions, I climbed a tree, and I waited until they went away. That's not really an incident."

Mom blinked. "To everyone else in the world, that is an incident. Write about that." And she went back to her tent to copy her data from the morning into the computer.

KEENA'S STUPID COLLEGE ESSAY DRAFT
AUGUST 21, 2001

Sample Essay Prompt: "Write page 72 of your autobiography"

I looked up from my notebook and realized I was lost, far in the north of the baboons' home range. There were no other monkeys with me except my small group; the rest of the troop was long gone.

I was sitting on a log under a big tree having a drink of water and thinking about what I should do next when I suddenly realized that the songbirds weren't singing anymore. The only sound in the woodlands around me was the harsh *krak-krak-krak* of the franco-lin birds calling out in alarm. This wasn't particularly worrisome—francolins are unbelievably paranoid and alarm call at virtually everything—but the silence of the songbirds was unusual. I stood up slowly and looked around. The baboons lazed about, seemingly unconcerned, but Balo walked over to the log where I'd been sitting and climbed up next to me. We both looked out across the plain in front of us, seeing nothing except grass blowing in the wind. Balo grunted.

"I don't see anything, do you?" I whispered. I knew she wouldn't answer but Balo is one of the smarter baboons in the troop and it felt reassuring to confer with an adult. She continued to stare at the plain, flicking her tail back and forth.

The chattering bark of a vervet monkey brought us both to complete attention, and Balo stood up on her hind legs on the log. Vervet monkeys don't alarm call unless they can actually see a predator, and if whatever they saw was a threat to them, it was likely a threat to us too. I shrugged off my backpack and stepped onto the plain, trying to figure out where the vervets were looking. I was staring intently at a patch of bright yellow grass when I saw the tiniest movement against the wind: a round, tawny ear.

Ever so slowly, I walked backward until I reached the tree, every muscle in my body screaming to move faster despite the voices of my parents in my head saying, "You never run from lions!" When I felt the tree at my back I kicked off my sandals and began to climb, endlessly thankful that the tree had thick bark with large nooks that I could jam my feet and hands into. The vervet monkeys continued to alarm, but the baboons hadn't seen the lions yet and were mostly ignoring them—all except Balo, who was looking alternately at the plain and back at me. Why was that girl climbing a tree?

Halfway up the tree, I paused. I had a good view of the woodland as well as the plain, and found a spot where I could sit with one leg dangling on either side of a thick branch. I was high enough to see over the tall grass and had a better view of the lions. There were five of them, all females, one with her head raised— it was her ear I'd seen twitch in the grass. I took a deep breath, since I knew I was safe in the tree. All I had to do was wait until the lions moved away, which I figured they would do sooner rather than later since it was now very hot, and lions, like all cats, hate to be uncomfortable.

The lion stood up, and Balo immediately saw it and alarm barked. She leapt into the tree, followed closely by the rest of our little group. They climbed much more efficiently than I had and were soon clustered in the branches around me, screaming at the lions on the plain.

"Oh, NOW you see them," I said, looking at Balo. "You couldn't have climbed this tree a little earlier and taken a look around?" The standing lion gave a big sigh and began padding through the tall grass toward our tree followed by the other four.

In a few minutes, the lead lion reached the shade of my tree and stopped. She lifted her head and looked directly up at me. I gasped. Her eyes were beautiful, and the rays of sun shining through the leaves made them glitter ever so slightly. I wasn't scared. I knew I was safe and the lions would soon be gone. I released my breath and smiled. I felt so proud of myself. I knew how to find the lions and what to do when I saw them. I knew where I was, generally, and even though I was completely alone (in terms of humans), I knew how to get home. I started to laugh. I was sixteen, trapped in a tree by five lions, and I was so happy I wanted to cry. Not everyone gets to have that kind of adventure!

I waited for another hour before I decided it was safe to look for the rest of the baboon troop. I climbed down from the tree, strapped my sandals back on, picked up my backpack (a lion had stepped on it!), and headed off toward Airstrip Island, where I guessed the rest of the troop might be. Balo walked along right next to me.

CHAPTER 18

THE LEOPARD ATTACK

WE RETURNED TO THE US in the blazing humidity of late August, a week or so before school started. The yard around our house was baked yellow from the sun and it was clear that it hadn't rained in weeks. The grass crunched under my sneakers at field hockey practice and the humidity filled my nose, making it hard to breathe. Since I was now seventeen, Mom and Dad let me drive myself to and from preseason practice in our old green Volvo station wagon. As we ran the interminable laps around and around the desert that was the field-hockey field, I dreamed of the moment when I would get to take my sneakers off and drive home barefoot. With the windows down and the South African singer Johnny Clegg blaring through the speakers of the CD player, I took the turns in the road just a little too fast and raced the sunset back to the house, imagining I was driving back into camp after a long day out with the baboons.

The Friday afternoon before Labor Day weekend, I trotted into the house after practice and dropped my sneakers in the front hall next to the baboon carved from a palm tree. As I was pouring a glass of water in the kitchen, the phone rang and I saw the crazy long string of numbers on the caller ID that meant the call was coming from the Baboon Camp satellite phone. The sat phone was an expensive piece of equipment that Mom and Dad had recently purchased for camp in case of emergencies. We'd never used it before.

I punched the button for the speakerphone and called out, "Hey everyone, Baboon Camp is on the phone!" Mom, Dad, Lucy, and I crowded around the phone and I leaned a sweaty elbow on the kitchen counter. "We're all here, Dawn; what's up?"

"Dorothy?" Dawn said, sounding very far away and slightly out of breath.

"Dawn? Are you okay?" Mom said.

"Jim and I are fine . . . but I have to tell you something."

"What happened?" Mom asked. Dawn took a deep breath, and began talking. Her usually upbeat voice was subdued.

The day before, Dawn and Mokupi had been out looking for the baboons on Airstrip Island. They were hoping to get an experiment done that day before letting Mokupi and Press go home early for the holiday weekend, so Jim and Press were bringing the playback speaker to her in a mokoro. When Dawn and Mokupi found the baboons, the whole troop was gathered around a bush, uncharacteristically quiet and vigilant. When Mokupi looked closer, he told Dawn that there was a leopard trapped in the bush.

We'd seen baboons with leopards many times before but never a situation that was so quiet and tense—even the time when Mom and I had found them in a similar situation. Usually if the baboons found a leopard, they erupted in alarm calls and tried to attack the leopard and kill it. Watching close to a hundred large monkeys go after a leopard was still one of the scariest things I had ever seen, and always made me remember that even though I counted them as my friends, they were still potentially dangerous animals that deserved my respect. This time, though, the leopard was completely cornered and there was nowhere he could go. Oddly, Dawn said that the baboons didn't seem concerned; they knew they had the leopard surrounded and just stared at him in the bush, where the leopard was crouched, growling. All the females with babies and young adults were there, including my buddy Domino. Every time the leopard moved, the baboons would leap at the bush screaming, pounding the ground, and lashing their tails.

Mokupi and Dawn were in the process of turning on their tape recorders and video cameras when the leopard made a break for it, bursting through the circle of baboons and heading down Airstrip Island to where Jim and Press had landed in the mokoro and were walking to join Dawn with the speaker. A tidal wave of baboons followed the leopard, racing through the trees and screaming. Jim and Press didn't see the leopard, but when Dawn and Mokupi joined them a few minutes later, the troop had cornered the leopard again and was relentlessly driving him down the narrow part of the island from bush to bush.

Finally, the baboons again cornered the leopard in a shallow hole under a termite mound. The adult males began running at the hole one by one, trying to drive the leopard into the open where they could jump on him. Realizing how close they were standing to the hole, Mokupi suggested that they move off to another nearby termite mound where they could get a better (and safer) look. This happened over the course of several seconds, but apparently it was a few seconds too long for the leopard: As Mokupi, Dawn, Press, and Jim made their way to the termite mound, the baboons suddenly gave one last group scream and all ran at the leopard at once. Clearly terrified, the leopard let out a huge roar and broke from the hole directly toward where Dawn was standing. Dawn jumped back a few feet, and Jim pulled her behind him as the leopard dashed past them and jumped on Press, biting him in the face, wrapping its front paws around him, and kicking at his chest with its back paws.

Before Dawn and the others could reach him, several of the baboons jumped on top of the leopard and chased him away into the bushes. Dawn didn't know whether they had killed him. According to her tape recorder, which was still on, it took only seven seconds from the baboons' scream to the leopard jumping on Press. Though Dawn and Jim were able to help Press stand up, he was gushing blood from his face, chest, and back.

Trying to keep Press as calm as possible, Dawn, Jim, and Mokupi helped him back to the mokoro and took him directly to where our motorboat was parked behind camp, grabbing the shortwave radio along

the way and calling down to Xaxaba to have a plane standing by to take
Press to Maun as soon as they arrived. They managed to control the
bleeding by using Jim's and Mokupi's shirts. Dawn said she planned to
find a phone as soon as they got to Xaxaba, but when they pulled into
the dock they found a truck waiting for them, along with a plane.

Dawn was now calling us from Baboon Camp. She and Jim were
back, and Press was safely in the hospital in Maun, though they weren't
sure when or if he would be returning to work. He'd survived the leopard
attack, but he also suffered a pretty severe concussion from a leopard
and at least half a dozen adult male baboons jumping onto him.

Mom and Dad listened quietly as Dawn told her story. Outside it was
an offensively perfect summer day: thick waves of heat rose from the
flagstones of our terrace and songbirds chirped as they splashed around
in the terracotta birdbath. Up the driveway, our annoying neighbor
was using his annoying leaf blower, and Mom's laptop pinged with the
sound of an incoming e-mail. Dawn spoke to us from another planet,
where people cared about things like leopards and monkeys, and where
bleeding to death in the woods on a Friday was a real possibility.

Dawn said she only had a few more minutes of battery left on the
sat phone, and after they'd reassured her that she'd done everything she
could do, Mom and Dad hung up, promising to check in again tomorrow
to see if there were any updates. By this time, we were actually able to
check e-mail in camp—sort of. We used the satellite phone to down-
load messages every few days but had to make sure no one sent us any
attachments or the system would crash. We could also only get a strong
enough signal by standing on top of the Land Rover in the middle of the
plain behind camp and holding the sat phone above our heads, which
in 2001 felt like a perfectly normal way to check e-mail.

After we disconnected, I walked through the house and threw open
the front door with a bang. The wooden planks of the porch were rough
on my bare feet and very hot from the sun. I hopped from one foot to
the other before jumping down onto the lawn, crossing the street, and
walking into the field across from our house. A stream trickled to my

Press out on Airstrip Island with Dawn's loudspeaker

right, and the sulfurous stink of skunk cabbages rose from the sticky mud in the low-lying areas by the water. Oblivious to the mud, I crossed the stream and climbed up on a large boulder on the far bank. The stone was warm and smooth and I crossed my muddy feet under me, relieved to feel a cool breeze push through the August heat and make it easier to breathe.

I was angry. Shocked and relieved, yes, but also angry. In my head I could hear the baboons' screams and feel the vibration in my ribs when the leopard growled. I knew these things; I'd heard and felt them both before. I knew exactly where on Airstrip Island Dawn and Mokupi had been, and exactly which termite mound they had been standing on when the leopard charged. I knew exactly the route they would have taken back to camp, and exactly how long it would have taken them to get to Xaxaba, given the height of the river at that time of year and the location of the hippo pools. If I had been there, I would have probably done exactly the same thing they did—Dawn and Jim had kept their cool and handled the situation perfectly. But I hadn't been there, and they hadn't needed me.

I didn't know much about myself as a seventeen-year-old. I liked being outside, running, and reading. School was terrifying. I didn't have many friends, and though I had figured out how to wear the right thing at school and not say anything too outlandish, every action was part of a conscious plan not to be seen or reveal anything about who I really was and the gay, wild, loud, Botswana part of me that just wanted to scream. If I knew anything about myself in absolute, clear certainty, it was that when those moments came, when it was just me and the lion, out in the wilds of nowhere in the Okavango, I was the one who could handle it—I was the one who would know what to do to keep everyone safe. I'd done it so many times before: from the boat trip to Delta Camp when I was ten to all the changed tires, lion escapes, and elephant charges that I was sure would have killed a less capable person than even teenage me. *That* was who I was—the one who would have helped Press up and kept him calm before he could get to the hospital. If there was a place for me in the world, it was right there on Airstrip Island with Dawn and Mokupi. I'd been waiting for moments like this for years, and when one had finally happened, they hadn't needed me; selfishly, I felt like that last, final place for me to be me had disappeared.

Don't make this all about you, I reprimanded myself. *This couldn't have less to do with you. You were literally on the other side of the planet when this happened.* I was very, very glad that Press was safe. Though I didn't know him well, he'd always been nice to me and was Mokupi's cousin. I wondered how Mokupi was handling this situation and whether he was in Maun with Press at the hospital. Did Mpitsang know? Had he gone to Maun to be with Press too? But I was still mad that I had missed it. I scraped the dried mud off my feet with my fingernails and scowled at the bushes around the boulder, feeling even more lost than before.

The next morning, I woke up to a dark sky heavy with rain clouds.

The air smelled like metal and made my skin prickle as distant thunder signaled an approaching storm. Though I had a field hockey tournament in the afternoon, I decided to go for a quick run anyway so I could enjoy the slow buildup before the storm hit. That was always one of my favorite times to be outside. I liked the sense of impending doom, which reminded me of the adrenaline spikes I'd always get out with the baboons when trouble was coming.

As the first drops came splashing down, I turned into our driveway and took the steps two at a time up to the front door. I was just reaching for the doorknob when I slipped on some wet moss and fell backward, slamming the side of my face on the flagstone step.

I screamed. Mom came running out of the house holding a dish towel and held it to my cheek as she helped me stand. Blood poured from a long, deep cut under my eye and Mom immediately decided I needed to go to the hospital. My last thought before I passed out in the back seat of the car was how ironic it was that when my own crisis finally happened, I was holding a Williams Sonoma dish towel to my face in the back of a Volvo station wagon.

When I next opened my eyes, I was lying on a gurney under the bright lights of a very clean-looking hospital room. I was still wearing my wet shorts and T-shirt, and my face throbbed like my arm had when I'd ripped it open on the fence at the ostrich farm. I vaguely remembered parking, talking to a nurse in pink scrubs, and throwing up in the waiting room of the ER until someone helped me onto the gurney. A white sheet was pulled up to my waist and Mom's purse sat on a chair next to me, though she was nowhere to be seen.

The curtain around my bed swished open and a tall, pretty woman with dark hair entered, carrying a clipboard.

"Hi," she said. "I'm Dr. Blake. So you hit your head, huh?"

"Yeah," I said. I tried to sit up but she put a hand on my shoulder and gently pushed me back down.

"Don't try to sit up," she said. "That was a pretty nasty fall you took and you need to take it easy."

"I'm fine," I said, ignoring the wave of dizziness that seemed to follow any movement of my head. I'd been hurt plenty of times before and never needed a hospital. This was all just an overreaction since we were in America and everything was overly dramatic here.

Dr. Blake raised an eyebrow.

"Oh, you're fine, are you?" she said. "What's the last thing you remember before I came in just now?" The lights overhead beat a staccato pattern in my brain and I vaguely remembered that I'd always hated fluorescent lights.

"I got sick in the waiting room and someone helped me onto this bed."

"So you don't remember the nurse taking you down for an MRI?" I blinked.

"No, not at all."

"Right, then. How about you do as I say, lie still, and let me take a look at this cut?" She pulled up a stool and began gently applying pressure all around my cheek and eye socket. Though I still thought coming to the hospital was an overreaction, I had to admit it felt nice to be taken care of by a professional, especially one as hot as Dr. Blake. I closed my eyes and sighed.

"So do you go to school around here?" Dr. Blake asked.

"Yeah. But I'm not from around here. I live in a camp in Botswana."

"Huh. Ever hit your head like this before?" She cleaned the cut with something cool and began stitching it closed. I'd never had stitches before and the tiny tugs on my skin as she moved across my cheekbone felt like the tiny pulls of wait-a-bit thorns.

"A couple of times," I said. "When I was five, the handlebars came off my bike when I was going down a hill and I knocked out two of my teeth. Then I fell out of the fig tree at our camp once or twice, and when I was twelve, a horse threw me into a fence. I'm not sure if any of those were concussions though because I never went to a doctor." I remembered from watching *ER* that doctors needed to know everything about their patient if they were going to correctly diagnose them. My head throbbed and I choked down a wave of nausea. I felt a sudden need to tell Dr. Blake everything she needed to know so she could help me feel better. The lights pounded.

"And this time you were running too fast on wet flagstones and slipped?"

"Yes."

She chuckled.

"You sound like my little brother," she said. "Always full speed, never thinking about your own safety."

I sighed again. Part of me wanted to correct her that I had been being careful, it was just an accident, but I was too tired and sick to care. Everything hurt and I just wanted to go to sleep.

"This isn't too bad," she said, closing the stitches with a quiet snip of the scissors. "But you definitely have a concussion. So no running or sports of any kind for a while, okay?" I glared at her.

"I don't do well sitting still," I said.

"You're going to have to try. I'll tell you the same thing I tell my little brother every time he ends up in my ER: I don't care whether you're from the suburbs or Botswana or the moon; you are not invincible."

"It was just an accident!"

"It's always just an accident. But you have got to be more careful—it only takes one thing going wrong for you to end up in serious trouble." She was right, of course. It's what I always thought as I headed out with the baboons: you can be as prepared as you possibly can be, and do all the right things, but there will always be a chance that something bad could happen. In the end, all you can do is your best—the rest is up to chance. I'd just never honestly believed that to be true until the leopard attack on Press.

Dr. Blake's hands moved softly across my face, cleaning the stitches and sticking Steri-Strips across the cut, while I stared at the equipment on the wall. I'd printed out a glossary of ER equipment and terminology so I could follow what the doctors on the TV show were talking about, and I tried to identify everything I saw in the exam room: Suture tray. Laryngoscope. Bag valve mask. Magill forceps. The equipment was shiny and clean, neatly organized, and ready for the next emergency to roll through the doors. I wondered what the Maun hospital was like, wishing that Press had been able to be treated at a hospital like this one. I'd never been to the Maun hospital but very much doubted it was anything like the one I was in. I was safe here, and was getting the best care I could possibly get. I was suddenly very glad to be in America.

Mom appeared a few minutes later carrying a blueberry muffin and a vanilla milkshake she'd gotten from the hospital cafeteria. Dr. Blake instructed me to stay off my feet for a couple of days, and to my surprise I felt no need to resist. Dr. Blake knew what she was talking about and I did feel pretty beaten-up. When we got back to the house, I carefully took a shower and lay down on the couch with a stack of books. Outside, dark clouds surrounded the house and shadowed the field across the street, but oddly, I felt no need to run. I sank into the pillows and closed my eyes, feeling clean and safe in a way I had never felt before and too tired to examine why.

CHAPTER 19

THE INFECTION RATE REACHES
36 PERCENT

I THOUGHT A LOT about Press, the hospital, and Botswana in the days following my fall. I wasn't supposed to do much besides nap and read when my head felt up to it, so I stared out the window and watched the leaves of the oak trees rustle in the late summer breeze. The temperature had mercifully dropped after the rainstorm and it was quite comfortable with the window open. Mom tentatively suggested studying for the SATs during my downtime, but after I shot her a glare that could have frozen water she retreated and said reading was probably just as good a use of my time.

Before flying back to the US that summer, we'd spent a couple of days in Maun with Bryony and Tim at the ostrich farm. This was unusual, since aside from the trip we'd made to Jack's Camp two years earlier, we never really spent any significant length of time in Maun or at the ostrich farm. Whenever we came back to Baboon Camp, we would immediately take a six-seater plane up to Xaxaba and then boat up to camp; we never stayed in town. Beyond seeing the progressive upgrades in size and efficiency at the Maun airport, I wasn't at all aware of what was actually going on in town. Anything I heard about changes going on in town, I heard through gossip from either Mokupi or the managers we saw at Xaxaba when we went to pick up our monthly shipment of fruits and vegetables. On holidays, sometimes Tim and Bryony would come up to visit camp with their daughters, Maxie and Pia.

Though we didn't see them often, I thought Tim and Bryony were some of the best people I knew, and despite the challenges of living in a town with few stores and no reliable doctor, they loved Botswana and, for most of the time I knew them, never thought of living anywhere else.

They were different during our last visit with them though. Bryony locked the doors at night and brought the dogs inside. Tim kept a rifle in the kitchen and hired several extra men to walk around the perimeter of the farm at night. He said a couple of his ostriches had been killed in the week before and eaten—he thought—by refugees coming in from Zimbabwe. Maun used to be a very safe town when we first arrived in 1992, but by 2001 we heard that the crime rate had risen dramatically, and Tim said that almost every day there were stories of carjackings, break-ins, and robberies. Most of Tim and Bryony's friends had installed fences around their houses and all had hired watchmen to keep an eye on their properties at night. More than a few had left the country entirely, heading for Cape Town or Mozambique, where they said it was safer to raise their children—including Henny the fearless bush pilot and Desmond the driver of the Leopard-Spotted Lorry, who had been key players in my boat trip to Delta so many years before.

Everyone in Maun, locals and expats alike, blamed refugees from Zimbabwe for the rise in crime. Robert Mugabe's oppressive regime and the incredible inflation in the country drove many Zimbabweans, both white and black, out of the country. Botswana was one of the easier places for them to get to, since refugees could pass through the Hwange National Park or across the minimally secure border crossing at Pandamatenga, where Lucy had lost one of her first teeth on our way to visit Victoria Falls. When the police in Maun did one of their periodic roundups of Zimbabwean refugees, they bused them back to the border only to see the same people turn up again in Maun a week later. It was impossible to stop the influx of people, and the government admitted that immigration control was not actually one of their priorities, given Botswana's rising problem with HIV/AIDS.

By the early 2000s, Botswana was in the epicenter of the rising HIV/AIDS epidemic in sub-Saharan Africa. Nearly 36 percent of Botswana's tiny population of less than two million people was estimated to be HIV positive—though the government admitted this estimate was rough, considering so few people would agree to be tested for the disease. Since HIV was first detected in the country in the 1980s, the government's emphasis had been on getting as many people tested as possible so it could get an idea of the scale of the problem. It had even entered into agreements with the Gates Foundation and the pharmaceutical company Merck to get people tested and into treatment with antiretroviral medications that were subsidized by the government and its partners. The government was internationally praised for having the right plan in place to control the spread of HIV, and it was widely expected that the country's incredible dedication of resources would prove to be the example for other countries on the continent on how to handle the disease.

Unfortunately, they were wrong. As the life expectancy in Botswana dropped into the low thirties by 2001, it was clear that Botswana's lack of medical infrastructure and the reluctance of the population to agree to be tested and undergo treatment were major roadblocks to the control strategy. Government officials and public health experts alike weren't sure what to do next, and even as more organizations pledged to help, it was clear that the problem wouldn't be solved anytime soon.

In Maun, if people weren't talking about the Zimbabwean refugees, they were talking about HIV/AIDS. Tour companies were losing employees at a rapid rate, and those who weren't sick were taking time off to attend the funerals of friends and family. Though the government's impressive education campaign about HIV and how it spreads made it pretty easy for people to understand how to keep themselves and their partners safe, it seemed like many people had a sense of inevitability about the disease: If everyone is getting it, then I'm going to get it too, and why should I change my behavior now? HIV is also a disease with a long timeline compared to something like malaria. Since it often takes years for the infection to manifest into full-blown disease, it was harder for public health experts to explain the relationship between infection, illness, and death in a way that was easy to understand.

Our beloved, beat-up Hilux posing in Maun

Press had recovered well from the leopard attack, but was under-standably not in any rush to come back to camp. When Dawn and Jim visited him in the hospital after the attack, he said he was fine and would like to keep his job at Baboon Camp, though he wouldn't be going out with the baboons anymore. They totally understood, and we were relieved to hear that he had sustained no long-lasting injuries from the attack, though he would likely always walk with a bit of a limp.

We didn't talk about HIV with Mokupi or Press. Dad had tried to on many occasions, and we even bought a big bag of condoms in Maun to keep in the kitchen in case Mokupi or Press wanted to take some. Ever the scientist, Dad made a heroic effort to explain how cellular infection occurred and why it often took years for HIV infection to turn into AIDS, but it didn't work. It wasn't that Mokupi and Press didn't understand; they just didn't want to hear it. Illness, in all its forms, was to Mokupi a generalized malady he called "the poison of Botswana" and it was all caused by some unnamed force that was out of his control. He didn't differentiate between flu, giardia, a cold, or HIV; it was all the poison of Botswana. No other explanation was possible. He refused to hear any different, and eventually Dad stopped trying.

Maun itself was more crowded than it had ever been too. When we first arrived in 1992, there was one supermarket that received a shipment of food from South Africa once a week. If you happened to be in line when the truck arrived, you could get fresh fruit and vegetables. If not, you were out of luck until the next week and had to make do with boxed and canned goods. There were no fast-food restaurants, no pharmacies, and only one bank, but its doors were broken and cows often wandered through. When cars got stuck in the deep sand on the unpaved parts of the road, they were often abandoned until the tow truck could come by, and goats often climbed on them to reach the leaves of the mopane trees.

By 2001, Maun was completely different. Trucks and cars (some only two-wheel drive!) roared through the town on paved roads. There were six traffic lights, three grocery stores, and half a dozen Indian big-box stores where you could buy things like plastic flip-flops, beach umbrellas, and cheap, mass-produced dolls that were only somewhat anatomically correct. Though cows still often hung out in the bank, they now shared the parking lot outside with shiny BMWs and Mercedes brought up from South Africa that looked fragile and delicate next to the Land Rovers and Land Cruisers of the locals. Overlander trucks passed through regularly, taking budget backpackers between Cairo and Cape Town and decimating the grocery stores like locusts descending on a cornfield. Though there was still no real doctor to be found, a few shady clinics sprang up on the outer reaches of town, run by immigrants from the Democratic Republic of the Congo and Zambia who advertised their abilities to treat conditions like "not being liked at work," "misfortune," and "misunderstandings." South African pop music blared from the shops and when driving through town my overwhelming sense was that of noise, noise, and more noise. Driving around town with Mom and Dad before Dad went to talk to Press, I was absolutely astonished at how quickly the town had changed, and how much I had missed in always bypassing Maun to go straight up to camp.

Tim and Bryony sold their ostrich farm that year and were leaving about the same time we were, to head back to the UK. Bryony had family in Wales, and while they wanted to be closer to them, they also admitted that the peace and quiet that had originally attracted them to Maun was gone. They didn't like the noise, the people, or the crime. When a friend of theirs had her house broken into while she slept, Tim and Bryony decided it was time to go.

These crises seemed far, far away as I lay on a striped couch from Pottery Barn in our living room in suburban Philadelphia, watching the oak leaves rustle in the wind. My face throbbed but I knew I would be fine; I had been treated at a clean, well-stocked hospital and cared for by a doctor who had probably studied at one of the best medical schools in the world. That I had all of these incredible resources available to me only twenty minutes away by car gave me a sense of security and, I had to admit, guilt. I imagined what kinds of conditions someone like Dr. Blake would see on a daily basis: probably ear infections, broken bones, accidental injuries, and maybe flu or pneumonia in the winter. Never what the health-care workers in the Maun hospital faced, or the diseases I knew Mokupi's friends and family dealt with under the umbrella of "the poison of Botswana." Schistosomiasis. Malaria. Tuberculosis. And, of course, HIV.

I closed my eyes and ran my finger along the tight, neat stitches that followed the arc of my cheekbone across my face. Dr. Blake had done a good job, and she said there likely wouldn't even be a scar. Then I ran my fingers across the smooth, rounded dome of scar tissue that still covered my left elbow from my horse injury. Here was the proof of what health care could do; I was a living example of it, and scars or lack thereof were the physical proof. What if I were in Botswana and caught something like tuberculosis? My parents would fly me down to Johannesburg or back to the US and I would likely survive. It was painfully unfair that the people I knew and had grown up with did not have access to the same kind of medical treatment, and I felt deeply, horribly guilty that I was able to take care of myself in a way that most of them were not.

It bothered me, too, that all anyone in the US seemed to know about Botswana were the statistics on HIV. Just as Botswana had been heralded on the international stage for implementing a model program for disease control, the eyes of the world had still been on Botswana as the plan faltered and, ultimately, failed.

"I can't believe you're still going back there," our friends and family said. "You're going to catch HIV and die!" Well, no, I patiently explained over and over again, you don't just catch HIV from being around people that have it, and we didn't even know if the guys that worked for us had HIV and we had no plans to ask them about it. Also, we didn't live in town. Baboon Camp was four hours away from town by car or boat, and the nearest human settlement to camp was the village where Mokupi lived and even that was more than an hour away. It's pretty hard to catch diseases from other people if you never see anyone, I explained. No mosquito carrying malaria would ever be able to make it to our camp. So we were fine.

And that's what struck me the most, sitting there on the Pottery Barn couch on a hot September day. I said I lived in Botswana, but I really didn't. Not at all. Not in the least. I lived in a world of campfires and tall trees and the scent of dust on the wind, where elephants shuffled quietly beneath palm trees and genet cats came out at night to eat figs, where the baboons sunned themselves on the cold mornings and fought over the wild mushrooms that grew on termite mounds after the rains came. That might have been "Botswana," at some point. But it wasn't anymore. Real Botswana was the tinny sounds of South African pop played on scratchy tapes in the mall in Maun, the roar of cars on the tarmac, and the ladies with perfect balance carrying jerry cans of water on their heads. It was goats standing on cars to eat leaves, kids running home from school in yellow-and-blue uniforms, and people selling carved hippos at roadside stands. I liked that world, what little I knew of it, but I had no claim on it, not the way I had on Baboon Camp. I had no more business saying I was from Botswana than someone who stumbled through the wardrobe into Narnia and had the audacity to say, "Oh yes, I love it here. This is now home! I am now *Narnian*." Because at the end of the day, whatever else happened, I was still a white girl born in the US, still the same girl that Masaku said shouldn't get a beating back in Amboseli because I was different from my friends—a white, American girl whose real home was far away from the elephants and the hyenas.

I took a sip of ice water and opened my eyes. Baltimore orioles called from the trees outside the window. Though they looked the same as the Okavango orioles back at camp, their calls were completely different. How strange that two species half a world away could look the same but be so fundamentally different? Idly I wondered whether there were orioles in Narnia, and then I fell asleep.

CHAPTER 20

I AM AMERICAN

IT WAS A BRIGHT, sunny morning in early September 2001 when Mom dropped me off at school. I was running a bit late that day, as we were coming from yet another doctor's appointment. The cut on my cheek had healed (though I started my senior year with a dramatic black eye), but I still had to go to several appointments with a dermatologist. Somewhere along the way in Baboon Camp I had picked up a nasty HPV virus and had thick, painful warts cropping up on my knee and forearm. Though the dermatologist burned them off with liquid nitrogen, the virus was proving to be stronger than the strains he usually saw in the US and I had to go back every few days to have the warts burned off again. Finally, it appeared that the treatment was working, but since the dermatologist was now effectively spraying liquid nitrogen onto raw scar tissue, it hurt tremendously. When Mom dropped me off at school after my appointment, both my knee and forearm were wrapped in gauze. Between that and my black eye, it looked like I had just left fight club on my way to study hall.

I headed down the carpeted hallway to the school library, where I planned to either get a jump on my homework or find a quiet corner to read Ursula K. Le Guin's *Tales from Earthsea*. Since people mostly ignored me at school these days, it didn't feel so unsafe to bring a book anymore, and I was very much looking forward to losing myself in a world of mist and runes. Turning the corner into the library, I saw a bunch of kids clustered around a television set. I'd never seen it turned on in the library before and it made me pause. The TV was usually stored in the front of the library and borrowed when we watched documentaries in history class.

"What's up?" I said to a small boy in my class named Dave, who was standing in front of the TV with his arms crossed. Dave stared ahead at the TV screen.

"A plane hit the World Trade Center in New York," he said. I looked at the TV and saw a thick column of dark smoke rising from one of the shiny towers. The anchors on the news were silent, and my first thought was how odd it was that there was no commentary to go along with the smoke. My second thought was, *Wow, that was stupid. Cessna pilots should know better than that.* The pilots who flew tourists back and forth between the game lodges and Maun were constantly getting in trouble with their tiny, six-seater Cessna airplanes, whether the engines were overheating or having pieces of their wings ripped off by baboons on the runway. The summer before, a pilot from a camp on the other side of the delta was just taking off when he ran into a giraffe as it suddenly crossed the runway—the giraffe and plane collided when the plane was twenty feet or so off the ground. The plane was completely totaled and the giraffe died. Though I knew, of course, that people weren't likely to be flying Cessna planes around New York City, the crash with the giraffe was the first thing that came to mind. There had been a lot of smoke then too.

On the screen, the smoke grew thicker. Against the sunny day and cloudless blue sky, the tower looked like a birthday candle someone had just blown out, only somehow awful in a way I felt deep in my stomach but couldn't identify. And then, as I stood in the library with my class-mates, I watched as a second passenger jet flew into the other tower, bursting into an explosion of flames and smoke and shrapnel.

First, there was nothing but silence. And then, someone screamed, and someone else began to cry. Dave's face turned pale and he looked away from the TV.

"I have to call my mom," he said. Vaguely, I realized that I had just

The Cessna/giraffe crash

watched a lot of people die, live on TV, right in front of me. One second they were there, and the next they weren't, just like that. I'd watched animals die before: lions killing buffalo, wild dogs hunting impala, and even the baboons, sometimes, when they found mice and other small animals. Most people thought baboons only ate fruit and seeds, but they were very proficient hunters and often ate smaller animals alive when they caught them. I hated it when they did this. Even with my hands over my ears, it was impossible to block the sounds of the dying animals and the crunch of bones as the baboons tore them apart. But, even though it was horrible, it was still part of the natural cycle of things in the delta: baboons hunted to eat, just like lions, wild dogs, and hyenas. Every animal had to get food from somewhere, and every animal had babies to feed that were just as cute as the babies of the animal they killed.

Not this though. This was different. There was nothing natural or cyclical or necessary about any of this. This was gratuitous and cruel. This was barbarism. This was watching hundreds of people die on TV live in front of me in study hall on a sunny Tuesday morning in fall, and it was not something I knew how to process. Around me, my classmates sobbed and one of the commentators on TV began to cry. The scene in front of me felt right next door and another world away all at once. I longed to find a tree to climb so I could get upwind of the danger, but instead I just stood and stared.

The bell rang for second period and no one moved. The crowd around the TV had grown larger, and when I felt someone at my shoulder, I looked up to see Brooke standing next to me, her face ashen.

"Doesn't your dad work in New York?" I asked gently. She nodded and gestured with the silver cell phone clutched in her hand.

"I can't get through," she said. "Everything is down." She was too tall for me to hug properly, so I reached out and squeezed her hand. She didn't move away.

The PA system buzzed. A voice said that classes were canceled for the rest of the day and that we should all go home immediately. The crowd around me began moving toward the doors, some still crying and others whispering to each other to find rides to wherever they were going. The usual noise and jostling in the hallway was gone and everyone moved quickly and quietly. Brooke and I were pushed to the side by the crowd leaving the library, and I grabbed the straps on my backpack and began to think about my next move.

Okay, I thought. *I'm scared, but I'm okay. What do I need to do when I'm scared but okay? I can handle this, if I think clearly.* Though Lucy was still in middle school, I knew she'd meet me by the car in the Upper School parking lot. That was our plan in case something urgent came up and we couldn't find each other. Neither of us had cell phones anyway; Mom and Dad said cell phones were useless things that no one really needed.

Brooke punched a number in her phone and watched helplessly as the number rang out.

"It's not working," she said.

"I'm sure he's fine," I said. "It takes a couple of hours to get to New York from here. Maybe he hadn't even gotten there yet."

She nodded numbly. "Yeah." The crowd streamed around us and I hitched my backpack higher on my shoulders so I wouldn't get knocked over.

"I gotta go get my sister," I said.

"Wait!" Brooke said, clutching at my hand. "Can you give me a ride home? My brother took the car today and I know you live near me." I blinked, wondering if I'd misheard her. She was talking to me like a normal human being?

"Sure," I said. "Come on."

Together, we pushed through the crowd of students in the hallway outside the library and climbed down the stairs to the main floor. Everywhere students were hunched against the walls, cell phones clutched to their ears, either trying to get through to someone who wasn't answering or crying to someone who had. A couple of teachers stood in the doorways of their classrooms, alternately staring into space or encouraging packs of students to disperse and go home. As Brooke and I exited the science wing and crossed over to the parking lot, I found myself distracted, ridiculously, by the thought that our field hockey game that day would probably need to be rescheduled.

Lucy was waiting at the car.

"Are you okay?" I asked, and she nodded, her blue eyes hard. Tougher than tough, my little sister.

"This is Brooke," I said. "We're giving her a ride home."

"Hey," said Lucy.

"Hey," said Brooke.

Brooke slid into the passenger seat next to me and Lucy settled into the back. I switched the radio to AM to try to find the news, and Brooke hunched over her phone, dialing and redialing the same number over and over again with no success.

The tree-lined suburban streets were deserted as we wound our way through town. The crackle and buzz of the AM radio station felt like a broadcast reaching us from a World War II bunker. Normally crowded intersections were devoid of traffic and no children were playing outside. We were listening as the first tower collapsed. The commentators mentioned a similar attack in Washington, DC, and I thought how strange it was that Brooke and I would be sitting side by side in a Volvo when the world ended. Who would have guessed?

Brooke's phone buzzed and she yanked it open.

"Dad?" she yelled. I wanted to look at her to see if the news was good but forced myself to keep my eyes on the road. *You have to get everyone home*, I said to myself. *One thing at a time, one thing at a time.*

"Is he safe?" I asked.

"Yeah. Yeah, he's fine," Brooke said breathlessly. "You were right; he hadn't even left for New York yet." She laughed. "He's at home. He's at home and he'll meet me there."

"That's good," I said. "That's really good." Lucy reached over the seat and squeezed Brooke's shoulder.

"I'm really glad your dad is okay," she said.

Brooke sighed deeply and let her head fall back against the headrest. Outside, the sun shone brightly and birds sang the way they do on beautiful days in the summertime.

"Hang on," Brooke said, her eyes snapping open. "What about your parents? Where are they?"

"They work downtown in Philly," I said. "I'll try to call them as soon as we get home but I'm sure they're fine. If they can't get home on the train then they'll probably go to a friend's house until the trains start running again. Either way, they'll let us know."

"You're not worried about them?"

I glanced at Lucy in the rearview mirror. She shrugged.

"No, not at all," I said. "It doesn't sound like they're in any danger where they are and I know they'll try to get home as soon as they can."

"I don't understand how you can be so calm," Brooke said. "This is all so scary."

"Yeah, it is really, really scary," I said. "But everyone whose safety I can control is fine. I'm getting you home and then we'll go home and I know that my parents are safe. That's all I can control."

Brooke stared at me silently and for a minute I was back on the lacrosse field wondering if she was going to call me Abu the monkey again.

"You really are as tough as you look," she said finally.

I smiled. "Thanks."

We slowed to a stop at the bottom of a delicately manicured drive-way about a quarter mile and a million dollars away from my house. Brooke climbed out and grabbed her backpack. A screen door slammed open and a tall man with gray hair leaned out of the house and called her name.

"Thanks for the ride," Brooke said.

"Anytime. I'm glad your dad is okay." I watched while Brooke ran up the driveway.

Lucy moved into the front seat and turned up the radio.

"She seems nice," Lucy said. "Are you friends?"

Ten minutes later, Lucy and I were sitting on an old oriental carpet in my family's living room, watching CNN. Mom and Dad had left a message on the answering machine saying they were fine and making their way home but didn't know when they'd be back. Outside, the leaves rustled in the late summer breeze and a chipmunk scuttled across the porch. On TV, we watched in silence as the second tower collapsed in a cloud of white dust that looked like it would blanket the whole world. People in Washington, DC, and New York were evacuating and there was talk of the US going to war, though with whom no one was really sure yet. What the commentators did agree upon, though, was that America and Americans were under attack.

I curled my legs under me and leaned back into the couch. *America and Americans are under attack.* My country was under attack. My family was under attack. I was under attack. This wasn't the same thing as being out with the baboons and having a leopard come after one of us, though that was certainly an attack on my Baboon Camp family. And it wasn't the same as being out with the baboons and having to run away from a lion when I was by myself with Balo the monkey, though that was certainly an attack (of a kind) on me. This was a cosmic reminder that I was part of something bigger than those things, something I had never really thought about before.

I knew I was American. I'd known it ever since I was a little girl in

Amboseli and Mom and Dad told me I had been born in California. I'd known it since Masaku told me I was different from Njaraini and Ma, and every day since then when I'd chatted with Mokupi or helped Mpitsang or Press with something around the camp. I was told over and over again that America was home, even though I was never there long enough for it to feel that way. I had all the trappings of being an American, from the clothes to the language and mannerisms, but actually spent all my time in a world where my identity was both the most and least important thing about me. I didn't need to be born in Botswana to love the delta as much as Mokupi did, but I would never be Botswanan, and I could never be African. Even beyond tangible differences like the ease with which my parents talked about college or how simple it was to access quality medical care, the most fundamental part of who I was had nothing to do with the places and people I loved and admired. I was not African. I was part of a different team. And I could feel any which way I wanted to about it—whether it be guilty at the privileges that my race and nationality afforded me or embarrassed at how my home country was sometimes regarded in other places in the world—but the fundamental truth remained: I was American.

My parents finally got home after dark, exhausted and drained. Lucy and I had pulled ourselves away from the TV and done the same things we always did in times of crisis: make a roast chicken for dinner and do our homework. I wanted to be useful, in whatever small way I knew how to be, and the first step in that process was making sure the people around me had enough to eat and drink. It wasn't until I started putting drops of iodine in the water, though, that I remembered that I didn't need to purify water in America, that this was a different kind of crisis from the ones I'd faced before. While the world was still coming to grips with what happened in New York, Washington, DC, and rural Pennsylvania, all I could do was keep myself and my family safe. Tomorrow would be another day, with new plans, new information, and new people to help, and I would be ready for it, along with every other American I knew.

*   *   *

There was also a crisis going on at Baboon Camp that fall, albeit on a much smaller scale. When Dawn and Jim returned to give Thore and Jacinta a break so that they could go home and visit family, Dawn wrote to us that Mokupi had stopped coming to work. Though he often did this, he was only ever gone for a couple of days, and his recent disappearances were stretching into weeks. Dawn and Jim didn't really need him in order to continue with Dawn's research, but we were all concerned about Mokupi and wondered where he was.

Mpitsang had moved back to the small staff village near Xaxaba, but no one from Baboon Camp had seen or talked to him since the fight with Mokupi about the hippo assassination attempt. Dawn went to see him one afternoon to ask where Mokupi was, but Mpitsang just shrugged. They hadn't spoken in a long while. Though she asked other staff members at Xaxaba, no one seemed to know where Mokupi was. They assumed he had either gone to see his family in Etsha or was in Maun—where, no one could guess. As far as anyone in Xaxaba knew, Mokupi didn't know anyone in Maun. He had just disappeared.

From the US, Dad e-mailed our friends at Xaxaba and Delta and told them to keep an eye out for Mokupi. Mokupi's health had been on a slow but steady decline in recent years and though we couldn't be sure it was HIV or AIDS, we were worried it might be. If he was missing, then it was also likely he wasn't receiving any kind of medical treatment or eating well enough for any medication to be effective. Not that he took medication from doctors anyway. Even getting him to take an aspirin for a headache was a challenge. He distrusted everything about the medication we brought with us from the US and didn't think anything from another country could address his health.

As the Baboon Camp family searched for Mokupi, and America and the world searched for meaning after the 9/11 attacks, my educational career plodded along. I began applying to colleges and took a road trip with Dad up the East Coast over one unseasonably cold weekend in

October, stopping at Princeton, Columbia, Yale, Brown, and Harvard. Dad was pushing hard for Harvard, his alma mater, and as we drove around New England, he discussed the pros and cons of various Ivy League institutions, mostly to himself, as I stared out the window and watched the snow collect on the lampposts.

I didn't really care where I went to college. I went through the motions of course, in the official way that one does with important life decisions, but it seemed so insignificant when there were much bigger things going on in the world, like leopard attacks, terrorist attacks, and Mokupi. Why should I worry about which university said it was better than the others? They all seemed basically the same to me, except for having different reasons why I didn't want to go there: At Brown, I watched the field hockey team struggle to run up an incredibly steep hill and decided Brown was not the place for me. There weren't enough trees at Yale, it was too loud at Harvard, and at Columbia our tour guide was shocked when he asked me if I wanted to be a Columbia University lion and I said, "No, I hate lions." Everything was too big and too crowded and so very far away from the quiet trees and wind of the places I loved. How could I ever survive in any of these places for four years? And what was the point? More work and all for what? More school and more work forever and ever and always? None of it would get me back to where I wanted to be. The idea gave me a headache.

I took the SATs. Then, because everyone at school was doing it and Mom thought she'd be a Bad Parent if she didn't follow along, I got an SAT tutor and took them again. My scores stayed exactly the same, proving my point that the whole process was a waste of time. At school, people talked to me even less than usual. College was the only thing on anyone's minds, and it seemed as though everyone I knew was either bragging about where they were applying or being so secretive about it that you'd think they were hiding nuclear codes in their lockers. At lunch and in study hall, my classmates clustered in small groups, clutching glossy college brochures in their hands and eyeing each other suspiciously. All I did was study. I knew I wasn't as naturally smart as people like Meghan and Nat, but no one worked as hard as I did. Before school, during school, after school, I was either running, studying, or sleeping.

I decided to apply early to Harvard. I didn't expect to get in, but I thought I might as well aim for the top and then go from there. I wasn't feeling very emotionally invested in the process, but it seemed to make my parents happy. I just wanted the application to be done and submitted so I could have some free time back; it had been weeks since I'd read a book, and not being able to run after field hockey practice made me jumpy and restless. My mind was wandering even more than usual and every pen in my backpack had been chewed to pieces.

Worst of all, we still hadn't found Mokupi.

CHAPTER 21

THE OTHER SPOT AT HARVARD

EARLY-DECISION APPLICATIONS WERE due on a Thursday, and on Friday morning, I walked into school feeling lighter than I had in a long time. Thank goodness that mess was finished! Now I just had to wait a few weeks to see if I got in. I very much hoped that I did, if only because it meant I wouldn't have to do all the work of applying anywhere else.

Since I was a senior, I was allowed to leave campus during my free periods. I was late that Friday morning because I'd gone to 7-Eleven to get coffee with a girl in my English class named Natalie, whom I was only getting to know senior year. I liked that she dyed her hair and that she agreed with me that *Heart of Darkness* wasn't necessarily a metaphor for human nature—it could also just be a story about a very stupid person who didn't know how to travel in the Congo. Natalie wore heavy black motorcycle boots and didn't laugh at me when I called it "a coffee" the way British people did. As the weeks passed, it became a tradition for us to go to 7-Eleven for a coffee on Fridays before English.

I dropped into a plastic chair in the cafeteria and slung my backpack onto the table, where it landed in its usual cloud of dust. Natalie sat down next to me and propped her heavy boots up on a chair. Ever since we started hanging out I had been dying to know what it felt like to walk in them. I imagined it would be like wading through the thick sand on White Island, but Natalie didn't seem to mind.

"So did you get your applications in?" a voice said. I looked up from rummaging through my backpack to see a couple of girls from my grade settle into the seats across the table from us. Two of the girls I knew from my math class, and the third was Jessica, the girl who'd made fun of my hair at the bar mitzvah party a hundred years before. They were all friends with Natalie. Jessica was generally a pretty grouchy person, but this morning she seemed even more pissed off than usual.

"I know you got your application done," Jessica said, looking at me. "Where did you apply? Or is it a secret?"

"It's not a secret," I said. "I applied to Harvard." Jessica snorted.

"I knew you would," she said. "And you'll probably get in too. It's *so* unfair."

"How is that unfair?" I said. "You could have applied there too. Anyone can apply anywhere they want."

"You're so fucking naive," Jessica said. "You know colleges won't take more than a couple of people from each school and it's completely unfair that you're taking one of the spots."

She didn't mention the other spot, and neither did I. We all knew who the first spot at Harvard was going to, and that was Meghan. Meghan had been destined for perfection since the day I met her in first grade and she got to play April O'Neil in Ninja Turtles at recess, and it was only natural that she would graduate as senior class president and go on to Harvard. It was fate. It was destiny. No one questioned it. This idea of "the other spot at Harvard" was a new one though, that had just started swirling around the senior class after someone came up with the idea that the best universities only took two students from any school's senior class. It was widely assumed that "the other spot at Harvard" would go to Nat or one of the other boys from the AP Physics class who was also a concert violinist or a Junior Olympic swimmer or something else impressive. The idea that someone else might have the audacity to even apply for one of these spots was somehow perceived as an insult to the most deserving among us. And it was an idea I thought was stupid.

"How is that naive?" I said. "I work really hard for my grades. Why shouldn't I get the same shot as anyone else?" Jessica rolled her eyes.

"You don't deserve to go to Harvard," she said. "We all know it. You have an unfair hook that no one else has and you're trying to use it to get something you haven't earned."

"Excuse me?" I said, my voice raising. Natalie put her hand on my leg under the table, but instead of calming me down, it made me even angrier. I didn't care that she was trying to be nice; I could defend myself just fine.

"You heard me," Jessica said. "You have this weird childhood that no one else had and you're going to talk about it in your college application and try to seem all different and special and better than the rest of us. It's like saying, 'Hey, I'm a weirdo circus freak, let me in to Harvard and I'll be your diversity.' It's bullshit."

"It's not bullshit," I said, making a conscious effort to steady my voice. "My childhood is not weird and I am not a circus freak. That's just me. That's just my *life*."

"Whatever," Jessica said. "You don't deserve to go there. You don't even deserve to apply there. We all think so. You'll just follow Meghan around and bother her like you've been bothering her since first grade, since you can't make friends on your own. I bet she hopes you don't get in, just like the rest of us."

"Fuck off, Jessica," Natalie said.

My breath caught in the back of my throat and the world telescoped down into the single pinprick that was Jessica's face, pale and pinched under her cascading chestnut hair that was always perfectly styled and never bleached by the sun. I blinked once, twice, and a third time, as Jessica turned away and carried on her conversation with her friends, completely ignoring me now that she'd said her piece about me and my future. Behind her, the windows looked out onto the quad between the Upper and Middle Schools, and across the lawn I saw the windowsill where I used to sit and read my dragon books. It was empty, but I knew that if I closed my eyes I could feel the cold aluminum under my legs and smell the swish of the pages. How was this conversation even happening? People like Jessica and the boys on the prank phone calls had spent years teasing me about my childhood and Baboon Camp and now here she was, in my face, resenting me for having it because she said it gave me an unfair advantage? What new nonsensical reality was this?

The bell rang and I snapped out of my reverie. Natalie looked at me questioningly.

"You okay?" she asked.

"Yeah, fine," I said, feeling anything but fine. I cleared my throat and focused on picking up my coffee cup and walking out of the cafeteria, one foot in front of the other. Stonily, I blinked the tears out of the corners of my eyes and clenched my teeth. This was not the time—and definitely not the place—to fall apart. I followed Natalie down the hall to the English wing, absently sidestepping other students and keeping my eyes glued on the ground, the same way I did when I was doing a focal follow on one of the baboons. No one was better at writing and walking than I was, though the scars on my shins were evidence of the occasional tumble into warthog holes.

In the classroom, I dropped into my usual seat in the back of the room, strategically placed along the windows so I could watch the squirrels in the trees and in the back row so no one could see the dragons I doodled all over my notebook. Some things were best kept private.

"Keena!" Meghan said, settling into the desk next to me in a cloud of Bath & Body Works. "Did you get your application in? Aren't you glad it's over?" I looked at her blankly, unsure of how to respond. Was this the girl I'd known since first grade, the desk friend who gave me *Calvin and Hobbes* books for my birthday and knew I liked owls? Or was Jessica right that this was the queen of the school and senior class president, who didn't want me to get into Harvard because she thought I didn't deserve to be there? I turned away and pretended to be writing in my planner. It was too risky to trust her. Meghan frowned and gave me an odd look, but the bell rang and saved me from having to respond. *All I have to do is avoid her for the rest of my life*, I thought. *Or at least until early-decision results come out in December.*

As it turned out, Meghan and I were the only two students who

Gifted at walking through melapo

applied to Harvard from our senior class. Once the rest of our classmates figured out it was just us and no one else, the conversation shifted from being about whether I even deserved to apply to how unfair it would be if I actually got in. Nat had chosen to apply early decision to Yale, which people seemed to think was fair but unfortunate, since he really should have been the other Harvard applicant along with Meghan. All attention was on the two of us, and it felt like the whole class was waiting to see what happened. What Meghan herself thought, I didn't know, as I was doing my best to avoid her.

Inevitably, and perhaps not surprisingly, I had another doctor's appointment scheduled for the week before the early-decision results were supposed to be e-mailed to us. I'd been finding my mouth guard very painful to wear during field hockey season that fall, and we finally figured out that my wisdom teeth were coming in and squeezing my jaw in a way that made the mouth guard cut into my gums. When I spat out a wad of blood after our final game of the season, Mom said it was time we finally dealt with the problem.

I spent the weekend after my operation lying on the couch watching nature documentaries and trying to eat soup through a straw. It turned out that all four of my wisdom teeth had been coming in sideways and the operation had taken much longer than it usually did. I woke up twice, and both times had to be put back under with laughing gas. My jaw throbbed and I could barely open my mouth wide enough to poke the straw through.

When I finally made it back to school on the day early-decision notifications were coming out, my face was still swollen to an unrecognizable degree and my jaw ached horribly. I found myself welcoming the pain since it distracted me from the roiling anxiety in my stomach. Now that my classmates had raised the stakes, I wanted to get into Harvard. I really did. I was proud of how hard I'd worked, and thought I had as much a right to go to Harvard as anyone else. As much as I tried to pretend it didn't bother me, the stares and whispers were really getting to me. I just wanted it to be over.

I was dozing in my usual corner of the library near the oak trees when I heard cheers coming from the row of computers by the librarian's desk.

"You did it!" Jessica's voice squealed. I sighed. Meghan must have gotten her acceptance e-mail. "You must be so thrilled," Jessica went on, all syrupy sweet in a way that even I—with my stilted social skills—could tell was insincere. "You really deserve it." *Such a suck-up*, I thought. But Meghan did deserve it. She had earned her place. She was smart and hardworking and had been since first grade with her perfect handwriting and perfect hair ribbons. I sighed again. *If dragons really do exist, now would be a great time for one to show up and eat me*, I thought.

I rose stiffly to my feet and tried cracking my jaw, which was a mistake and sent me staggering against the bookshelf in a wave of pain.

"Are you okay?" Meghan asked. She knew where my library corner was, even though she never bothered me there.

"Yeah," I said, as I brushed a tear from the side of my puffy and misshapen face. "You got in, huh?"

"Yes."

"That's really awesome. I'm so happy for you." I gave her an awkward hug, breathing in the Bath & Body Works. *She even smells perfect.*

"Your turn," she said.

"Do I have to?"

"You shouldn't be so hard on yourself," she said. "What if it's good news?"

"Mmph."

I followed Meghan to the row of computers, where Jessica stood with her arms crossed, already glaring at me. I sat down on a blue plastic chair and opened my e-mail inbox. There it sat, one new e-mail, black and unopened, from the Harvard University Admissions Office. Blood pounded in my ears and I tried to think about grass, sand, and monkeys, swords and princesses and pirate queens, boats and crocodiles and cold beers. Quiet trees, soft wind, and birds flying home at sunset. *Don't be scared*, I said to myself. *You are not in danger and nothing is attacking you. There is nothing scary here.* I clicked the e-mail.

"Dear Applicant," it read. "We are delighted to inform you..." I coughed out a laugh. Was this a joke? Meghan squealed and hugged me around my shoulders.

"You did it!" she said. My hands shook and my face pounded. I squinted at the screen. I didn't even remember what the rest of the e-mail said. Carefully, I wiped more tears off my swollen cheeks and laughed again.

"I guess so," I said.

"I should say congratulations," Jessica said. "But you don't deserve it."

"Honestly, what is your problem?" I said, Meghan's hand still on my shoulder. "Why do you care where I go to school? It's not like you even wanted to go to Harvard; you applied early to Georgetown. And you got in! This has literally nothing to do with you." Jessica shrugged.

"No, it doesn't," she said. "I just think it's bullshit that Harvard let you in because of how you grew up. Your parents took you somewhere weird and you lived there, but it's not like you actually DID anything yourself." Never did anything? I should have spent more time at school talking about what I did in Baboon Camp. Maybe then at least if she still didn't like me, she might have the decency to be scared of me. Did she even know how fast I could gut a fish?

"Our grades are exactly the same," Meghan said quietly. "Also, shut up."

"It's fine," I said. "Thanks, but I don't need your help. I can take care of myself."

"I know you can; it's just so rare I feel like being a bitch to someone." Meghan had never said anything like that in her entire life.

I laughed aloud. "Anyway, congratulations," Jessica said, picking up her backpack to go. "Enjoy a whole new school where everyone thinks you're a freak and you have no friends."

"Well, at least in a few months we'll never have to see her again," Meghan said as Jessica walked away, already texting on her cell phone. "And where no one knows you used to be known as Abu the monkey." I jerked my head up, causing another spasm of pain to reverberate through my jaw.

"You knew about that?" I asked.

"Everyone knows about that," Meghan said. I groaned, and only partly because of my jaw.

"Hey," she said. "At least with your face like this you look more like the genie than Abu."

I shoved her away gently while she laughed, remembering that this was still the girl I'd known since we were six years old.

"Shut up, Harvard," I said.

CHAPTER 22

A BEAR JUST DOING HIS BEAR THING

SIX WEEKS AFTER I graduated from high school, I found myself sitting cross-legged on the floor of a freshman dormitory at Harvard, being asked a series of questions about how comfortable I was in the wilderness. We hadn't gone back to Baboon Camp that summer since my parents had work to do at the university, and they claimed that I had to spend all my free time getting ready for college, which just meant putting all my clothes in a box, then pacing my room and worrying about how much everyone at college would dislike me. My entire senior year had been hijacked by the drama around my admission to Harvard and it felt like that had destroyed any progress that I had made trying to fit in. Even though Meghan promised we'd still be friends when we got to school, I wasn't sure I entirely believed her.

I'd spent all of high school trying to mold myself into this image of what I thought an American girl should be, only to end up more alone and confused than before about who I actually was and what was important to me. Botswana Keena wasn't safe in America, and American Keena was disliked and lonely, so what was I supposed to do now? Go to college and remake myself again? Run away to a mountain to live on acorns and talk to the squirrels? That summer, I lost my appetite completely, drank gallons of Diet Coke (it was so easy to get in America!), and paced and paced and paced.

Among the tsunami of orientation materials I received before college was a pamphlet for something called the First-Year Outdoor Program, or

FOP. FOP was a weeklong hiking and canoeing trip in Maine that was designed to bring groups of incoming freshmen together, to get to know each other before school started by bonding in the wilderness. I'd never been to Maine before but liked the idea of being outside for school. I immediately signed up for the program and chose the most difficult trip they offered: ten miles a day of rigorous hiking and canoeing. Just the thought of all that physical activity quieted my mind, though I tried not to think about the fact that there would be other students on the trip too. If we were hiking all day, how much talking could we really do? Maybe I'd be safe if they were all too exhausted to ask me questions about who I was and where I came from, since I had no idea how I would even begin to answer them.

Two minutes into my orientation day conversation with a Harvard upperclassman, however, I knew I was in trouble. This guy was way too cheery for 8 a.m. on a hot August morning and wanted to know every last little thing about me—and not just my medical history and whether I was okay with eating peanut butter. He wanted to know what I thought and felt and hoped to get out of this outdoor experience and whether I expected to be a changed person on the other side of it.

"Not really," I said. My throat was dry and my head swirled with the realities of actually being on a college campus and talking to an upperclassman. The buildings were unnaturally huge and it was very loud. I hunched my shoulders and crossed my arms, trying to hide my sweaty palms against my T-shirt. Why was it so sticky in Boston in the summer? It was hot in Botswana but never a wet heat like this. I couldn't breathe. The upperclassman, who was to be one of the leaders on my hiking trip, flipped to a new page on his clipboard and looked at me eagerly.

"So no dietary restrictions and no expectations. Okay! Let's talk about the trip itself. We'll be gone for a full week, and hiking or canoeing all day every day. Do you have any concerns about the level of physical activity?"

"You mean walking all day with a backpack? No, not at all," I said. My backpack usually held a radio and test tubes for collecting baboon fur and blood, but at least this was still familiar territory. The boy made a note on his clipboard.

"Great! What about sleeping in a tent? Does that concern you at all?"

"I've been sleeping in a tent for ten years," I said.

"Great! Wait—what?" he said. "Hang on, did you say ten years? In a tent?"

"Yeah. I live in a camp, and we use tents for our rooms."

"And you've been living there for ten years?"

I frowned. Was he not listening to me? "Yeah."

"Where? I don't think there's anywhere in America you can do that."

"I wasn't in America; I was in Africa. A place called the Okavango Delta in Botswana."

He blinked. "What were you doing in Botswana?"

"My parents are primatologists. They study the evolution of social communication in nonhuman primates. I grew up in their research camp in a game reserve in Botswana."

"Like . . . among the animals? Were there lions and tigers and monkeys there?"

"Well, yeah, of course there were, but no tigers. Tigers don't live anywhere in Africa; they live in Asia," I said. This conversation was getting weird. "It was a game reserve so there were lions and elephants, and hippos and giraffes, and zebras too. And yes, a lot of monkeys—baboons specifically."

"And you were just there. With the animals. Just wandering around."

"Yes." For a long minute he did nothing but stare at me, and I fidgeted. Why did people always react so strongly to this stuff? At least people in high school already knew my story. Now that I was in a new place I'd have to tell my story over and over again until it was just something people knew about me. I wasn't really looking forward to it either, especially when it was inevitably followed by questions like whether I rode elephants or kept monkeys as pets. Why did people always ask me that? It was insane to keep a monkey as a pet; everyone knew that. The boy glanced down at his clipboard.

"So if I asked you if you were scared about running into any animals the answer would be a 'no,' right?"

"Right," I said. "Are there animals in Maine I'm supposed to be scared of?"

"Well, there's . . . bears, I guess," he said. "People are usually pretty scared of bears."

"How come?"

He shook his head and smiled, still staring at me. I wished he would stop. "Because they're bears? And people are usually pretty scared of bears? I thought that was kind of obvious."

"Oh," I said and shrugged, trying to act nonchalant and regain control of this conversation that had rapidly moved into uncomfortable territory. "Well, no, I'm not scared of bears. Or any other animal in Maine. So I think I'll be fine."

"And you picked a Level C trip, the hardest one."

"I had to," I said. "You didn't have a *Jurassic Park* level."

He laughed again and shook his head. "I have six other campers I need to talk to but I want to come back to this Botswana thing," he said. "I need to know everything about you now." Damn it. That's exactly what I was hoping to avoid. I laughed nervously.

"Okay," I said. "But you've already kind of heard it all."

"No way. This is too cool. But you can tell me more about it on the trip."

I retreated into the common room my group was using to store our gear and took a seat in the corner, my back pressed against the wall. We were going to "camp out" in the common room in our sleeping bags before taking a bus to the trail the next morning. The other campers swirled around the room making small talk before going to sleep, and as I watched them my heart started to race. They were all so tall and looked so mature and confident. Weren't they as scared as I was? Would they like me when they knew who I was, or would they think I was weird and uncivilized like everyone in high school did? I curled into a tighter ball and rubbed the scar on my elbow. *I can't hide forever*, I thought.

My usual hiking buddies

And they'll all find out about me soon enough. I closed my eyes, took a deep breath, and blocked out the conversations around me. *Quiet is a good place to start*, I thought.

I let my mind wander and found myself high above the clouds, walking into the castle in my head. I hadn't been there in years, not since I was the girl sitting in the windowsill at school reading my book about dragons. Surprised it was still there, I pushed open the door and found the inside of the castle just as warm and inviting as it always had been. And full of some familiar faces. Laurana Kanan the elf princess was there, as was Lessa the dragonrider of Pern. Captain Nancy Blackett was there too, of course, and had a new friend by her side: my buddy Domino the baboon, the feistiest little monkey in the whole Okavango Delta.

"Hello, Keena," Captain Nancy Blackett said. "Where have you been? We've been waiting for you."

I laughed a little and a couple of the other campers in the common room looked at me questioningly.

"Sorry," I said and closed my eyes again. I was dizzy with relief and thought I might really be going out of my mind. They were still there! All of them! Even after I put my books away and told myself I couldn't be or want or have those things! The castle was still there, and so were my heroines, princesses and warriors and baboons, all together. I wiped my hand across my eyes and sniffed, still giggling to myself. If they were still there, then that meant that Botswana Keena was still there too. All I needed to do to find her again was close my eyes and go to the castle in my head. Suddenly, this trip seemed like a piece of cake as long as I had Botswana Keena with me again, Pirate Queen of the Okavango Delta. She wasn't scared of anything—not even Harvard freshmen.

We spent a hot, stuffy night in the dorm room, which reeked like teenage boys by the time we woke up in the morning. We gathered up our packs, and our trip leader, the boy whose name I learned was Andy, divvied up the group camping supplies among us. When he suggested it might be a good idea for the boys to carry more because they were bigger, I made sure that he saw me packing my backpack with just as much gear as the boys were carrying. No one was going to treat me any differently just because I was a girl. I could do so much more than these boys could anyway. They looked so nervous!

We piled onto a school bus to head to Maine and I slid into a seat by the window. A girl with curly dark hair paused next to my seat and then asked if she could sit with me.

"Sure," I said, making room. She looked pale and I patted the seat to seem more welcoming. She sat down and gestured with a brown paper bag clutched tightly in her hand.

"In case I throw up," she said.

"That's...one way to introduce yourself," I said. "Are you worrying about getting carsick or about the trip?"

"The trip," she said. "I've never been to Maine before. I've never even been hiking before."

"Where are you from?"

"Montclair, New Jersey."

"Never heard of it." She laughed.

"Seriously? That's funny. It's outside New York." She gestured with the bag again, this time pointing at a boy across the aisle with dark, floppy hair and glasses. "That's Jonathan. He's from New York too. And I'm Erika." Jonathan leaned across the aisle and held out a hand.

"Are you the girl from Africa?" he asked.

"Botswana," I corrected him.

"Right. Good. I'm staying near you in case you need to save me from a bear."

"Oh, can you fight bears too?" another girl said from the seat in front of me. She was very tall and blonde and just for a second reminded me of Brooke, before I realized that this girl was heavier in the shoulders and looked like a much more serious athlete. She propped her chin on the back of the bus seat and smiled brightly. "Great," she said. "None of us have the slightest idea what we're doing, so as far as I'm concerned you're officially in charge of bear safety."

"Okay," I said. Everyone was being so nice and no one had said a single nasty thing to me yet. What new planet was this?

Somewhat to my surprise, I was disappointed that there wasn't more time to talk on the actual hike itself. The Level C hike was actually fairly difficult, and we were up before the sun every morning, walking or canoeing until the sun went down again at night. Everyone was so exhausted that they fell asleep right after dinner, and usually only our leader, Andy, and I stayed up, sitting around the fire listening to the birds and watching the stars glitter overhead. Though it was very hot during the day, it felt no different from Botswana in the dry season, and when the temperature fell at night the air was crisp and cool.

It took me a full five days to convince myself that there were no lions in the bushes and no hippos in the lakes. Every time we walked through the tall grass of a mountain field, every muscle in my neck went rigid and my eyes darted from side to side, watching for movement against the wind and listening for the alarm calls from francolins or vervet monkeys that meant there were lions nearby. My heart pounded, and even in the cool mountain air, I sweat through my T-shirt almost immediately. Every time we got into our canoes and set off across another body of water, I thought about just how epically stupid it was to paddle through the reeds where at any minute a hippo could rise up and bite our canoes in half. What were we thinking? Did we have a death wish? No one in the Okavango would ever be dumb enough to put themselves in this kind of danger. My jumpiness didn't go unnoticed, and I finally had to explain to my canoe-mate, the tall blonde girl named Katy, exactly why I was so jittery when we were supposed to be having fun.

"There are no lions in Maine," Katy said. "That's your new mantra. Just repeat it to yourself in your head every time you get freaked out." And that's what I did, over and over and over again, as my canoe paddle sliced through the water and I tried to familiarize myself with a whole new world of trees and birds and plants that I didn't recognize: *There are no lions in Maine, there are no lions in Maine, there are no lions in Maine.*

The last night of the trip, we camped on a rocky island in the middle of a lake. The wind had picked up during the day, and the waves on the lake rose almost to the sides of the canoes that rested on the shore. Andy was concerned about us being able to leave the island in the morning and whispered anxiously to someone on the other end of a cell phone he'd been pretending he hadn't brought with him. He'd been too busy to make a fire, so I had done it, enlisting my new friends Erika and Jonathan to gather kindling, after I explained to them what kindling was.

"What are you looking at?" Jonathan asked, jolting me out of my reverie. I'd been staring across the lake and watching a dark shape trundle along the shoreline.

"Oh, there's a bear over there."

"A WHAT?!" Jonathan scrambled backward off his rock and Erika grabbed my arm.

"A bear? There's a bear over there?" she asked. I frowned.

"Yeah, he's just moving along the shore, doing his bear thing. Why, are you scared?"

"It's a BEAR!" Jonathan squeaked again. "What should we do? Where should we go?"

"Nowhere," I said, smiling. "Don't worry. I promise he's not going to hurt you."

"How do you know?" Erika said. "I know you know everything about animals but there aren't bears in Africa."

"That's true," I said. "But that bear is just looking for food. He's not going to come over here unless he knows we have food, which he doesn't since Andy bear-bagged it. And even if the bear could smell our food, why would he swim across this cold lake to get it? There's plenty to eat where he already is."

Jonathan climbed slowly back onto his rock and Erika released her death grip on my arm. They were silent for a minute or two, watching the dark shape move along until it disappeared into the trees and out of sight. The stars twinkled and smoke from our campfire rose through air that smelled like stone and pine.

"Well," Erika said finally, "you were right about that bear. But where there's one bear, there are more. Until we get back to Boston, you aren't leaving my side."

"Even after we get back," Jonathan added. "Who knows what crazy stuff happens in college? We're going to need you around."

"Absolutely," Erika said.

CHAPTER 23

EXTREME DRIVING IN A BROKEN TOYOTA

ONE OF THE BEST parts about being in college was how early classes ended in the spring. At the beginning of May I would wrap up my final exams and was ready to head back to Botswana, where my parents would meet me with Lucy.

Despite the looming dread of my finals and the fact that I was still in a city, I found that I liked spring in Boston. People in New England were always so grateful for the end of the cold weather that as soon as anyone could physically wear shorts and flip-flops without getting frostbite, they all did, and then found every excuse to try to tan themselves on the quad in between melting piles of snow. I thought it was hilarious.

One by one my final exams passed in a haze of flash cards and Diet Coke until, finally, on a chilly morning in May, I found myself standing in Boston's Logan International Airport with my dusty backpack, ready to head back to Botswana.

"Can I check my bag to my final destination?" I asked the gate attendant. "I'm actually flying through Frankfurt and Johannesburg before I get to Maun in Botswana."

"Mm-hmm," she said. "Frankfurt, Johannesburg, and back to Boston."

"No, Botswana, not Boston."

"Right, back to Boston."

"No," I said. "I'm not coming back to Boston until September. I'm flying to Botswana, not Boston. It's a country in Africa." The gate attendant looked at me blankly.

"It's a real place, I promise you," I said, trying to be helpful. "I go there all the time."

"I need to get my supervisor," she said, and I fought not to roll my eyes.

Finally, two hours later, I was on the plane and on my way back home, a crisp, fresh new Dragonlance novel in my backpack. As the sun set over Boston harbor and I watched the coast of the US slowly disappear behind me, I closed my eyes and let my head fall back against the seat. I took stock. How was I doing? Physically, I was okay. That was a good start. Mentally, I felt okay too. I had made a couple of friends and discovered that there were some parts about life in the US that made me smile, even though they were hours away from school. It didn't matter so much that I couldn't see the mountains and streams and bears every day; even knowing they were there if I needed them was good enough. I took a long, deep breath, opened my eyes, and grinned. Time to forget about all that stuff. Botswana Keena was on her way back home. Hell yeah.

Though I was still planning to spend a lot of time in Baboon Camp that summer, especially on the weekends, I actually had a side project that would mean living in Maun for part of the time. We still didn't know where Mokupi was, and the HIV/AIDS epidemic in northern Botswana had only gotten worse: in 2002, the World Health Organization estimated that close to 40 percent of people in Botswana were HIV-positive, but that number was probably closer to 50 percent in the Ngamiland province in the northwest, where Maun was. I couldn't wrap my head around that number. The idea that one out of every two people I saw in town could be sick with an incurable disease was unfathomable to me. I didn't know a lot of Batswana since we lived so far away from other people, but the few I did know had been friends of mine since I was eight years old. When I read the local Maun newspaper online (Maun had a newspaper now! And it was online!), all I saw were funeral announcements and stories of families driven apart by the stigma surrounding testing for HIV and caring for individuals who were sick. It was heartbreaking and did not at all fit into the image I held in my head of what Botswana really was. I recognized that this was just another example of "real Botswana" knocking on the door of what I had always thought Botswana to be: my idyllic bubble of Baboon Camp's game reserve, which existed a literal world away from the troubles of the country itself. I very badly wanted to understand this other world. I loved Botswana and its people too much to sequester myself in my magic kingdom and ignore what was going on outside its walls. Inasmuch as it was possible for a white American girl to understand what was going on in real Botswana, I wanted to. And I wanted to find Mokupi. I was worried about his health and every day out with the baboons I missed him.

So, I was going to spend two months in Maun, volunteering at an orphanage for children who had lost their parents to AIDS, and interviewing health-care workers and doctors about the country's response to the epidemic—what was working, what wasn't, and what their concerns were for future intervention efforts. At this point there were dozens of aid organizations working in Maun, and their programs overlapped so much that there was a great deal of confusion among the district health officials as to who was doing what, where, and with what resources. When I went to the district Ministry of Health office in Maun to introduce myself and ask for permission to volunteer in town (since I had no official affiliation and no work permit), the district official told me that if I could even put a list together of what was going on in Maun it would be a tremendous help.

Mom and Dad said I could use our old Toyota truck for my project, since it was now a "town" car, being too beat-up and structurally unsound to make the drive from Maun to camp in one piece. I had to sit on a cushion to reach the pedals and figure out how to drive a stick shift on the opposite side of the car from our Volvo in the US, but after lurching around the parking lot of the Maun Airport for a while, I decided that I had it well enough figured out. The fact that it had no windshield wipers or door locks was a small problem, but something I would just have to deal with. I had also convinced our old friend Tico, who I had met more than ten years before on our first boat trip to Baboon Camp, to allow me to camp out at his house. He kept a few cots available for the transient graduate students who worked at his wild dog research camp.

Every morning as the sun came up, I had a cup of tea with Tico and his wife, Lesley, and set off into town, starting at the orphanage where I volunteered. Though the orphanage was technically funded by a much larger nongovernmental organization, it was clear that no money had been allocated for the center; the building was half constructed and had no running water. The electricity was sporadic, though that wasn't surprising since electricity was spotty all over Maun. No staff was there on the first morning I arrived, and after making a few calls to the NGO that was supposedly funding them, I learned that no staff had arrived because they had no transportation to the center, and even if they got there they had no way to pick up the children from their relatives' houses. A sleepy-sounding finance officer said they were discussing whether they had the resources to purchase a bus or a van, but that decision had been put off until the chief financial officer returned from vacation in four weeks' time. Until then, if I wanted the center open, I had to go pick everyone up.

Fine. I asked where the staff members lived.

"The lady in charge," the sleepy finance officer said, "lives in Botshabelo Ward down a long road and behind a house with a tin roof."

"Do you have an address?" I asked. "Or maybe a phone number where I can reach her?"

"If you want to phone her," the man said, "you will have to purchase a mobile phone for her since she does not have one."

"So you don't know how I can reach her and only kind of where she lives?" I asked.

"The people over there, they know her," the man said. "You can ask."

Off I went. Dodging herds of goats, cows, and donkeys, I swerved through town, holding my breath at every stoplight as cars and trucks careened through with no regard for signals or staying on their own side of the road. Overlander trucks teetered on tiny wheels and the minibus taxis raced between them at top speeds, with ticket collectors hanging out the window yelling for stops and fares. By the time I finally reached the center of town and found a cheap electronics store, I was drenched in sweat and covered in dust. The driver's side door didn't work properly since one of the baboons had snapped off the door handle, so whenever I stopped I had to climb in and out through the back seat, which was harder than I expected.

I bought a mobile phone and a SIM card and asked the clerk where I could find Botshabelo Ward. Without looking up from his own mobile phone, he gestured vaguely toward the airport and said I could ask someone over there.

I parked behind the airport and approached two elderly gentlemen sitting under a mopane tree in white plastic chairs.

"Dumêla borra," I said. "I am looking for the lady who works in the orphanage over by the Matshwane School."

Incredibly, the men knew who I was taking about and summoned a small child who agreed to take me to the lady's house.

"Thank you!" I called as the child led me away down a winding path between the houses.

"We know you!" the men called back. "You are from the baboons!" and they burst out laughing. I was shocked that they recognized me.

"You know the baboons?" I said, and one of the men waved his hands.

"Yes, we know the baboons!" he said. "And you, we know you. You are the girl with the baboons!" I laughed and waved back as we walked away.

It turned out to be quite a long walk to Mma Lesedi's house, and when I did finally get there it was already early afternoon. She was glad to see me, if a bit confused, since she had been told that the center could not open until they secured the funds for a vehicle. But if I had one they could use, she said, then she would get to work immediately.

"Tomorrow," she said, "you will come get me and then we will fetch the children from their grandparents' homes. Then, we will take them to the school. And when school is over, you will take them home and then take me back here to my home."

"Okay," I said. "But my car isn't in the greatest shape and I can't take more than two or three kids at a time." She said that was no problem; I would do as many trips as I needed to do. And if I wanted to speak to other health-care workers or doctors, I could do that either before I picked everyone up in the morning or after I dropped them off at the end of the day. That sounded like an awful lot of driving to me, but I signed up to volunteer, and if this is what they needed me to do, then that's what I would do.

It was dark by the time I drove back to Tico's house. He lived on the outskirts of town, past the beginnings of what was to be a soccer stadium. Tracks led off the main tarmac road in every direction—deep treads in the dust that would sometimes be reshaped or redirected during the day, depending on how many cars had driven down them since the morning. The track to Tico's house left the tarmac road at a sharp left after a donkey crossing sign and wove through the mopane trees toward the river. I had to write on the back of my hand all the turns it took so that I would not get lost. Very few houses were lit and the headlights of my car dipped through clouds of mosquitoes as I lurched down the track. My back ached with the strain of hunching my shoulders and my palm was slippery against the gearshift. Everywhere there was dust, dust, dust: down the neck of my shirt, up my pants, and in the back of my throat. My eyes were full of the stuff.

Finally, a small, cozy house pulled into view. I parked behind Tico's Land Rover, the vehicle bristling with antennae for tracking radio collars on wild dogs and dented on one side from being charged by a hippo many years before. Tico thought it was a cool story and had never gotten the dent fixed, which I appreciated. It still looked as badass as it had to me when I was eight years old, and though I'd never said it out loud, I still secretly thought that Tico might really be Han Solo. One never knew.

On the porch, Tico's wife, Lesley, sat in a canvas chair, feet propped up on a wooden stool, reading a book. Winged termites circled the lights overhead, and distantly I could hear their two sons playing with

Legos at the back of the house. Something fell over and there was a shriek followed by laughter. Outside, the cool night air vibrated with the sounds of frogs, crickets, and owls. Down by the river, a hippo bellowed. There weren't as many hippos in town as there were up in camp, but Tico said this one had established a territory down by an area they called the Old Bridge and refused to move. I wondered if Tico ever thought about the hippo charging his car and if it made him respect them just a little bit.

"How'd it go?" Lesley asked. I sank down onto the porch step and wiped a gritty hand across my forehead.

"Fine, I think," I said. "Tomorrow's going to be pretty different. And probably the day after that too."

"I bet," Lesley said. Lesley worked for Tico's project too, but her research was about working with local communities on ways to coexist with wild animals instead of hunt them. Predator species like lions, hyenas, and wild dogs were often poisoned by locals who thought the animals might be a threat to their livestock. In the time I had known Tico, he had lost at least three dogs to poisoning, and in every case the social structure of the group had been completely shattered by the loss of that individual; it took years for them to rebuild their pack society. It was Tico and Lesley's hope that by getting local communities invested both financially and emotionally in the well-being of the wild animals, they would see that tourism and conservation were legitimate ways to earn a living that didn't come at the expense of an endangered species. It wasn't easy work though, and Lesley was often shouted at or threatened by farmers who'd lost livestock and didn't want her or her agenda anywhere near their properties. I thought she was the coolest person on earth.

"You want to help me make Easy Mac for the kids?" she asked. Before flying out, I'd e-mailed Tico and Lesley to ask what I could bring them from the US, and Easy Mac was at the top of their list—impossible to get outside the country and something every American kid wanted. It was the ultimate cultural touchstone for anyone who wanted to be reminded of America, right down to its last delicious, fatty bite. After the day I'd had, the idea of sitting down with their kids and sharing some Easy Mac sounded both completely bizarre and immensely comforting.

"I sure do," I said.

In the weeks that followed, I developed a new routine: Up before the sun in the icy winter morning, I headed off to Botshabelo Ward to pick up Mma Lesedi, sometimes dropping Tico and Lesley's sons at school on the way. Then Mma Lesedi and I would circle through the wards on the outskirts of town, picking up the children to take them to the center. Though I worried that I would spend all my time ferrying children around, it turned out that only a handful or so actually attended day school at the center; many of the children's grandparents thought it was unnecessary for the children to be taken somewhere else to play when they already had full-time care from their grandparents at home. Mma Lesedi didn't seem to mind since it meant fewer children for her to watch, and it meant that I had more time to drive around town interviewing health-care workers about HIV/AIDS.

I hated driving around town. Maun's road system was certainly better developed than I remembered, but only in the sense that more roads were paved. The complete disregard for traffic laws made it impossible to predict what other drivers were going to do, and I seemed to be the only person in the entire city who looked both ways before crossing an intersection. I only partially trusted the ancient Toyota to actually move fast enough to avoid being flattened, and the clouds of smoke and dust that billowed behind the trucks made it extremely hard to see. My car had no airbags and no rearview mirrors since the baboons had ripped those off, so I already felt vulnerable and exposed next to the massive cross-continent trucks shuttling between South Africa and Zambia. Every time I clambered through the back and settled into the driver's seat, I felt like a *Star Wars* fighter pilot preparing for a final run on the Death Star, but without a friendly droid in the back to reassure me that, yes, I probably would be alive by the time I got to my destination. And whenever I got where I was going, I collapsed in my seat, drenched in sweat, hands shaking, and wondering why I thought this would be a good idea in the first place.

The interviews did not help improve my mood. Many health-care workers were too busy to talk to me, which I understood, and those who did have time painted a bleak picture of treating HIV and AIDS patients in the area. No one wanted to be tested in the first place, since most people equated getting tested with being diagnosed (though to be fair, the odds weren't exactly good). And since there was no lab to conduct blood tests in Maun, all the blood samples had to be flown to either Johannesburg or the capital of Botswana, Gaborone, which took an average of three weeks. By the time the results made their way back to Maun, most patients had been lost to follow-up or were impossible to reach because they didn't have phones or permanent addresses. Of the people who did get tested and were diagnosed with HIV, only a very few agreed to take the medications, despite the fact that the government provided the medicine completely free of charge. Antiretroviral medications had to be taken in a complicated cocktail of pills several times a day and supplemented with a healthy, balanced diet in order to be maximally effective. Many patients didn't see the point of the pill regimen, and even fewer had watches with which to track what pills should be taken when. Hardly anyone could afford healthy fruits and vegetables, though I did hear that the Ministry of Health was so desperate to get HIV patients to eat a healthy diet that the government sent a fruit basket to every patient who agreed to take the medication. Every clinic was full, every health-care worker was overworked, and everywhere there were posters from the Ministry of Health championing safe sex and condom use. Everyone was trying so hard, but from the number of minibuses at the clinics and endless lines of patients waiting to be seen, it was clear that the effort wasn't working.

Every night, after I took the children and Mma Lesedi home, I drove back to Tico and Lesley's house in a fog of dust and truck smoke, my eyes red with grit. Most nights, Lesley was reading on the porch when I drove in, and after I washed my hands and got a beer, I sat silently with

My beloved Hilux in its younger days

her on the porch step, trying to square the desperation of the sick town with the quiet bellows of the hippo in his pool near the Old Bridge. Baboon Camp had always felt like another planet when compared to America, but that made sense to me since the differences between the two places were so extreme. What I didn't understand was how it could be possible that sitting on Tico's porch, a mere one hundred kilometers from the beauty of Baboon Camp, there could be such hopelessness and despair. The birds and trees may have been the same, but nothing else appeared to be. *This* was real Botswana, not my tent next to the mangosteen tree or reading in the sun while guarding a frozen chicken. That was an impossible place where no one else lived because it's not how real people live. It was too pristine, too precious. It was too perfect to exist. But I had grown up there, and it felt real to me. None of it made any sense.

As the days went by in one never-ending cloud of dust and lines upon lines of patients at the clinics, it became clear to me that running away to Baboon Camp was an escape that existed only for me and my family, not for anyone else in the world, even the people who actually called Botswana home. The reality of the country's people and their future was here, in the HIV support groups and the patient nurses working night and day to get people the care they needed, not in a camp in a game reserve where only I, an American, was privileged enough to live. Reality seemed very close and Baboon Camp so impossibly far away.

CHAPTER 24

BLOOD AND DUST AND BOTSWANA SKY

DAD WASN'T SPENDING MUCH time in Baboon Camp either that summer. While Mom and Lucy kept the camp running, Dad was flying back and forth to the capital, Gaborone, to give a series of presentations on his and Mom's work in an attempt to convince the Department of Wildlife and National Parks (DWNP) to extend the project.

The DWNP had no real objection to my parents' work itself, but since the beginning of the project in 1992, the DWNP had been pressuring my parents to move Baboon Camp to a location outside the Moremi Game Reserve. No other camp in Botswana was located inside a game reserve, including the tourist lodges, and we'd only been able to set up Baboon Camp because it had already been established by my parents' predecessor, Bill Hamilton, and was basically grandfathered in. Even Tico's wild dog research camp wasn't in a game reserve, and his research was much more high-profile and fancy than my parents', since for some reason people tend to think that wild dogs are more charismatic and sexy than baboons.

In theory it wouldn't have been terribly difficult to move Baboon Camp, since "outside the game reserve" was as close as across the river from where it already was, but logistically it would have been a long, expensive mess. The area on the opposite side of the river was unleased as far as we knew, but at any time it could be rented by a tourism or hunting company that would also have to sign off on our location. More importantly, we'd already looked pretty hard and couldn't find any islands that would have been suitable for a campsite. A proper site had to be close enough to the river to allow easy access to the baboons, permanent enough that it wouldn't flood every year, and have enough big trees to provide shelter for the camp. All the structures would have to be moved and rebuilt, and a channel would have to be created to link our lagoon with the new campsite on the other side. We would waste a huge amount of time looking for the baboons since we wouldn't be close enough to hear where they were in the morning, and we would be way too far away from camp to do anything if someone was attacked while in the field, as had happened with Press and the leopard. No one wanted to move, but it was starting to become our only option if we wanted to continue our work.

The pressure from the DWNP was one reason why the time had come for my parents to make a decision about the future of Baboon Camp, but another was that my parents were having a problem with their research grant. The US National Institutes of Health (NIH) had been the biggest funding source for my parents' and their postdocs' research for many years. Keeping Baboon Camp operational required a lot of money; in addition to paying the postdocs' salaries, it had to support two cars, Mokupi's and Mpitsang's salaries (and later Press's), all the equipment and data analysis in Botswana and the US, as well as expensive travel to and from camp.

In 2003, the NIH initially decided to renew my parents' grant, which was excellent news—and what prompted Dad's trip to Gaborone to talk about whether the camp would have to be moved. Dad had just returned from his trip, however, when we got the news that the director of the NIH had instead decided to rescind their grant. He declared that research with the baboons was not "translational," a jargon term that meant it wasn't directly related to the development of a new human product—in this case, some kind of pharmaceutical product or therapy that could then be licensed and sold for a lot of money. Scientific studies into the evolution of human behavior fell outside that category, and my parents' grant was canceled. Just like that, their funding was gone.

I don't know how my parents felt about losing their grant. I only heard about it through an e-mail from Lucy, since at the time I was in Maun trying not to die. I never asked them, but I'm sure it was frustrating and demoralizing though not entirely unexpected, given the US administration's stance on research that didn't have a clear end goal, such as it was. Speculative research—or, science purely for the general sense of advancing human knowledge and learning a little more about why we are the way we are—had always been a difficult sell to most people, particularly when taxpayer funding was involved. What upset me about this news was that their research *was* translational, if you actually let them explain it: through their research with vocalizations and hierarchy manipulation, they added a crucial puzzle piece to the story of how humans developed awareness of each other as individuals, and how having to keep track of who everyone was and how they related to each other in a community as large as a baboon troop is one of the reasons our ancient relatives had to develop such large brains.

Many times I'd overheard my parents say self-deprecating things about how silly it was to study monkeys when other people we knew were doctors or lawyers or doing other things to actually help people, but they worked so very hard at it. Despite the fact that their work was highly technical and involved a lot of data, in my mind they had always fallen in the same category as painters or singers or writers: creative, thoughtful people whose passion helped make us become smarter, better humans. We needed those people just as much as we needed anyone else.

There was also a third reason why my parents had to finally sit down and think about the future of Baboon Camp: walking around with the baboons was becoming much, much more dangerous. There had always been the risk of running into lions and buffalo, but by the early 2000s the main danger was the elephants. Botswana had experienced an explosion in the elephant population since we arrived in the early 1990s, particularly in Chobe National Park and the Zambezi basin to the northeast of the delta. As the number of elephants grew, they began moving south into the Okavango, where before they had been only in small numbers. It was relatively rare to see an elephant when I was little, but by 2003 we saw them every single day. And not just isolated males, but giant cow-and-calf herds of mothers and babies too. Cow-and-calf herds are vastly more dangerous than lone males because the females charge humans to keep them away from the babies. The herds are enormous, and there is no way to skirt around them to keep up with the baboons. If the baboons went into an area where there was a cow-and-calf herd, we had to end the workday and go home.

There were increasingly more buffalo and lions too, as well as more hippos in the river. Even on a day when we didn't run into elephants, we were almost guaranteed to run into lions or buffalo or both—sometimes at the same time. Seventeen hippos took up residence in the lagoon in front of camp, and it was so dangerous bringing the boat in and out of the river that we moved it to the other side of the island where there were fewer hippos and they were less likely to attack us as we drove by. Every night, lions called from the laundry area and buffalo shuffled around in the water by the fig tree. One night, a pride of nine lions killed a buffalo behind the shower, only fifty meters or so from my bed. The screams of the dying buffalo and the sounds of the lions crunching bones kept me up for hours as I lay in my cot trying to convince myself I didn't need to pee.

Since the very beginning of the project, people had asked my parents why we didn't carry guns when we went out with the baboons. All the game reserves in South Africa and many in Botswana require that armed rangers accompany any guests on foot, and people were shocked and horrified that we would wander around on foot so far away from camp without a car nearby and without any gun at all, much less one capable of taking down a buffalo or a lion. And it's true: as sensational as the stories of escaping from buffalo and lions are in retrospect, it was incredibly dangerous to do what we did and to do it every day for so many years.

Dad always said there were two main reasons why we didn't carry guns, and the first is that we weren't trained to. No one had any military experience, and if we wanted to be serious about using a gun to protect ourselves from animals as big as lions, we would have needed some really serious weaponry, not something that could be comfortably carried on our backs as we walked. I met rangers in South Africa who said their AK-47s were essentially useless against animals the size of buffalo and lions, so I could only imagine what kind of gun we would have needed.

The second reason we didn't carry guns is that if we got to the point of needing to defend ourselves with a gun, it was already too late. When we ran into animals, we did so because we stumbled upon them (or they on us) on foot, within a matter of meters, not kilometers. We would be intently following a baboon or catching up with the rest of the troop, round a corner, and BAM, there would be the elephant, buffalo, or lion immediately in front of us. Even if we had a gun, we wouldn't have time to use it before the animal got to us—we'd need to find a tree and climb up as fast as we could or it was all over.

The best way to keep this from happening was not to get ourselves into this situation in the first place. When we were with the baboons, this was relatively easy: there were so many baboons that there were eyes everywhere. If lions were around, we would probably know because the baboons would tell us—that is, if they could see the lions themselves. They wouldn't necessarily alarm call to elephants or buffalo, but those were easier to spot than lions. For this reason, we felt much, much safer when we were with the baboons. Even so, I got to be highly attuned to signs that dangerous animals might be nearby, even tiny changes like in smell or birdsong. It was when we were walking out to the baboons in the morning or home in the afternoon that we really felt at risk. We tried to be loud and vigilant, but most of the time it didn't matter: we either saw the threat from a far enough distance that we could figure out how to get around it, or we didn't and we had another near-death experience that left us shaking all over and somewhat hysterical for the rest of the walk.

This kind of thing was happening much too often now, and it wasn't like in America, where you could make safe decisions like driving more slowly or looking both ways before you crossed the street. At a certain point, it didn't matter how careful you were; there was absolutely nothing you could do about a lion appearing in the bushes right next to you.

In the back of our minds I think we always knew how dangerous the research really was. After more than ten years in Baboon Camp, it was statistically astounding that the worst thing that had happened to anyone in camp was Press's leopard attack. Given the frequency with which we saw snakes, elephants, buffalo, hippos, and lions, and the sheer number of times we would get back to camp and say, "Whew, almost didn't make it," I think we all began to believe, deep down, that maybe our luck was running out. Maybe next time would be the time when someone died. Going out with the baboons used to be my favorite thing in the whole world, but as the near misses grew more and more frequent, even I began to feel tense and uneasy away from camp.

One hot day in late August, I went out with my parents to find the baboons on the far side of an island called C16 behind camp. Press had fully recovered from the leopard attack (now almost two years in the past) and was back at work, but didn't go out with the baboons anymore, as per his request. So, that morning, it was just my parents and me. We found the baboons sunning themselves in the woods, but they seemed unusually jumpy for what was typically a quiet time of day for grooming and socializing. Wondering what was making the monkeys so anxious, I climbed up a termite mound next to a big male baboon named Betelgeuse, who was staring into the woods on the other side of a small floodplain. I didn't immediately see anything, but the *krak-krak-krak* of francolin alarm calls meant that something was over there, and Betelgeuse knew it. A few vultures circled overhead, so I assumed that something had been killed in the woods overnight and the surrounding wildlife had just found out about it. That didn't necessarily mean whatever killed it was still there—that depended entirely on the predator. A leopard would have dragged the kill somewhere else and hyenas would have gone back to their den. Lions, on the other hand, often ate and then slept by their kill, guarding it from scavengers like jackals or hyenas or the circling vultures. They might still be there. Silently, Betelgeuse and I scanned the shoreline, looking for movement. We saw nothing.

Trying to see what the vultures are circling

The baboons relaxed a little as the morning wore on. It was clear from their behavior that they really wanted to cross to Airstrip Island but were nervous about it. They milled around on the shore, grunting to each other and waiting for someone to decide that they were ready to go. This was usually one of the older females, and when Sylvia eventually gave a chorus of grunts and began to cross the floodplain, the rest of the troop followed in a tidal wave of tails, feet, and fur, running after Sylvia as fast as they could and disappearing into the woods. I hated when the baboons did this, since it was impossible to keep up with them and I inevitably got left behind and had to track them to wherever it was Sylvia decided to go. Though Mokupi had taught me well, it wasn't easy to track running baboons because they kicked up sand and scuffed their footprints in a way that made it difficult to tell how old the tracks were. And, ever since Balo and I had run into the lions, I had to admit I really didn't like being left alone in the woods.

Mom and Dad were nowhere to be seen, and I guessed that they had either already crossed to Airstrip ahead of Sylvia or were behind me with some stragglers. In any case, I didn't know where my parents were, so unless I wanted to be alone (I didn't), I had to run when the baboons ran. I yanked my backpack straps tight and took off with the troop, wading through water that was up to my knees and filled with spiny hippo grass. On the other side of the water, I thought I might have smelled a recent kill but didn't have time to stop and investigate. On we ran, down the narrow part of Airstrip and through the palm tree grove, all the way to the far side of the island where there was a particularly tasty jackalberry tree. Here, the baboons began to calm down and regroup. Mom and Dad, who had been behind me, finally arrived at the jackalberry tree almost an hour after I did.

We had a normal, peaceful remainder of the morning with the baboons and, as usual, began to walk home around one thirty in the afternoon. The sun climbed high in the sky and my T-shirt clung damply to my shoulders as we walked back toward camp. My legs were criss-crossed with dirt, scratches, and bruises from my sprint down Airstrip

Island, and it was *so* hot by midday that my hair rested on my head like a helmet.

After about an hour of walking, we reached the spot where we'd seen the vultures earlier that morning. I held up a hand and Mom and Dad stopped behind me without a word. Vultures still perched in the leadwood trees all around us, and I sniffed to see if I could smell whatever it was I'd smelled before. There was a metallic blood scent in the air, but it was faint. Maybe the kill had just been a small animal.

"What do you think we should do?" Mom asked.

"There was definitely something here," Dad said. "But now? I don't know."

"The vultures are still here," I said. "But I don't see any tracks. The baboons must have run over them earlier." We looked at each other in silence. Were the predators still nearby?

"It's probably fine," Mom said.

"I'm starving," I said.

"Let's just be careful," Dad said. We decided to skirt around the patch of woods and cut through the leadwood trees to a trail that looped around the end of the island. I led the way, with Mom behind me and Dad bringing up the rear. Out in the full sun and away from the woods that smelled like blood, the day felt glorious. A cool breeze whipped through the waving yellow grass and sent ripples scurrying across the floodplains like water bugs in the lagoon. Okavango orioles darted through the trees in flashes of yellow, and Meyer's parrots shrieked to each other as they flew high overhead, blue on blue against the sky. Deeper in the bushes, flocks of babblers muttered as they picked through leaves on the forest floor. Distantly, a hippo bellowed from the river. I could still hear francolin birds alarm calling, but I didn't pay them any attention. They alarm called so often it barely registered anymore.

Coming around a blackthorn acacia bush, I pulled up short as a blast of noxious odors hit me like a truck. Mom gagged and took a step back.

"I guess we found the kill," Dad said. About thirty meters away, under another blackthorn acacia, a patch of wet, dark dust indicated where at least part of the animal had been eaten. I saw a few bone fragments but no hooves or horns to indicate what had been killed.

"Oh God, do you think it's that baby giraffe we saw here yesterday?" Mom asked. "That would be horrible."

"Only one way to find out," I said. "Let me go check it out."

"You sure?" Dad said.

"Yeah, it's fine," I said brightly. "If something was still here, we'd know it by now." I slipped out of my backpack and crept forward quietly, stepping around tussocks of grass and moving slowly closer and closer to the bush and the wet spot.

I was more than halfway to the kill site when a young male lion exploded out of the bush and charged me. I knew it was a male because he had the start of a mane, and also because every single detail of that lion's appearance seared itself into my brain in one moment of pure terror. I instantly forgot everything I ever knew about not running from lions and stumbled backward, trying to get back to the path or my parents or a tree, though I knew there was nothing behind me but grassy plain without a tree in sight. The lion roared and charged again, tail whipping from side to side and claws extended, digging into the sand.

I stumbled backward again, but this time I felt my leg give way as I tumbled sideways into a warthog hole, wedging my sandal at the bottom. I tried to pull my foot out but it was stuck. I couldn't move. I twisted my torso around and got one last look at fur and dust and bloody teeth against a perfect Botswana sky before I squeezed my eyes shut and prepared to die. My last thought was that the doctor back in America had been right: I wasn't invincible after all.

An eternity later, I opened my eyes. The lion had stopped about three meters away from me and just stood there, growling low and staring at me with his ears flattened against his head. And just as quickly as he'd charged, he turned away and walked back to the bush, where I now saw several other lions lounging around in the shade, sleeping with full bellies. Breathlessly, I twisted my foot around until I could pull my sandal out of the hole and limped back to my parents, who were standing exactly where I'd left them, faces white.

"Let's get out of here," I said, shocked that I could speak at all, my throat was so dry. Quickly, quietly, we walked the rest of the way down Airstrip Island, crossed to C16 where we'd found the baboons that morning, and back onto Camp Island.

I thought about nothing as we walked. It hurt to breathe, and my legs moved on autopilot. Sweat dripped down my back and the birds sang so loudly I wanted to hold my hands over my ears. Bile rose in the back of my throat and I gagged as I tried to swallow it back down. When we finally reached the shore of Camp Island, I sank to my knees in the dust and burst into tears. My entire body shook and I threw up in the hippo grass, feeling suddenly small and fragile. I wiped my hand across my face and tasted blood—where from, I didn't know. I pushed my fingers into the ground and took one gasping breath after another as tears dripped one by one off my nose and into the dust. Mom and Dad didn't say anything, and I was glad. We all knew what had happened. There wasn't anything more to be said.

When I walked into Baboon Camp, it could have been any other day. Press was sweeping the path and humming to himself. The kitchen door creaked as Lucy closed it behind her and carried a cup of tea to the table. Small purple flowers drifted down from the fig tree, as starlings, orioles, and robins danced through the branches and the occasional vervet monkey passed by, making the branches dip. The sand was soft and cool on my feet, and across the distant melapo, giraffes walked through the water in graceful succession, dipping their heads with each step and carving delicate silhouettes against the bright blue sky beyond. My world was perfect beyond what earthly perfection is meant to be: a magic castle for a brave little princess with a head full of pirates and dragons to live and run and sleep under the stars as the birds fly home to roost and the hippos call from the river. But it wasn't real. And I didn't belong there anymore.

That fall we closed Baboon Camp.

GOODBYE, NARNIA

I STILL WALK AROUND with my head down. I'm not being unfriendly; I'm just looking for snakes. When a big truck comes around the corner, I still think it's an elephant and my first reaction is to look for the nearest dumpster to hide behind. I don't like being predictable; predictability in a daily schedule is how lions know where you're likely to be when it's dark outside and makes it easier for them to hunt you. They're smart like that. Though I will happily spend hours at the zoo, I will never go into the reptile house, and you can forget the lion enclosure. I dream about lions almost every night: chasing me across the lacrosse field, stalking me during a final exam in graduate school, or lurking in my bedroom closet, twitching their tawny ears and growling so low and deep it makes my bones vibrate.

I love it when it rains. At the beginning or end of a rainstorm you can always smell that indefinable and unmistakable scent of rain on dust. It doesn't matter if there isn't any dust where you are; that's one of the magical things about this smell, that it reaches all over the world, even in the places where there is no dust and there are no songbirds to sing when the sun comes out.

Baboon Camp is where I lost my first tooth, shot my first snake, and learned about fractions. I've cleaned its paths, replaced its roofs, and moonwalked through it in the slippery mud after rainstorms when the shongololo millipedes come out. It's where we had Christmas and where

Home

we celebrated our birthdays. It's where I learned to love all the things that make me who I am, and where I learned all those things over again when I made the mistake of putting them away. It's where I discovered bravery and self-confidence and that a wild imagination is one of the best things a child can ever have. It's where I learned to sing Christmas carols when I pee to make sure no lions are nearby. I believe my initials are still carved into the fig tree, though I will never know whether the elephants have torn it down.

That's the thing about Baboon Camp: I'll never really know what happened to it. It appeared from nothing, a clearing in the trees on an island in the delta that could really have been anywhere. And just as easily as it appeared, it disappeared. When we packed up our tents and took apart the buildings, the grasses and bushes and trees came back, just as they had been before we arrived, and slowly, over the years, all the signs that humans were once there faded away until it looked exactly the way it did before we got there. The impala and giraffes and baboons move through, never knowing that where they now eat and sleep and play with their babies, I once read all of Harry Potter and guarded frozen chickens from a clever baboon. They still see the same sunsets from the same tree where I wove my own bow and arrows and flew a pirate flag I'd sewed myself from one of Dad's T-shirts.

I think about Baboon Camp every single day, but American Keena has given me some important experiences as well. American Keena has seen *Game of Thrones*, *Friends*, and *The X-Files*, knows not to put metal in the microwave, and has begrudgingly admitted that air-conditioning feels really good when it's one hundred degrees outside. She loves the snow, the changing seasons, and not having to wash her clothes by hand. She's proud to say she's American. And when she puts her nieces to bed, she feels a warm swell of pride when they say, "Aunt Keena? Tell me about the monkeys." She's fortunate to still call Nat, Meghan, Katy, and Erika her friends.

At this point in the story, you may be asking yourself: What, in the end, happened to Mokupi? No story about Baboon Camp is complete without Mokupi. Sometime in the year after Baboon Camp closed, we got an e-mail from a contact who worked in Xaxaba telling us that one of their staff members had seen Mokupi at a local clinic and that he was very sick.

Dad flew back to Botswana to find him and take him to the hospital. He found Mokupi at a friend's house, lying underneath a thin blanket, skeletal in his thinness, and coughing. Dad was so upset he did what white people working in Africa should never do: He took Mokupi to the hospital, right to the front of the line of people waiting in the sun, and demanded that a doctor see him immediately. He insisted that Mokupi be tested for HIV—also something he should not have done, but something he couldn't not do, under the circumstances. Though the doctor didn't tell Dad what the results were, the number of pills the doctor gave Mokupi to treat his illness was enough of an indication that it was AIDS and that it was very advanced.

I don't know exactly when Mokupi died, but I remember where

I was when Dad called to tell me he was gone. I was sitting on a cafeteria bench in Johns Hopkins Hospital, reading a textbook about the epidemiology of the HIV virus. I was six months into a master's program in international public health, focusing on HIV and AIDS in southern Africa and what was being done at a global level to address the epidemic. When I hung up the phone, I stared at the maps and charts in my book and saw only the smiling face of my old friend, the man who talked to the baboons every day and whose face lit up when it rained. The last day I remember spending with Mokupi, he led me far away from the baboons to show me a Pel's fishing owl, one of the rarest birds in the world and one that only lives in the Okavango. It has always been my favorite bird, and when we found not one but two Pel's fishing owls sitting with a small chick, Mokupi told me it was one of the happiest days he could remember. No one loved the delta like he did.

I now work in global public health. I've worked in some of the fanciest, best-equipped hospitals in the world, and I've worked in clinics where no one is trained, and old, broken equipment is used and reused because there isn't any other option. The knowledge that the places with the biggest health challenges are also the places where health care is the hardest to come by enrages me.

Though I live in the US now and go to work every day in a tall, shiny building that smells like nothing, my heart lives far, far away, where the sun is just rising over the swamp and the birds are waking up the forest with their calls. While I miss my wild world with a fierceness that is sometimes painful, what I have learned is that it's not the place that makes the adventure—it's the person. No world is free of danger; it's just that sometimes, the lions walk on two feet and sit next to you in the cafeteria. You may not need to climb a tree to get away from them, but you will always need a strong cup of tea, a calm head, and a plan. Though I still wish that the trees around my house were filled with monkeys, and that the things that go bump in the night could be hippos and not backfiring cars, I know that every time the sun rises, it rises with the same possibility for adventure that it does on Camp Island, thousands of miles away. The wardrobe door may have closed on Narnia, but that doesn't mean the story is over.

My favorite activity in my favorite place

ACKNOWLEDGMENTS

The story of Baboon Camp is one I've wanted to write since first stepping off Dan Rawson's boat in the summer of 1992. "How did you survive?" people have asked us for years. "What was it like?"

I used to say, "Well, that's a very long story. How much time do you have?" Though it's been great fun to talk about poisonous beetles and monkey fights to shocked faces over and over again (you'd be amazed at how quickly I can kill polite conversation at a cocktail party), I'm so glad to be able to put these stories down on paper in a more permanent way. Want to know what it was like? Here, read this. It's all there.

First, thank you to my family. Thank you for sharing quiet afternoons on the river drinking beer, and raucous evenings around the campfire. I know they were the happiest times for you too.

Thank you to Meghan and Nat: my first friends. Thank you for your letters, your kindness, and for still wanting to publicly acknowledge me when I said things like "I'm going to go be a bat!" and ran into the woods. Thank you to Brooke, who—I want to point out—isn't one person but a combination of three people. I'm glad we all ended up being friends too.

Thank you to Masaku, Mpitsang, Press, and Mokupi. Our homes in Kenya and Baboon Camp would have been impossible without your help. Thank you for teaching me so much and for showing me how much magic a place can have if you just know where to look. I miss you.

Thank you to all the people who have called Baboon Camp home over the years. We share something that is hard to put into words, but I hope this book can be a comfort to you when you miss staring out across the melapo and listening to the birds.

Thank you to my agent, Jeff Kleinman, for pulling an incredibly disorganized story out of his slush pile and patiently helping me mold it into something book-shaped. I will never be able to express how integral you've been in this book's journey and how thankful I am for your advice. Thank you to the Best Editor of Editors (stet, capitalization intended) Millicent Bennett: your enthusiasm and wise input made this book what it is, and I'm so lucky to have had the opportunity to work with you. Thank you to the rest of the team at Grand Central for all your hard work and tolerance for bad *Star Wars* jokes: Carmel Shaka, Karen Kosztolnyik, Ben Sevier, Brian McLendon, Anjuli Johnson, Albert Tang, Evan Gaffney, Staci Burt, and Morgan Swift.

Finally, thank you to Laura. It must have been weird when we just started dating and I handed you a giant stack of printed pages and said, "Here, read this. It's my life story." Thank you for your endless patience and encouragement to chase my dreams. None of this would have happened without you. I love you.

ABOUT THE AUTHOR

Keena Roberts graduated from Harvard with a degree in psychology and African studies. She was deeply affected by the impact the HIV/AIDS epidemic had on Botswana when she lived there; at Harvard, she studied Botswana's response to the epidemic. After graduation, she spent two years working in the US House of Representatives on issues relating to foreign affairs and health policy, and later earned a dual master's from Johns Hopkins University in international public health and development economics. Most recently, she has worked at the US Department of Health and Human Services in HIV/AIDS and LGBT health policy and for a government contractor on implementation of the Affordable Care Act in the United States, and she now works for an international market research company examining consumer health in more than one hundred countries around the world.